To a group of young people visiting her home:

"...your life is before you... it will be what you choose to make it...stand always on your own foundation. But you will have to make that foundation. There will come times when to make this stand will be difficult, especially to you of Hawaiian birth; but conquer you can...if you will."

Bernice Pauahi Bishop

Kamehameha Summer Ethics Retreat

2002

PAUAHI
The Kamehameha Legacy

PAUAHI

The Kamehameha Legacy

GEORGE HUʻEU SANFORD KANAHELE

Kamehameha Schools Press
Honolulu Hawaiʻi

KAMEHAMEHA SCHOOLS

Inquiries should be addressed to:
Kamehameha Schools Press
1887 Makuakāne Street
Honolulu, Hawai'i 96817

The paper used in this publication
meets the minimum requirements of
American National Standard for Library Sciences—
Permanence of Paper for Printed Library Materials,
ANSI Z39.48-1992 (R1997)

Printed in Canada

ISBN 0-87336-005-2

Library of Congress Cataloging-in-Publication Data
Kanahele, George H.S.
Pauahi: The Kamehameha Legacy

Includes bibliography and index.

1. Bishop, Bernice Pauahi, 1831–1884
2. Hawaiian–Princes and princesses–Biography. I. Title.
DU627.17.B4K36 1996   996.9'02'0924 [B]   86-19981

12 11 10 09 08 07 06 05 04 03 02   7 6 5 4 3

CONTENTS

ACKNOWLEDGMENTS

I wish to thank the Trustees of the Kamehameha Schools/Bernice Pauahi Bishop Estate for allowing me the freedom to think and write as I pleased.

I must also express my debt to all the members of the Kamehameha "family" who helped me in numberless ways, often going beyond the call of their regular duties.

Also, if I could award a medal for empathetic listening, it would go to Kaupena Wong who heard every word I wrote and then some. More often than not, I did the listening, thanks to Namahana Lydia Maioho, John Dominis Holt, Edith McKinzie, and many others who were willing to share their knowledge and time with me.

Needless to say, I alone am responsible for any errors of commission or omission in this book.

George H. S. Kanahele
June 3, 1986

PROLOGUE

Two centuries ago, when Hawaiian prophets were still honored for their insights, Kapihe was one of the most gifted. A *kahuna* or priest in the court of Kamehameha I and a descendant of the famed Napua line, he had prophesied the downfall of the *kapu*, the ancient religious system and the 1819 Battle of Kuamo'o which decided the course of modern Hawaiian history.

One of Kapihe's last great prophecies may have been the one recorded in the *Journal* of the missionary William Ellis. Although Ellis branded him a "false prophet," he still thought enough of his calling to preserve for posterity the following prophecy:

"Kapihe ... informed Tamehameha that when he should die, Kuahiro would take his spirit to the sky, and accompany it to the earth again, when his body would be reanimated and youthful; that he would have his wives, and resume his government in Hawai'i; and that, at the same time, the existing generation would see and know their parents and ancestors, and all the people who had died would be restored to life."[1]

What did Kapihe mean? Was he referring to the literal resurrection of Kamehameha and his future return to earth, as some have suggested? If so, this meant that he had digested Christian eschatological dogma and grafted it on to his own traditional beliefs. While this kind of intellectual synthesis is not beyond the realm of possibility, it forms the basis of only one interpretation.

There is another view, perhaps more credible because it is more compatible with Kapihe's Hawaiian antecedents. That view is that Kapihe was referring not to any bodily resurrection of Kamehameha along with the *maka'āinana*, much too egalitarian a notion for Hawaiians of the time. Rather, he was referring to Kamehameha's symbolic return in the "reanimated" form of Hawaiian youth who would by some instrumentality carry and perpetuate his name and honor through their words and deeds.

According to this view, this prophecy could have been fulfilled only with the founding of the Kamehameha Schools. Over the past one hundred years, the Schools have educated thousands of Hawaiian youth each of whom, in a sense, bears Kamehameha's name and perpetuates his memory through their ongoing achievements. Kamehameha, therefore, has returned and continues to dwell among his people by the example of the youthful beneficiaries of this and future generations.

The instrumentality through which all this was realized was *ke ali'i* Bernice Pauahi Bishop, the great-granddaughter of Kamehameha I, who founded the Schools not to honor herself, but to honor the ideals and achievements he and his successors represented. It was her destiny to bring this to fruition.

Genealogical Table Showing Connections of Ali'i with Pauahi

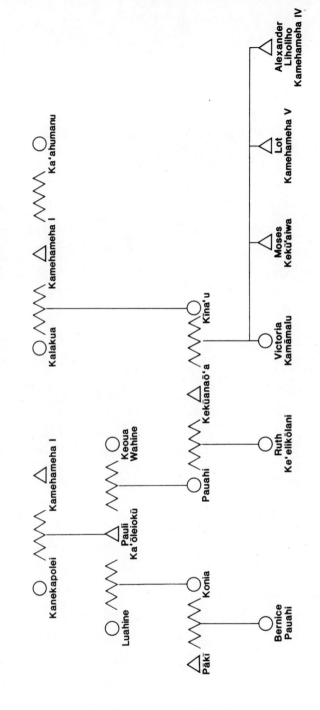

△ = Male
◯ = Female
∿ = Marriage

DEDICATION

This book is dedicated to the founder of the Hawaiian Kingdom, Kamehameha I and his descendents, the last of whom we honor in this book; and to the Native Hawaiians and Hawaiians-at-heart — through their accomplishments and support — this uplifting biography of ke aliʻi Pauahi was made possible.

1

HAWAIIAN ROOTS

To Hawaiians of the time 1831 was not an auspicious year. Civil war was narrowly averted that year when Liliha, the popular widow of Boki, the tragic entrepreneur-chief, was dissuaded from launching an armed revolt against the Regent Ka'ahumanu. Now a fervent convert to Christianity, Ka'ahumanu imposed new *kapu* regulating gambling, drinking, dancing, and the Sabbath with such severity that many Hawaiians felt oppressed, if not disillusioned. The non-missionary foreign residents were appalled and threatened retribution of their own. Economically, the chiefs were awash in the sea of debt caused by the collapse of the sandalwood trade which had ruined the fortunes of many of the *maka'āinana* (commoners). *Haole* (white) merchants like James Hunnewell and Henry Peirce were already laying down the foundations of economic control of the Kingdom.[1] And like the years before and after, 1831 saw hundreds of Hawaiians dying from strange diseases like syphilis and smallpox. In some places, as the writer Kamakau would say, the ground had already become "white with the bones of the dead."[2] No wonder that Kathleen Mellen was moved to write: "As the tumultous year of 1831 drew to a close it found the Hawaiians sunk in spiritual gloom ... Despair had come to the Hawaiians as a sickness comes, moving slowly through the veins and over the spirit. A miasmal melancholy hung listlessly over the land."[3]

Hawaiians reportedly gave 1831 a name: *Ka makahiki o ka pilikia nui* or "The Year of Heavy Trouble,"[4] which may have prompted Ralph Kuykendall, modern Hawai'i's historian, to call the ensuing decade "The Troubled Thirties."[5]

Yet, looking at it from our perspective today, 1831, for all of its *pilikia*, was not entirely an inauspicious year. It produced an event that has affected and will continue to affect the intellectual vitality and cultural integrity of modern Hawaiians like no other event of its kind. For it was in Honolulu on December 19th, at ʻAikupika, the home of her chiefly parents, that the royal child, Bernice Pauahi, was born. Destined as the heir of the Kamehameha lands and founder of the Kamehameha Schools, she was the instrument through which the aspirations and ideals of the Kamehamehas would be fulfilled. The story of this enormous legacy begins with two things inseparable in the telling of the origins of Hawaiian royalty: her birth and sacred lineage.

Birth and Sacred Lineage

Even in the 1830s when the mythological and political underpinnings of the chiefly class were being seriously eroded, a royal birth was still a moment of significance. The miracle of a royal birth or the addition of a newborn chief was not only a blessed event in itself, but also an affirmation of the continuity of a lineage going back ultimately to the gods. In the Hawaiian belief system, the *aliʻi* or chiefs were not mere *Homo sapiens,* but supernormal *akua* (gods) by virtue of their genealogy, their inherent *mana* or "divine force," their ritual sanctity, and, to a lesser degree, their generally superior physical and intellectual attributes, honed and developed through centuries of selective breeding and training. While the biblical theology of One God and the egalitarian notions of New England democracy may have undermined somewhat the old faith in the *aliʻi,* still many Hawaiians believed in the sacredness of their person and callings.

Thus, when the High Chiefess Konia gave birth to Princess Pauahi on that Monday in December, the event was celebrated in the time immemorial fashion by *haku mele* or poets composing and reciting *mele inoa* (name chants) or *mele hānau* (birth chants). These chants honored the newborn, recognized her genealogical links to mythological as well as earthly progenitors, and enriched the event with ceremonial power. Listen to the one *mele hānau* that has survived to this day, as it was recited more than a century and a half ago:[6]

Kulia kalani e Uli
Kulia ka pule ia Ku
Wahia ka lani e Kane
Oa ka moku ia ka ihi
O paʻihi ka lani ke aliʻi
Ninau o Kane, Kanaloa
Eia ka hoaka o naʻliʻi
Eia ka eu o ka laʻi kapu
Ke kupua nana i hele ke kai uli ke kai kea

Ke kai ka popolohua a Kane-honua-mea
Eia kalani ka haku ko'i alamea
He kapu he moe wai no ka uka
Nona ke ka nani ula i loa'a

Or

The Royal Princess is desired by "Uli" (Eternity)[7]
The prayer of supplication for her was desired by "Ku."
Break the heavens O "Kane"
The islands are crashed by "Kaihi."[8]
"Paihikalani"[9] was the chief.
When "Kane" inquired of "Kanaloa:"
"Here is the symbol crescent of chiefs!"
Here is the urchin of the still atmosphere of Kapus!
The one that sends the white sea
And the dark blue sea running.
The dark green sea of "Kane"—foundation of that someone.
Here is the heaven, the star, the hard volcanic stone,
The water bed for a man!
"She is sacred!" answered "Kaihi."

Though the passage of time has made the meaning and symbolism of
some of the poetic metaphors unclear, what is clear is the involvement of
the major mythic gods Kū, Kāne, and Kanaloa in affirming the nature of
the *ali'i* child: "She is sacred!"

Then, in a few dramatic lines, reminiscent of descriptions of events at
Kamehameha's own birth,[10] the *haku mele* tells of the cosmic omens
heralding the child's birth:

Hanau kalani ke kani nei ka pahu
Ku'i ka he kili lapa ka uila
I ho mai kaua koko ka a lewalewa
Ka punohu ka ha'o wale i ka moana
Ua ikea ka lani me ka malama

Or

The Royal one is born, the drums are sounding,
The thunder resounds and the lightning is flashing.

The blood rain is falling and is moving along with the floating clouds
The wondrous rainbow pillar stands alone in the ocean.
The Royal one is acknowledged warmly.

We don't know for sure whether the skies roared and flashed on that day, although December can be a stormy time in Honolulu. Perhaps more important is that the *haku mele* recognized these as the appropriate signs of the appearance of an *ali'i* child.

The *mele* continues on to reveal Pauahi's chiefly ancestry, but except for a few vital names, much is woven into a tapestry of poetic imagery that is layer upon layer deep with allusions and meanings that only Hawaiians of old could truly understand. Nonetheless, we can easily identify the illustrious ancestors described in the following passage:

He a hua ku no ke kai hohonu
O ka lani nui i mamao
O ka keawe hiapo kapu no ia
Oke kulu o ka hinu o ka hou o ke kapu la ho'i ia ia
Or
A great standing billow of the deep ocean,
Of Kalani-nui-ia-mamao
Who was "Keawe's" Kapu first born
The sheen of the sweat of the Kapu was his.
Desired from heaven and by earth.

Kalaninui'iamamao and Keawe are the two obvious names (the others being most likely disguised) in the entire chant, and they are the key to Pauahi's links with the Kamehamehas.

Keawe or, more properly, Keaweikekahiali'iokamoku, was the *mō'ī* (king) of the island of Hawai'i. The nineteenth century historian, Abraham Fornander, described him as "an enterprising and stirring chief who ... obtained a reputation for bravery and prudent management of his island ... and during his lifetime ruled the island peaceably and orderly, without rebellion, tumult, or bloodshed occurring to be chronicled in song or legend."[11] Kalaninui'iamamao was the "Kapu (sacred) first born" of this great king. The mother of Kalaninui'iamamao, Lonoma'akanaka, also had strong roots on the island of Hawai'i. She was a chiefess of the district of Ka'ū and belonged to the powerful 'I family of the Hilo area. When Keawe died, he established Kalaninui'iamamao as the *ali'i aimoku* or ruling chief of Ka'ū, while to his younger son, Ke'eaumoku, he assigned the districts of Kona and Kohala. We do not know much about the character and reign of Kalaninui'iamamao, but history says he was killed in a quarrel or deposed by the "notoriously and proverbially turbulent people" of Ka'ū.[12]

For our immediate purpose in tracing Pauahi's links to the Kamehamehas, Kalaninui'iamamao is pivotal, for he is the father and "stepfather" of two men who shaped the origins of the Kamehameha dynasty as no other could have. These men were the High Chiefs Kalani'ōpu'u and Kalanikupuapāikalaninui Keōua, respectively the uncle and the legal father of Kamehameha I. They were half-brothers because they had the same mother, Kamaka'īmoku, but different fathers. Kalaninui'iamamao sired Kalani'ōpu'u, while Kalanike'eaumoku fathered Keōua. Significantly, Kalanike'eaumoku was also a son of King Keawe by his second wife Kalanikauleleiaiwi. He was thus the brother of Kalaninui'iamamao. The one common ancestor in all these relationships is Keawe, which undoubtedly explains why his name stands out in the *mele hānau*.

Keōua, along with his brother, lived in the service of (some say, in the shadow of) the then reigning king of the island of Hawai'i, Alapa'inui. As one of the top commanders of the king's army, he was noted for his bravery and intelligence. He died in his prime, before he could demonstrate fully some of the qualities he had passed on to his son Kamehameha.

It is said in the footnotes of Hawaiian genealogy that Keōua was not the blood father of Kamehameha, but rather that his true sire was the gifted king of Maui, Kahekili. Keōua's wife, the High Chiefess Keku'i'apoiwa, was the niece of King Alapa'inui and was famed for her beauty and grace. The story goes that she went to visit Kahekili's sumptuous court at Wailuku, where the king became "enamored" of her. Not long after returning to her residence in Kailua, she was known to be pregnant with the child Pai'ea (the boyhood name of Kamehameha).

Whether the story is true or not, so far as is known, Keōua always acknowledged the boy as his own and loved and protected him. Furthermore, in the official royal genealogies, he is the recognized father of Kamehameha. But if Kahekili had been known for a fact to be the biological father of Kamehameha, the Hawaiians of old would have regarded the child's dual parentage as a matter of good fortune. To the Hawaiians, such dual parentage (being the biological child of one great chief and the acknowledged child of another) was a matter of good fortune that bestowed upon the child a greater status and *mana*. In pre-Christian Hawai'i, it was neither uncommon nor unacceptable for high chiefs and chiefesses to have extramarital liaisons leading to the birth of royal children. Such mating was sanctioned or condoned so long as it could "satisfy the demand for a pure-blooded lineage."[13] There was certainly no moral stigma attached to it. In any event, whether or not Keōua was his biological father, Kamehameha still inherited the genes of Keawe, because his mother was Keawe's granddaughter.

In a sense, Kamehameha had still another "father" in his uncle Kalani'ōpu'u, who raised him after Keōua met his untimely death. Kamehameha was still in his youth when his father died and spent the greater part of his young manhood under the care and tutelage of Kalani'ōpu'u. At the time (the 1770s) Kalani'ōpu'u was *mō'ī* of the island of Hawai'i, as his grandfather Keawe had been. He ruled with an iron hand but wisely, delegating responsibility widely to his subordinate chiefs and *konohiki* (land managers). He selected and surrounded himself with good people, "wise counselors and soothsayers," and *kāhuna* or specialists skilled in canoe-making, fishing, building, and other fields.[14] But he was above all a warrior-king marked by enormous physical strength, courage, discipline and a never-say-die attitude. Kamehameha must have learned well from his mentor-uncle because he exhibited many of these same attributes and skills later on when he became king.

A touching scene between Kalani'ōpu'u and the young man Kamehameha showed the bonding of their father-and-son-like relationship. Reports had reached Kalani'ōpu'u that some of the chiefs were threatening to do away with Kamehameha, whom they feared. He took Kamehameha aside and warned him, saying: "My child, I have heard the secret complaints of the chiefs and their mutterings that they will take you and kill you, perhaps soon. While I am alive they are afraid, but when I die they will take you and kill you. I advise you to go back to Kohala." And then he added, "I have left you the god; there is your wealth."[15] He was referring to the god Kūkā'ilimoku (the famous war image of Kū) as a source of spiritual strength and faith. Kamehameha did go back to the land of his birth, with his god, to await his future.

In this star-studded, *mana*-laden genealogy of Pauahi, no one, of course, surpasses Kamehameha the Great in leadership, historic achievement, and lasting impact or in having a transcending vision for his people. If Keawe is the Genetic Fountainhead, Kamehameha is surely the Emulative Model for his descendants. He personified many of the qualities and skills that his people esteemed from ages past: physical prowess, fighting spirit, excellence and achievement, industry, integrity or *pono*, courage, discipline, wisdom and intelligence or *na'auao*. He demonstrated abiding faith in the sacred traditions, yet understood the forces of change; he brought about political stability and national unity; he maneuvered the ship of state skillfully through the turbulent seas of Western technology and commerce. Giants among men are recognized everywhere, so it is no wonder that this *"Ka Liona o ka Pākīpika"* or "Lion of the Pacific," as Joseph Poepoe, the early twentieth century Hawaiian historian called him, has been ranked by foreign visitors and writers alongside Alexander the Great, Napoleon Bonaparte, and General Marquis de Lafayette.

Considering the many *mele* in praise of Kamehameha and the volumes written about his life and accomplishments, this is but a cameo view to remind us of the larger-than-life dimensions of the man who dominated the *ku'auhau* or genealogy — and future — of the royal Pauahi. Ironically, her *mele hānau* does not specifically mention him or his exploits, although the subject was surely covered in other *mele*.

From Kamehameha the Great, Pauahi's bloodline flows through the veins of his first-born son, Pauli Ka'ōleiokū. Joseph Poepoe calls him *ke keiki kamaha'o* or "the love child" of Kamehameha.[16] The child's mother was Kanekapolei, who was married to Kalani'ōpu'u. Mary Kawena Pūku'i, the celebrated Hawaiian scholar from Ka'ū, tells us how this happened. "Among the chiefs, a boy was not only trained in warfare and government but when he was grown physically, a matured chiefess was chosen to train him in sexual practices. This was part of his education. Should a child result, he or she was reared by the mother. Thus it was that Kamehameha claimed Ka'ōleiokū as 'the son of my beardless youth,' at the dedication of the *heiau* of Pu'ukoholā. This was the son born to him by Kanekapolei, one of the wives of his uncle Kalani'ōpu'u."[17]

Hawaiians placed extraordinary importance on ancestral purity, so much so that this was often a cause of rivalries within the chiefly class. Not surprisingly, claims and counterclaims were commonly advanced about the parentage of this or that *ali'i* child. As we have seen, such was the case with Pai'ea or Kamehameha. Such was the case too with Ka'ōleiokū.

The question arose out of the famous incident at Kawaihae, Hawai'i Island, involving Kamehameha and Keōua Kuahu'ula, the high-chief son of Kalani'ōpu'u. Keōua, who had been at war with Kamehameha, was induced to go to Kawaihae where Kamehameha awaited him to parley for peace. Keōua took several canoes filled with his trusted chiefs and warriors from Ka'ū. Dividing the company into two groups, he took command of the first and placed the young warrior-chief Ka'ōleiokū in charge of the second. According to Abraham Fornander, who described this event in detail, Keōua somehow knew that he would not come out of the meeting alive and even "prepared his own body for the sacrifice." He deliberately placed in his canoe only those "whom he wished to be his companions in death, his *moe-pū*." He ordered all the others to follow in the group "under the charge of his half-brother, Pauli Ka'ōleiokū, whose life he supposed Kamehameha would at all events spare, the young man being the natural son of Kamehameha."[18] This assumption proved correct, for Keōua and his companions were indeed killed. Ka'ōleiokū and his group were saved when Kamehameha stopped the slaughter, saying, "He shall not die; he is the child of my youth."[19]

What manner of person was Ka'ōleiokū, grandfather of the "royal child" Pauahi? What qualities of intellect and character did he receive from his father? Which of these did he exemplify? Unfortunately, these questions are difficult to answer because our knowledge of his life and accomplishments is quite sketchy, partly because he seems to have lived much in the shadow of his father. Since he was apparently raised by Kanekapolei and then by Kalani'ōpu'u, it is reasonable to assume that the values and skills he acquired were not unlike those acquired by Kamehameha himself: those of the warrior-chief. His traditional world-view must have been significantly altered, however, when as a young boy he met Captain Cook. Ka'ōleiokū boarded Cook's ship the *Resolution* when it first appeared off Maui in November 1778, and was frequently on board the ship throughout the following month because he was supposed to have been "a favorite" of Cook. He was a witness to "Lono's" (or Cook, who was thought by some to be the reincarnation of the god Lono) death at Kealakekua Bay and even accompanied the body back to the ship. We can only guess about the impression these events made upon his youthful mind, but, like his father, he must have grown up with a healthy respect for the *mana* and technology of the new world.

We do not know much about Ka'ōleiokū's whereabouts and experiences between the death of Captain Cook in 1779 and his dramatic encounter with Kamehameha at Kawaihae in 1791. Apparently, he joined forces with his half-brothers Keōua and Kiwalaō and fought with them against Kamehameha's armies in a series of battles over a ten-year span. In this period Ka'ōleiokū must have developed his fighting and leadership skills and attributes to a high degree, or Keōua would not have chosen him to command the second group at Kawaihae. I'i, for example, said that Ka'ōleiokū was "famous for his spear throwing. Because he knew just where to strike a dodging person, his spear did not miss."[20] Kamehameha no doubt recognized his abilities, for after their reconciliation, Ka'ōleiokū fought with his father throughout the campaigns of conquest on the islands of O'ahu, Maui and Hawai'i. In the years of peace and stability that followed, Kaʻōleiokū was apparently given responsibility for Kaʻū, where his family estates were located, and assigned other governmental tasks by Kamehameha. On one such mission to Honolulu, having to do with the construction of the fort there, he became ill and died, shortly before the death of Kamehameha.[21] Had he lived beyond his father, he might have played an even more important role in the early years of the Kingdom.

Pauli Kaʻōleiokū was married at least twice. His first wife was Keōua, by whom he had a daughter, Pauahi, the namesake of Bernice Pauahi, and one of the wives of Liholiho or King Kamehameha II. His second wife was Kahailiopua, more commonly called Luahine, by whom he had Kanaholo Konia, the mother of Bernice Pauahi.[22]

We have now completed the genealogical linkage of *Kalani* (royal) Pauahi with Keawe, the common ancestor of the Kamehamehas. Thus, when the *haku mele* (composer) of Pauahi's birth chant tells of the "Royal ladder" of the chiefs, the metaphor may be illustrated in the following way:

Keawe
Kalanikeʻeaumoku
Keōua
Kamehameha I
Pauli Kaʻōleiokū
Kanaholo Konia
Bernice Pauahi

Ultimately, the ancestral line ascends back to Papa (Mother Earth) and Wākea (Father Sky) and to the great *akua* (gods).

Her paternal line is less illustrious, but this is probably due more to an accident of history than to lack of noble standing or genetic superiority. It is said that Pauahi's father Abner Kaʻehu Pākī, "was born at the wrong time...when the Maui family kapus [powers] were down and the glories of the Maui royal family had passed."[23] Pākī was the son of Kalani-helemaiiluna whose father was the great eighteenth century king of Maui, Kamehamehanui. Kamehamehanui was in turn the brother of Kahekili, the same man who may have been Kamehameha's blood father. It is also noteworthy that Pākī's mother, Kawao, was a direct descendant of Keawe as were the Kamehamehas. Thus, in this circuitous way, both Pauahi's mother, Konia, and father, Pākī, have the same common progenitor. In fact, Kawao, who was a high chiefess from an *aliʻi* family on the island of Hawaiʻi, had named her son Pākī after an incident involving Kamehameha. On the coast of Puna, Hawaiʻi, Kamehameha was attacked by some fishermen and in retaliation threw showers of stone or *kaʻehu* (throw) *pākī* (stone) at them. They would have killed him had he not been rescued by his men. Years later Kamehameha commemorated this incident in the "Māmalahoe Kānāwai" or "Law of the Splintered Paddle," designed to protect the innocent and helpless from wanton attacks similar to the one the fishermen had made on him.[24]

Names, relationships, alliances, places, achievements, qualities—such is the fabric out of which the *haku mele* composed their birth and name chants honoring the newborn princess. Since these were recited at or near the time of birth, some of the first words the royal child heard were those naming and praising her *kūpuna* (ancestors). And as Pauahi grew up, she heard more of the same, for it was part of the education of the *aliʻi* to learn their genealogy. An *aliʻi's* social, political, ritual, and *kapu* (sacred) status as well as prestige were predicated on such knowledge. Without it the *aliʻi* had no claim to their *mana*. Indeed, Hawaiians believe that to be ignorant of one's lineage is to shame one's ancestors and oneself: To know where you come from is to know who you are.

Konia-Pākī and Pauahi's Separation

The royal baby was delivered in "Egypt" or ʻAikupika, as the home of her parents was named. It was a native-style house with a grass-roof that if located in modern Honolulu would be somewhat *ma uka* of (inland from) the corner of Bishop and King Streets in the heart of the downtown area. The house was not large and, on the nineteenth of December, may have been quite crowded with midwives, ladies-in-waiting of the High Chiefess-mother, family and other *aliʻi* observers, for it was customary for the newborn *kapu* child to be viewed by such a crowd.

What they saw was a "pretty little lady" with delicate features and a light complexion. Her facial features, especially her eyes, seemed to have come from her mother, Konia, and her fair skin from her father, Pākī, who was of "a very light (*ʻehu*) complexion." When compared to the darker hues of other Hawaiians, he was always a little more noticeable. The *ʻehu* type, with their reddish hair, long-headed and tall, as was Pākī who was six feet four inches in height, stood out among fellow-Hawaiians. There were not many light-complexioned Hawaiians, but there were enough to have attracted the attention of Fornander and other observers of early Hawaiʻi.[25] This point is made because the child's light skin color was to prompt whisperings among some Hawaiians and *haole* that her real father was not a Hawaiian.

Konia and Pākī were married in 1830, she for the first and he for the second time. By then both were courtiers at the court in Lahaina. Pākī, in fact, had been chosen as a boy to be one of the playmates of Prince

Kauikeaouli (Kamehameha III), and later had been a member of the Hulumanu, an organization of youthful favorites of the Prince who were known for "drinking rum, rioting, playing billiards and dancing."[26] Sometime in the 1820s, however, he abandoned his high-living ways and found the new religion. Pākī became a convert, partly through the influence of the Queen Regent Ka'ahumanu and Kīna'u, both of whom were fervent Christians. Konia had also become a Christian and because of "a good steady disposition," we are told, she became a good "influence upon Pākī."[27]

It was quite a suitable match: both were *ali'i*-born, intimates of the reigning monarchs, Protestants, with complementing personalities. But physically, they were quite a striking contrast. Pākī was tall, with "massive arms and legs, a handsome body and the litheness of a good athlete," while Konia was short, with a delicate, intelligent face, and quite plump. Their marriage would endure until their deaths in the mid-1850s.

Following the delivery of the child, one of their most urgent tasks was to give it an *inoa*, a name. This was no casual exercise, for naming was a ritual of power. Hawaiians believed that every name had *mana*, a force of its own, that could influence and shape the character, personality and even destiny of the bearer. A good name could bring good fortune while a bad *inoa* could bring a person bad luck.[28] It was also common in naming the *hiapo* or firstborn to choose a name from an ancestor. So it was a solemn moment when Konia and Pākī gave the name Pauahi to their *hiapo*. The name belonged to Konia's half-sister, the child's aunt. The name Pauahi seems to have come from an incident in which the original Pauahi was nearly burned to death as a child. An accidental explosion of gunpowder killed five men, destroyed her mother's house, and injured her badly. To commemorate her lucky escape, she was given the name: *pau* or finished and *ahi* or *fire*, which liberally translated means "the fire is out." The original Pauahi was the mother of Ruth Ke'elikōlani. The lands Ruth would later leave to Bernice Pauahi Bishop would form the bulk of the Bishop Estate. Thus the choice of the name Pauahi had more significance than perhaps anyone at the time realized, for Ruth's mother made possible the legacy of the Kamehameha Schools.[29]

Meanwhile, as the mother and baby were being tended to indoors, a tamarind tree was being planted outside for the proper disposition of the *'iēwe* or placenta. Hawaiian custom required that it be buried, preferably under a tree or in a hole cut in its trunk. As the tree grew it protected the *'iēwe*. Because it was identified with the person whose *'iēwe* it guarded, the tree was *kapu* (sacred).[30] Since there were no suitably large trees growing on the premises the 'iewe was buried and a tamarind sapling planted over it. The tamarind, a species introduced to the Islands from India, had become popular and was one of the few trees that could grow on the almost waterless and treeless plain of Kou (the original name for Honolulu). The sapling grew into a large tree where, in later life, Bernice Pauahi would meet with many of her people, who regularly sought her advice. It was a tree that gave both shade and *mana*.

The young parents must have cherished the next few days with their newborn, for it was the only time in the next eight years that the child would live with them in 'Aikupika. In keeping with prevailing custom, Konia had promised the child to her aunt Kīna'u. Konia probably did not have much more than a week to suckle her first and only baby before she had to let her go. Upon meeting Kīna'u at the bedside of Konia, Laura Fish Judd, wife of an influential missionary doctor, wrote: "We make the toilette of the pretty little lady. She is to bear the name of Bernice Pauahi and will be taken from her mother in a few days."[31] Anticipating the separation must have been a wrenching experience for Konia. Kīna'u must have understood the feeling, for almost exactly a year before she had given up her newborn son (the future Lot Kamehameha) to Ulumaheihei Hoapili, Governor of Maui. Both Konia and Kīna'u fully understood the binding nature of the *hānai* promise: *Nāu ke keiki kūkae a na'au.* "I give you this child, intestines and all."[32]

Perhaps there was consolation for Konia in knowing that Pauahi would be nearby. Kīna'u's home was a stone's throw away in an area known as Pohukaina.[33] Also located there were the homes of several prominent *ali'i,* including Ka'ahumanu; her niece Pauahi; Kekāuluohi, one of Liholiho's wives; and their guardian, Luanu'u Kahalai'a. Not too far away were the residences of Liliha and Lilia Namahana, Ka'ahumanu's sister.[34] Honolulu was but a large village of about four thousand inhabitants, with only one road, King Street, and the rest merely footpaths. Almost everyone was in hailing distance. So on a quiet night Konia could well have imagined hearing the cries of *ka lani* Pauahi, so near yet so far away.

Childhood Under a Second Kamehameha

For the next eight years, until 1839, Pauahi was to be mothered, nourished, loved, protected, clothed, and taught by her foster mother Kaho'anokū Kīna'u. Kīna'u was the eldest daughter of Kamehameha the Great and was but 26 years old in 1831. Standing six feet tall and weighing "over four hundred pounds," she was said to bear "a remarkable resemblance" to her father.[35] She had also inherited many of his fine qualities. As Kamakau states: "She had the courage of a man. Had she been one, she would have been a second Kamehameha."[36] Elizabeth Kīna'u Judd compared her to other chiefesses and judged her to be "far superior" and "a woman of strong character and a firm friend of progress."[37] Of Kamehameha's daughters, she came the closest to exemplifying his character and leadership.

Though still relatively young, she had already experienced the joys and sorrows of being a wife and mother. At an early age she was one of the wives of Liholiho, who died tragically while touring London in 1823. She then was married to the Chief Kahalai'a who in 1826, along with many other chiefs, died during an epidemic of whooping cough. A few months later, she met the High Chief Kekūanaō'a at the funeral of his wife Pauahi, the half-sister of Konia and Bernice's namesake. Chiefesses sought after Kekūanaō'a as a husband because, as I'i noted, he was "well supplied with tools for farming and fishing."[38] Kīna'u married him the next year and by 1831 had borne three sons: David, Moses Kekūāiwa, and Lot Kapuāiwa (or Lot Kamehameha). Kīna'u also bore Kekūanaō'a another son, Alexander 'Iolani and a daughter, Victoria Kamāmalu. When the baby Pauahi entered her embrace, it could be said, as Mrs. Judd did, that Kīna'u was already "a loving, exemplary wife" and "a tender mother."[39]

By this time, Kīna'u was also a confirmed member of the Protestant faith. She had been baptized in 1825, at the same time as Ka'ahumanu. As we will see by the kinds of policies she promoted as *kuhina nui*, Kīna'u was a staunch supporter of religious belief and conformity, particularly as it involved her new-found Congregationalism. It is hard to tell how much she allowed Jehovah and Christ to replace the Hawaiian gods Kāne, Kū, Kanaloa or Lono and the beloved *'aumākua* (ancestral spirits), but she could not have abandoned completely her traditional beliefs and practices. After all, she still believed in her *ali'i* status and its sacred prerogatives which were rooted in the ancient myths and values.

While she still clung to many aspects of her old culture, Kīna'u adopted a progressive stance toward the inevitable changes, precipitated by Cook's arrival, that were already reshaping the social, economic, political, and cultural character of Hawai'i. By 1831 she had already learned to read and write and to appreciate the *mana* of the *palapala* (or written word) and its enormous implications for change in the education and thinking of Hawaiians. Like all the other *ali'i*, she enthusiastically supported the founding of the first school, Lahainaluna, in the earlier part of that year. "The chiefs were all eager for education," says Kamakau, so much so that "educated people were like chiefs...because the chiefs treated them as chiefs."[40] This high premium placed on knowledge, in this case gained through Western schooling, was a reaffirmation of a standard that prevailed throughout the history of *ka po'e kahiko* (the people of old).

Less than seven months after Pauahi's arrival in Kīna'u's household, the Queen Regent Ka'ahumanu died. This event thrust Kīna'u into the office of *kuhina nui* or prime minister of the kingdom. She retained the position until she died in 1839, though she had to maintain an uneasy balance of power between herself and King Kauikeaouli (Kamehameha III), who was only eighteen years of age, and other contending political forces. Pauahi was raised by a prime minister in a home that was at times at the vortex of Hawaiian politics, with all of its excitement and pathos, idealism and intrigue, glory and failure.

Although Kīna'u was indisputably the central figure in Pauahi's life during this period, another who played an important role was Kekūanaō'a, her foster father. By 1831 he had already gained considerable respect in royal circles. He was a favorite of Liholiho whom he had accompanied to London and served in various responsible capacities. As a result of his travels, Kekūanaō'a had experienced first-hand the advances made by Western science and technology and had no illusions about what needed to be done if his people were to adapt to the new world. He, too, had learned how to read and write and had an immense regard for education. Many years later he would become the equivalent of a minister of education in the Hawaiian government. Like Kīna'u, he had joined the church and eventually became one of its chief defenders. John Papa I'i said of him: "All truly admired Kekūanaō'a and loved him for the many good things he did and for his unlimited kindness."[41] Finally, as mentioned earlier, his relationship with the child Pauahi was influenced by the fact that he had once been married to her aunt and was also the father of her only cousin, Ruth Ke'elikōlani.[42]

No doubt, there were other persons during this period who exerted an influence on Pauahi and her development. These included her *kahu* or attendants, who hovered over her constantly anticipating and providing for every possible want. All *ali'i* children were looked after by a bevy of *kahu*, and those of the highest rank usually had the largest number of attendants. Sometimes one person would be assigned the role of principal *kahu*, which made that person almost a surrogate parent. We are not certain about how this part of Pauahi's life was organized, but it seems reasonable to believe that as a child she learned a great deal by observing or imitating her *kahu*. In addition, Pauahi must also have come in frequent, if not daily, contact with her royal relatives and family friends, since the Hawaiian household was an *'ohana* or extended family rather than a nuclear one. Lastly, she would have also had a select group of playmates of *ali'i* rank with whom she would have spent a great deal of time over this period of years.

If the child is father to the man or, more appropriately in this case, mother to the woman, then these persons, along with the events and activities of which they were a part, were all critical to Pauahi's upbringing. As educational psychologists like to tell us, early experiences have an important bearing on the attitudes and values of the individual as an adult. This modern insight was also a fundamental premise of the traditional Hawaiians' understanding of human behavior, clearly revealed in the principles and practices followed in rearing and training children. In other words, Pauahi was undoubtedly influenced and molded by her foster parents, royal relatives, friends, playmates, and her *kahu* — by their feelings, attitudes, values, aspirations, opinions, and perceptions. The only question is how and to what extent.

Even under the best of circumstances, if we had complete information and understanding of all the personalities and factors involved, trying to answer this question with precise cause-and-effect explanations would be difficult. It is doubly difficult when we have so little information, especially documented evidence about Pauahi's personal experiences and impressions of her childhood. Nonetheless, we know enough to make some reasonable suppositions that will help to explain certain aspects of her character, as well as the origins of some of the attitudes and ideas that marked her adolescent and adult development.

Given the religious convictions of Kīna'u and Kekūanaō'a, it is easy to understand why Pauahi became a Protestant. The influence of the missionaries, the *Paipala* or Bible, the Church and its sanctions, was rather pervasive. She must have been exposed to biblical stories, principles, and standards, if not taught them by the missionaries. Mrs. Judd was a frequent visitor and confidant of Kīna'u, and John Papa I'i, a stalwart Christian and confidant of *ali'i*, was Kīna'u's private secretary. Pauahi must have learned to sing simple melodies, memorize Gospel truths, attend Sunday services, or somehow participate in the life of the Church, however minimal her involvement at that age. Though she might have heard or seen "ungodly" things associated with traditional Hawaiian beliefs or non-Protestant ideas, in her protected environment she was imbued with the Word. By the time she left to be enrolled in the Royal School in 1839, she was an embryonic Christian.

Not just a Christian, Pauahi had to be a Protestant or a Congregationalist. This was not only because of the missionaries, but also because of Kīna'u's political and religious philosophy. Like her predecessor Ka'ahumanu, Kīna'u believed that the state or government and the people should have one common religion and that "the people should follow the religion of their chiefs."[43] Having many religions, she believed, would generate family disputes, cause dissension in society, and make more trouble for government. Both she and Ka'ahumanu insisted on this course because they were trying to keep the kingdom unified in the face of political in-fighting and the immense changes going on in Hawaiian society. This is why she objected to the establishment of the Catholic mission, even declaring "that chief or commoner who turned to the Catholic Church was a traitor against the Hawaiian government."[44] Persecutions of Hawaiian Catholics were severest during the "Troubled Thirties." Since the child Pauahi could not have been totally unaware of Kīna'u's attitude toward Catholicism, her later attitude of seeming intolerance toward Catholics may have begun here.

If becoming a Christian was the least traditional thing she could do, being an *ali'i* was the most traditional thing she could be. When the *haku mele* intoned her sacred birth and traced her genealogical ties back to Kamehameha and Keawe and to the gods, he merely confirmed her predestined status as a chiefess. To be, to feel and think and act like an *ali'i* was as natural for the *ali'i*-born as it was for the *maka'āinana* to be a commoner. In a society as structured and as disciplined as Hawaiian society, conforming to one's genealogically and socially defined role was necessary for acceptance, if not survival. Those who were most bound by this system were the *ali'i* themselves. Everything important about Hawaiian society was designed to validate, maintain, and perpetuate the chiefly class along with its mythological underpinnings. Pauahi was a captive of the most powerful tradition of her society.

It is impossible to tell how early *ali'i* children began to sense their special role, but it must have been among the first things *ke keiki* (the child) Pauahi sensed, if only intuitively. "*Ka lani* Pauahi" or "*Ke ali'i* Pauahi" — words that she would hear continuously for the rest of her life — would have been among the first sounds she heard. Her *ali'i*-hood would have been affirmed and reaffirmed in a thousand ways — by the treatment she received from her *kahu*, by the deference showed her by the *maka'āinana*, by her relationships with Kīna'u and other *ali'i*, by the rituals and symbols of Hawaiian society. Everything about her childhood in Kīna'u's household validated the reality of her royal status. She could not nor would she ever forget who she was.

She was a sacred child born to power and its exercise. As an *ali'i*, by virtue of her lineage and the *mana* or spiritual force she had inherited, she possessed the primordial right to power, if and when she chose or was chosen to exercise it. The quintessential idea in being an *ali'i* was the possession and use of power. In Hawai'i the power of the *ali'i* was ultimately extraordinary or sacred, and the Hawaiians revered and deferred to their chiefs and chiefesses. Pauahi no doubt came to understand the nature of *ali'i*-hood very early in her life, although members of an egalitarian society would find the concept difficult to comprehend.

Given this mind-set it is reasonable to conclude that the child Pauahi developed a powerful sense of personal worth and self-esteem which in turn generated feelings of confidence, independence, assurance, and pride. True, the same mind-set could transform such feelings into the arrogance, selfishness, condescension and ruthlessness of which many *ali'i* were guilty. But the system had built-in safeguards in the form of social, political, and religious sanctions aimed at minimizing such abuses. The spirit of the system was conveyed by an elaborate set of moral injunctions which stressed such values as reciprocity, *mālama* or caring, *ha'aha'a* or humility, and *lokomaika'i* or generosity.

We can imagine the growing child Pauahi being taught sayings such as these, which were all addressed to aspiring *ali'i*: *"E mālama i ke kanaka nui, i ke kanaka iki"* or "Take care of the big man and the little man," and its corollary, *"I ali'i no ke ali'i i ke kanaka"* or "A chief is a chief because of his subjects."[45] Both emphasized the reciprocal nature of the use of power, that ruler and followers have mutual obligations. This sense of reciprocity, of giving back something of a worth equivalent to what you receive, was so deeply embedded in the psyche of every Hawaiian, that every child understood it. Pauahi would have also heard the admonition: *"Ku'ia ke hele a ka na'au ha'aha'a"* or "A humble person walks carefully so he will not hurt those about him."[46] In other words, don't misuse people. The *ali'i* who inspires respect and allegiance is the one who doesn't throw her weight around. *Ha'aha'a*, she would have learned, is the *ali'i*'s defense against the excesses of pride and egotism. She must have learned these lessons, because in later years *Ke ali'i* Pauahi would be known and praised for her caring and humility.

Another important standard she would have learned is encapsulated in the words *"E 'ōpū ke ali'i"* or "Be as kind and as generous as a chief should be."[47] Generosity was one of the building blocks of the Hawaiian social

order, and the chief was the ultimate measure of generosity. The chief had
the greatest amount to give and the greatest motivation; in giving generously the chief reaped honor and prestige and accrued *mana*. Chiefly
generosity was a way of redistributing goods and services throughout the
community and of "investing" in the overall development of the realm,
since economics, and not altruism, defined the role of the *ali'i*. This
economic theory was elementary to traditional Hawaiians. If not the
theory, the value of generosity or *lokomaika'i*, as an obligation that went
along with chieftainship, must have been instilled in the child Pauahi and
reinforced in many ways in her later years. This early training in the value
of giving as an *ali'i* responsibility led to the many acts of generosity that
culminated in her last will and testament.

Even as a child Pauahi willingly or unwittingly learned other things
about the use of power that helped to shape her attitudes as an adult. One
was that *ali'i* sometimes paid a heavy price in the exercise of their power.
She was a firsthand witness to this, for there were many times when she felt
the tension, frustration, and disappointment that showed on the face or in
the voice of her prime minister mother. Kīna'u presided over the Kingdom
in tumultuous times of "heavy trouble." There was the struggle, which
nearly came to armed combat, between the *kuhina nui* and Liliha, who
sought the governorship and control of O'ahu. There was the fight
between Kīna'u and the young king, who wanted to expand his own
authority. There were the conflicts with chiefs who opposed her overly
strict regulations on drinking, gambling, and keeping the Sabbath. And
there were other troubles with the *haole* merchants who demanded better
conditions or terms, with Catholic priests and their French backers, and
with some of her own "backsliding" Hawaiian constituents. The child
Pauahi may have been too young to understand all the underlying reasons
for these problems, but she was not too young to store up memories and
emotions about the trials of leadership which would later be reinforced by
her own experiences. Perhaps these early recollections of unhappy times
provide part of the answer to why she refused King Lot Kamehameha's
offer of the throne in 1873.

In this aristocratic society of *ali'i* endowed with divine power, rank and
privilege were carefully protected by a palisade of do's and don'ts. While
every child was taught these rules and their underlying values as a matter
of *hana pono* or right behavior, the *ali'i* child was subjected to the most
thorough indoctrination. "The royal child mastered an intricate code
governing the prerogatives of rank and the prohibitions or *kapu* that
accompanied privilege."[48] Although some elements of this system (such as

prostrating oneself before a high *ali'i* with the penalty of death for failing to do so) had disappeared by the early 1830s, the code and its spirit were still very important. For example, how you held yourself, whether kneeling, squatting or sitting, in the presence of ranking *ali'i;* or the distance you kept from them, whether in conversation, processions or ceremonies — these were still considered essential in the etiquette of the times. There were no special schools or courses on royal manners, so the child Pauahi was taught these by the best of mentors, her parents and *kahu*, in the best of all schools, her home at court.

Perhaps, more important than the mechanics of the code were the underlying principles and values. The cardinal principle Pauahi learned was that the space around the sacred *ali'i* was *kapu* and that to intrude on it would be to diminish an *ali'i's mana*. She could not forget that the vital element of *ali'i*-hood was power. Power, that is, the transcending extraordinary *mana* of a sacred chief, demanded respect and deference. The elaborate code of conduct and protocol was designed to maintain that attitude. As she grew up, changing times may have forced her to compromise the letter of the code, but she never forgot its spirit.

As children naturally seek models to imitate or emulate, so did Pauahi, consciously or unconsciously, seek in Kīna'u her model as an *ali'i* and a woman. We do not know how completely she may have tried to pattern her attitudes and values after her *kuhina nui*-mother, but some things seem to stand out. Kīna'u's religious feelings, a sense of the sacred, spirituality and faith; her independence, confidence and pride, but not her reported condescension and sometimes arrogance; her great sense of responsibility and especially her courage and generosity — these attributes all seem to have been part of Pauahi's own character. There were certainly others, both positive and negative, that shaped Pauahi's thinking and behavior. Kīna'u's impact on Pauahi the child was long-lasting, the cumulative result of a variety of experiences repeated many times over a period of eight years.

Of equal importance to Kīna'u's personal impact is the effect that the events of the "troubled thirties" had on Pauahi's feelings and perceptions of the life of her people. Though she may have led a somewhat sheltered existence, by 1839 she must have sensed that life was not easy for Hawaiians, that there was a great deal of death and sickness, despondency and disillusionment, loss of pride, esteem and spirit, and not much tranquility or brotherly love in a rapidly changing and divided land. Her feelings and perceptions were not shaped by particular events happening at one moment of time, but by the cumulative effects of activities that took place with increasing regularity. Hawai'i was not merely in a state of transition but decline.

Pauahi's nearly eight-year sojourn with her prime minister mother came to an end on April 4, 1839, when Kīna'u, only thirty-five years old and still "young, beautiful and unwrinkled," died of mumps. She left behind her baby daughter, Victoria Kamāmalu, whom she had given birth to only five months before — and Pauahi, whom she had loved as her own. John Papa I'i informs us that "When Kīna'u started on her journey from this world, she left behind much to grow and the affection and tears of her children" — excepting "the two girl babies, Kamāmalu and Kamaka'eha (Lili'uokalani)" who "did not understand weeping."[49]

Both Pākī and Konia joined in the mourning. Konia was particularly grief-stricken, for she had held Kīna'u in high regard. Just a few months earlier, she had named her newly adopted baby girl Kamaka'eha or "Sore eyes," after a time when Kīna'u was ill with "a dull headache and sore eyes."[50] It was Kīna'u who took Kamaka'eha to her breast and fed her as she did her own Kamāmalu, an act that embarrassed Konia but endeared Kīna'u to her.

The grief felt by Pākī and Konia was shortly followed by the joy of anticipating Pauahi's return to their home. Apparently, they had never completely gotten over the separation and now were "very desirous" of getting Pauahi back. Kekūanaō'a, however, was not very willing to part with Pauahi because "he and the other chiefs had become very proud of the promising child."[51] Intelligent, pretty, sensitive, determined, strong yet humble, Pauahi was viewed by many as a child of promise. Kīna'u must also have perceived Pauahi's potential. She seems to have happily envisioned Pauahi and Lot eventually being married, since she had apparently revealed their betrothal, at least to her sister, Kekāuluohi, who succeeded her as *kuhina nui*.[52] Death saved Kīna'u from the disappointment of Pauahi's later refusal of Lot's offer of marriage.

In any case, Pākī persevered and soon prevailed over a very reluctant Kekūanaō'a, and Pauahi was restored to her natural parents. Yet, for the next ten years she would hardly spend a day with them, as she would live as a boarding student in the newly established Chiefs' Children's School, also called the Royal School. She would live these years without direct parental influence and, instead, accept the affection and guidance of another woman in her life, Mrs. Juliette Montague Cooke, her teacher and confidant.

2

AT THE CHIEFS' CHILDREN'S SCHOOL

The ten years that Pauahi would spend at the Chiefs' Children's School would be a critical period in her life. This decade of maturation from childhood to womanhood — a period that would see her learn a new language, develop her intellectual and aesthetic capacities, make new friends, strengthen her faith, acquire new attitudes and values, and discard some of the old — would form the crucible of experience from which she would extract the elements of much of her later life.

Neither people nor schools are born full grown, and so the first part of this chapter focuses on the Royal School's antecedents in the life and minds of the chiefs, their aspirations and those of the Cookes, and how these aspirations were transformed into a building and a curriculum. For Pauahi and the other royal children, life away from their homes, parents and *kahu* was a trial of adjustment. Some did not succeed in surviving it, but Pauahi triumphed perhaps as none of the others did. Her triumph was not only academic, but aesthetic, physical, moral; and in the end spiritual development marked her as Kekūanāoʻa and others had foreseen: as a child of promise.

The Setting

Traditionally, *aliʻi* children were taught and trained by specialists or *kāhuna* either at home or at the court. Kamehameha, for example, underwent a "rigid system" of training for the first seven years of his life at the court of King Alapaʻinui, and then was specially trained by the famed warrior-chief Kekūhaupiʻo. Some of the major subjects of instruction included oratory (which was considered one of the "higher arts"), astronomy, geography, myths and rituals, military tactics, fishing, and others.[1] Each high chief or chiefly family furnished and managed the education and training of its own children. The most powerful and prosperous, who had access to the greatest number of best qualified specialist-teachers, would have provided their children the best education. But all chiefs, whatever their economic or political circumstances, attached high priority to the proper education and training of their offspring and potential successors. For power and knowledge were synonymous in the world of the *ali'i*.

The chiefs were educated but not schooled. That is to say, they were taught largely on an individual basis by one or more specialists: expert fishermen, craftsmen, orators or warriors. The method was "tutorial," an ideal teaching and learning approach because it is the most efficient and focused form of education. The chiefs were not taught in a school, a place for teaching and learning where a large number of students are gathered from one or more communities to be taught in classes by teachers who may be less than masters or experts of their subjects. In contrast to the tutorial method, today's school is based on the "collegial" method of teaching, which is clearly less efficient and less focused. The collegial system is largely a concession to numbers, useful when there is a disproportionate number of students to master teachers, and to economics. Because the chiefs were educated by the tutorial rather than collegial method, we can say that they were efficiently if not well educated, although they were never schooled.

By the 1820s the chiefs were aware of schools, because by then the institution was commonplace in Hawai'i. Between the missionaries and the government, hundreds of schools, though fairly primitive, had been organized throughout the islands. By 1828, in fact, virtually the entire Hawaiian adult population of about 37,000 had been to school to learn reading and spelling. Even the chiefs had attended such schools. As the adult educational movement subsided in the 1830s, attention was turned to educating the children. A variety of schools were established: so-called "common" schools taught by Hawaiian teachers, and "select" schools, usually for boarders, taught and controlled by missionaries. By the end of the decade, as many as 12,000 to 15,000 *keiki o ka 'āina* (native children) were being schooled.[2]

The Chiefs' Children's School was unique because for the first time *ali'i* children would be brought together in a group to be taught, ostensibly, about the ways of governance. Apart from this educational purpose, there was an equally, if not more, important political consideration. John I'i tells us what it was: "In conformance with Kīna'u's wish that the royal children be educated, a consultation was held to decide the best way to build a school for them. It was desirable that they remain together, thereby retaining the harmony among them and discouraging rebellion of one against another. Such things as rebellion and constant wars in the land were known in olden times, because, as William Richards taught, the children of the chiefs were reared apart."[3] In other words, the School was to act as another important unifying force among the ruling elite, instilling in their children common principles, attitudes, and values as well as a shared vision. This was of critical importance because the Kingdom was facing the constant threat of attack by more powerful foreign governments and interests. Only a unified leadership and a unified people could ensure the survival of the Kingdom. This fact would never be lost on the School's alumni when the reins of leadership were passed on to them.

Once the chiefs decided on the best way to proceed, things moved swiftly. Within two weeks, they had secured the cooperation of the missionaries (who had debated interminably about the School's financing and elitism), hired the missionary couple Amos Starr Cooke and his wife as principal instructors, located a temporary classroom, and enrolled six students. Apparently, the hasty startup did not allow time to develop a curriculum or to clarify the purposes of the School. This haste accounts for some of the subsequent confusion about the School's mission as seen by the missionaries, on the one hand, and the chiefs, on the other.

On the morning of June 13, 1839, Pauahi began her first day at school, along with her three brothers (Moses Kekūāiwa, Lot Kamehameha, and Alexander Liholiho); William Charles Lunalilo, the son of Kekāuluohi; and James Kaliokalani, the adopted son of High Chief 'Aikanaka. Over the next ten years, she would be joined by Victoria Kamāmalu, Emma Rooke, Lydia Kamaka'eha (Lili'uokalani), David Kalākaua, Peter Young Kaeo, Abigail Maheha, Jane Loeau, Elizabeth Kekaaniau, Polly Paaina, and John Pitt Kīna'u—all told, sixteen children. They ranged upon entry from age two to eleven, and differed widely in their temperaments and abilities, goals and destinies. But they all had one common bond: their genealogical sanctity and *mana* as ali'i-born. They did not represent all of the children of the ranking chiefs of the time, but from their ranks would come all of Hawai'i's kings and queens between 1855 and the fall of the monarchy in 1893. Pauahi was in august company.

The Cookes were not fully prepared for the opening day of school. Mr. Cooke wrote in his journal on June 13: "After I had been to meeting Bro. Judd came to me informing me that Kekuanaoa had come with the children and thought I had better have a school with them. I came home and found them here, six in number ... I sent for a desk ... and placed it here in my study and had the children seated. Kekuanaoa left and I kept the children about an hour."[4] Given less than two weeks notice and the unusual circumstances, perhaps no teacher could have been prepared. But in a real sense the Cookes were never completely prepared or, more precisely, qualified to do justice to the chiefs' hopes for the School and its pupils.

In the first place, the Cookes had no extensive experience in teaching either in Hawai'i or their native New England. Before arriving in Hawai'i in 1837, Mr. Cooke had worked as a bookkeeper and clerk in a general store. He had failed his entrance exams to study for the ministry at Yale. He had not taught a day. What experience he had was limited to on-the-job training as a teacher in the Congregational Mission's select schools in the Islands.[5] Mrs. Cooke had taught in a school for a nine-month period before her arrival. Neither had any special teacher training nor the command of specialized knowledge in any subject. In the second place, we can also say they were ill prepared because they had little understanding of *ali'i* ways and even less sympathy for them. In truth, their entire philosophical and theological background stood in fundamental opposition to the basic political and religious foundations of the *ali'i* system.

If the chiefs had applied the same standards traditionally used in engaging *kāhuna* for similar tasks, the Cookes would never have passed muster. Why did they select the Cookes? Why didn't they apply their usual standards of excellence? Why didn't they conduct a longer, more thorough search for the most qualified persons? Was it simply because they had no choice since good teachers were not available? These are questions of hindsight easier asked than answered. Whatever the reasons, in the end the choice may have come down to character. The Cookes exhibited qualities which the chiefs deemed necessary for the experimental venture: self-discipline, faith, stick-to-it-iveness, courage, practicality, and compassion, among others. Whatever their professional or cultural limitations, the Cookes certainly had the strength of character to see the School through to its end. Perhaps it is also these qualities that Pauahi admired most in them.

The Cookes were best prepared to teach the Gospel of Christ according to Congregationalism, and they wanted to convert people "until Christ be formed in them."[6] This was, after all, their sacred calling, the only thing that gave meaning to their lives in a "benighted" land, and the School was but a special means to fulfill that calling. They perceived the purpose of the School as being synonymous with their mission and they would ultimately measure their success in terms of Christian conversion rather than worldly scholarship. In short, the Cookes were interested in saving heathen souls; the chiefs were interested in saving their Kingdom on earth.

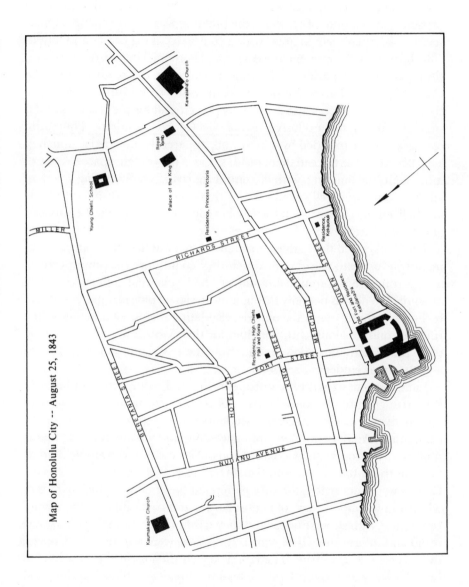

Map of Honolulu City -- August 25, 1843

The building that was to be Pauahi's school, as well as home-away-from-home, was completed within a year. Located at about the site of the present State Capitol of Hawai'i, the building was square-shaped, about seventy-six square feet in area, with a courtyard in the center and a well. The thirteen or so rooms included a large classroom, kitchen, dining room, sitting room and parlor, and living quarters for the students and the Cookes. Pauahi shared one of two rooms reserved for girls, each ten by sixteen feet. There was also a spacious playground for the students and a smaller one for the exclusive use of the Cookes' children. The entire complex was surrounded by a high wall, apparently intended as much to keep people out as to keep them in.[7] If the idea is to design space to control movement, the building, with its central courtyard commanding a view of all the rooms, was well suited to constant observation and supervision. It symbolized the regimen that the Cookes sought to impose on the students and their education.

The Cookes and their advisers sought to create at the school an environment conducive to learning in which they could have maximum control and permit the minimum amount of "bad" external influences. They attempted to do this not only through the design of physical space, but also by limiting contact with the outside, regulating the use of time, imposing rules of conduct along with penalties for their violation, and prescribing the types of activities allowed. This was the environment which Pauahi and the other students had to adapt to.

Limiting contact with the outside meant eliminating the troublesome *kahu*, reducing interaction with parents at home, curtailing relations with the "natives," in effect, keeping students away from distractions in the community. Among the "bad" influences, the students' army of attendants ranked at the top in the Cookes' minds. Alexander, for example, had as many as thirty *kahu* in tow, and Pauahi had several of her own. As far as the Cookes were concerned, the *kahu* pampered the children, satisfying every whim and whimper; they told ghost stories and contaminated their innocent minds with superstitions; and they tried to find as much fault as they could and inform the whole world. If the *kahu* were a trial to the Cookes, the reverse was also true. The *kahu* resented the loss of their traditional (and for some hereditary) role. This loss threatened their standing and livelihood, and they also feared, rightly, that the children would lose one of their most direct ties with the Hawaiian people and be further isolated. In the end, while the Cookes did not succeed in eliminating them, the *kahu's* presence was drastically reduced. This made the children more dependent on their mentors the Cookes and, at the same time, on each other.

Parents were allowed to visit the school as often as they wished. Konia and Pākī visited Pauahi and later Lydia Kamakaʻeha as well. Kekūanaōʻa, who was now Governor of Oʻahu, was also a frequent visitor. But the children were not permitted to visit their parents at home. They were "tabued," in Cooke's words, from leaving the school without permission, even when it was not in session. Of course, some of the students ignored the tabu and left the School's grounds for reasons of nocturnal dalliances, homesickness, and so on, as we will see.

In addition to parents, other aliʻi, foreign dignitaries, sea captains and ships' officers, and other guests were allowed to visit the School and its pupils. Toward the midpoint of the School's existence, there were many such visitors, including young haole men who eyed the fair princesses of the realm. The students also participated in the community at large, attending Sunday services at Kawaiahaʻo Church and making trips to other parts of Oʻahu and the Neighbor Islands. But, all in all, the students still led a fairly cloistered life within the School's white adobe walls.

To control the students, the Cookes regulated their time more strictly than it had ever been regulated before. The daily routine included awakening at 5:00 a.m., morning devotions at 6:30 followed by breakfast at 7:00, then class work from 9:00 to 12:00 when lunch was served. Another three hours of class work filled the afternoon. Supper was at 5:30 p.m., followed by evening prayers. The younger children went to bed at 7:00 and lights were out for everyone no later than 8:45 p.m.[8]

Occasionally, this timetable was suspended for special events, such as the opening of Parliament, the arrival or departure of a ship, the visit of the King, or a funeral. Despite many breaches by students and parents, the Cookes tried to abide by this schedule. The discipline of regularity and punctuality was an essential part of their psychology. The young chiefs were being taught to live by the clock, quite a deviation from the ways of their forefathers, who had no clocks and lived by their own measure of time.

Naturally, this new order came with a host of rules—the new kapu. Boys and girls were not to fraternize in each other's rooms. No one was to enter the kitchen or to fight. Each pupil was to eat three meals a day and no snacks in-between. Anyone late to dinner simply went without. Everyone had to respond immediately to the sound of the school bell. Everyone went to church twice on Sunday. No improper language was to be used. Lying, cheating, gambling, drinking, dancing, fornicating, and so on, were all summarily proscribed. The list of rules was long and grew longer as time went on.

In brief, the environment in which Pauahi and her peers were placed was one that no other group of Hawaiian *ali'i* had ever been subjected to before. The School represented a profound break with the past, ending centuries of tutorial tradition among the *ali'i*. Because it was an experiment never to be replicated, the School was not the start of a new tradition of chiefly education. But it tested its students' abilities to think and learn, and also their character, values and attitudes. As such, it was an environment fraught with risks for everyone involved, particularly for the students who were, in effect, the royal guinea pigs.

A Triumph of Adjustment

As in any environment, those who adjust well tend to do better. By adjustment we mean bringing one's thoughts and actions into harmony with the existing or changing conditions of the environment. Being well-adjusted does not necessarily imply a state of conformity nor a wholesale modification of the self. A person who, chameleon-like, changes his colors to suit every alteration in his surroundings, or who mindlessly surrenders a vital attribute or standard merely to accommodate something new, is probably maladjusted. In the Hawaiian ideal expressed in the word *lōkahi*, harmony implies not perfect equilibrium but a dynamic balance, a blending of opposites or differences. The person who achieves this also achieves a state of mind conducive to performing at his potential best. Achieving a dynamic balance requires the ability to assess and learn from one's environment, on the one hand; on the other, to know and understand one's essential self; and then to make the necessary adjustments — the harmonious blending.

Pauahi had this ability, the sense of *lōkahi*, which formed an important part of her character and thinking. At age eight she may not have been able to rationalize or articulate it, but she must have acted intuitively on that basis. This assumption fits the traditional Hawaiian theory of child psychology, that the average child reaches the age of accountability by seven or eight years, having sufficient understanding of herself and surroundings to take responsibility for her behavior. In any case, Pauahi exercised that ability, because the record shows that she consistently made appropriate adjustments throughout her stay at the school that enabled her to perform as well as, if not better than, most other students.

Take, for example, the new *kapu*, the host of rules instituted by the Cookes to regulate the students' behavior. Obviously, all the students had to adjust to these rules, with some difficulty, considering their somewhat overindulged upbringing and the nature of the rules themselves. Not surprisingly, the boys seem to have had the most problems. The three brothers, Moses, Lot and Alexander, broke the rules with regularity, if not impunity. They earned the dubious title of "nightwalkers" for spending so much time sneaking off at night to try drinking or smoking, or to hang around the dance halls. Moses and Lot committed even graver sins by visiting the girls in their rooms and getting into bed with them. The girls included Emma, Jane, Polly and Abigail, but no mention is ever made of Pauahi. Although such sexual behavior would have been tolerated in traditional Hawaiian society, the Cookes viewed it as a cardinal sin. Accordingly, they took the matter to the King and even made the culprits sign a "purity pledge." Still, Abigail left the school having to get married to a "scholar" from another school, and Moses was eventually dismissed, to the chagrin of his father, Kekūanaōʻa.

Pauahi did not entirely escape the snare of the rules. She was once caught laughing in church along with Moses, Lot, Alexander, Jane, and Abigail, and was "shut up." On another occasion she was part of a gang made up of Moses, Alexander, Peter, and Jane who "threw dirt into Mrs. Dowsett's yard and some went into the house and some struck her and fell into some bread she was making for breakfast."[9] At still another time the three brothers were caught eating "poi and fish" in Pauahi's room. She may have been guilty of other infractions, succumbing perhaps to the influence of Jane, her bosom friend, and her brothers. This would be understandable, for Pauahi, too, had to pass through her own "storm and stress" of adolescence.

The detailed chronicles of the Cookes provide no evidence that her transgressions were any worse than these minor lapses. We have, in fact, the assurance of Juliette Cooke that Pauahi was "seldom giving cause for any reproof" because she was "extremely prudent."[10] She never said this of any other student. Being prudent means having wisdom as "in the exercise of reason, forethought and self-control" or of having shrewdness as shown in "the skillful selection, adaptation and use of means to a desired end." To be prudent is to be practical, cautious, sensible; to be imprudent is to be impetuous, careless and unreasonable. Everything we know about Pauahi tells us she was prudent.

We should not confuse her extreme prudence with lack of courage to act or to take risks. On the contrary, the process of coping with the challenges posed by her compliance with the new *kapu* reinforced the sense of independence and courage which she had inherited or acquired from her Kamehameha forebearers, including Kīnaʻu. She exhibited enormous courage in choosing her future husband, when she faced the rejection of her parents and the royal establishment. She did not shy away from taking chances, but her risk-taking was always based on careful calculation of the consequences. The nature of the prudent person is to take only those risks over which she can have some meaningful control. Excessive caution and deliberateness, however, tend to smother spontaneity and creativity. Pauahi may perhaps have paid this price for her prudence, but we do not have any evidence to demonstrate that this was so.

One of the adjustments required of Pauahi and her peers was something no traditional Hawaiian would even have dared to think about. The Cookes wanted their students to think and act more like egalitarian democrats. They insisted, for example, that the young chiefs respect all older people, without regard for their social or genealogical status. While acceptable among the *maka'āinana*, this value was not for the *ali'i*. Hawaiian custom required that all *maka'āinana*, old and young, defer to all *ali'i*, including the young. Not age, but birth and rank determined the order of deference in the traditional aristocracy. The Cookes themselves treated all of their students alike, ignoring any distinctions in position among their young princes and princesses. They taught the students a new democratic philosophy to demonstrate the superiority of this behavior over the old native ways.

The Cookes, like the other missionaries, came from anti-royalist republican New England where individualism and the ideal of the dignity and equality of all people reigned supreme. They eschewed all notions of the "divine right of kings" and all nobility, rank and title, which were outlawed in the American Constitution. The principles of democracy, they supposed, were divinely based in the Bible, which declares that all people are the children of One God, a Heavenly Father who loves everyone equally.

What the Cookes were trying to do in their efforts to democratize Pauahi and her chiefly peers was to demythologize the *ali'i*, that is, to remove their sacredness. What distinguished chiefs from ordinary people was their *akua* status, which came from and was legitimized by the ancient *mo'olelo* or myths. If the sanctity of the *ali'i* were undermined, they would lose their mythical status. Whether or not the Cookes were fully conscious of what they were doing, the results were the same.

Perhaps, the most dramatic and painful portrayal of this desanctifying process can be seen in the punishment Mr. Cooke and his assistants administered to any wayward prince. Some examples: he struck David (Kalākaua) on the face in a public church service for making noise, and on another occasion whipped William, Kali, David and Alexander for "pumping," and William again for "impudence." Moses was the most frequent victim of Cooke's discipline, once receiving a severe lashing. Other types of punishment applied to the girls and boys included withholding food and keeping them locked up in their rooms or confined to a grass house in the school yard for several hours or even days.[11] But corporal punishment was the most demeaning because it violated the *kapu* nature of the physical body of an *ali'i*.

The royal victims of Cooke's corporal punishment understandably resented such treatment. Moses expressed their collective indignation when he said to Mr. Cooke, who had just struck Alexander on the head: *"He keiki a ke ali'i oia nei."* "He is the child of a chief."[12] Clearly, the message was that even if he deserved to be punished, it is wrong to strike a chief. Cooke's recorded reply betrayed his attitude: "I am king of the school." In fairness to the Cookes, we should remember that corporal punishment was quite respectable in American education then and for a long time after. The rod may have been the great equalizer for Mr. Cooke, but for the young chiefs it was more a prod for anger and rebellion.

Pauahi was probably an innocent but not an indifferent bystander to these happenings. Since she was close to the boys and a naturally empathetic person, she must have felt sorry for them. But, by the same token, she may have felt sorry for the Cookes too, since she trusted in their basically good intentions, however misguided some of their methods may have been. She must have also felt there was something *hewa* or seriously amiss with the act of physically abusing an *ali'i* child and may vicariously have shared in the physical and psychic hurt of the boys.

Of one thing we can be fairly certain: the democratizing process drove a wedge of doubts into her tightly structured *ali'i* belief system and forced her to ask questions. Some questions she might have asked herself: Were *ali'i* really the sacred heirs of a long line of *akua ali'i?* Did they possess such extraordinary *mana* as to make them truly sacred? Were they superior and everyone else inferior? Or was there something right and good about all people being equal? But even if so, how could everyone be equal? If questioning is the start of the process of intellectual change, Pauahi may have started that process here.

We need to keep in mind, however, that other factors may already have predisposed Pauahi toward that change. These factors include her prior exposure to Christian notions; the snippets of conversation she overheard from *kahu,* visitors, Kīna'u, John I'i, and others; the sermons of Hiram Bingham, Amos Starr Cooke, William Richards, and other missionary preachers; and, of course, her own ruminations about these and other life questions young people tend to ask. By this time Hawaiians had already been in the throes of westernization for at least fifty years, and of Christianization for more than twenty years. But it was the school—ten years of dancing to the same drumbeat—that forced Pauahi and her peers to make the adjustment, in part at least, to viewing their *ali'i* status as secular rather than sacred.

This was not an easy or quick process but rather only a gradual and bumpy transition, partly because of the inherent contradictions in the process itself. At the intellectual level, the contradiction that Pauahi had to resolve was this: How can you be a Hawaiian *ali'i* and not be sacred? What complicated matters further was the fact that she was also undergoing a conversion to Christianity. How can you believe in your own sacred origins, while at the same time accepting the idea of One God? The way Pauahi may have resolved this contradiction was to *lōkahi*, to blend the seeming opposites. Ultimately, it can be reasoned, the *mana* or god force of the Hawaiians and the Christian God are but manifestations of the same universal, immanent, transcendental divine power that energizes all things. When Hawaiians speak of *mana* as being available to everyone or when Christians speak about the divine spark in everyone, are they not pointing to the same force? The Supreme Reality is the same for all people; the differences and contradictions people may have are due to their different perceptions. As for Pauahi's own sacred nature, it was part of the universal *mana* made extraordinary by the continuous maintenance from generation to generation of genealogical, hence genetic, purity and of high performance and achievement. In other words, she inherited her sacredness as a gift from her royal ancestors and *'aumākua* (ancestral gods) but enhancements to it would come from her own work and accomplishments, through the use of her own talents. And conversely, her sacredness could be reduced by the abuse and misuse of her talents. As paradoxical as it might seem, the sacred nature of the *ali'i* was maintained through the exertions of their humanity — their ordinary, secular selves — in consistently extraordinary ways.

If Pauahi had resorted to *lōkahi*, to a blending of Hawaiian and Christian beliefs, then this raises a question about the nature of her Christian conversion in general and the depth of her theological commitment in particular. It was stated earlier that Pauahi was already an "embryonic Christian" by the time she entered the Royal School. While this statement is somewhat imprecise, we still can ask how much more of a Christian she became during the next ten years. One way to answer this question is to examine the religious training she encountered at the School.

The Royal School was not intended to be a religious seminary, but it had many of the same trappings. "Seek first the kingdom of God and his righteousness" was its injunction to its students. Religious combined with moral training took precedence over any other subject. As a matter of fact, religion, often in the guise of character building, permeated the textbooks on subjects such as geography, reading, spelling and history,[13] so that much of the students' secular curriculum was loaded with Christian messages. Like the Cookes, all of the assistant teachers were Christians. So was the highly respected John Papa I'i who served as the chief guardian or *kahu* assigned to the School by the chiefs. Sundays were set aside entirely for attending church services, and there were daily devotionals.

Pauahi gives us a good idea of how full of religious ceremony a Sunday could be. On July 21, 1844, she wrote in her journal: "Yesterday we went to church. Mr. Whitney preached. His text was in Luke 16:5. We went down to the chapel. Mr. Hunt preached. His text was in Matthew 10:21. We came home and ate our dinner. At two o'clock we went to church again. Mr. Armstrong preached. His [text] was in Ephesians 4:27. In the evening Mr. and Mrs. Cooke, Moses, Lot and Jane and I went down to the chapel. Mr. Pogue preached."[14] On this particular Sabbath Pauahi attended four services and heard four sermons given by four different preachers. (The sermons, particularly in the "native" meetings in the afternoon, were often given in Hawaiian.) She was diligent in attending church, but so were all the other students since they didn't have much say in the matter. Mr. Cooke wrote: "The habit of always attending church has become so fixed that they do not imagine that they can stay at home."[15]

Pauahi's attendance at church may not be a good measure of her faith, since the students' attendance was mandatory. Then too, attendance is only an outward manifestation and can often be more mechanical than meaningful. But we have no inkling that it was for her. Pauahi may not always have been as attentive as Mr. Cooke wanted, but she invariably recorded in her journal the scriptural theme of each sermon. She must have enjoyed the spiritual, ritual and social content of church, because she remained a church-goer for the rest of her life.

Prayer, both in the morning and evening, was another dominant feature of her religious life at school. Like church attendance, the morning prayer or devotional, at least, was required and failure to participate was penalized. Pauahi writes that one morning she along with a few others "missed breakfast" because they did not attend the "morning prayer." A few days later she says that Moses "did not ate [*sic*] breakfast since he was late at prayers."[16] On the surface, the Cookes' practice of penalizing the students for not praying does not seem to make sense. Forcing someone to pray would seem pointless since prayer is efficacious only when it is a voluntary act. But to the Cookes, who obviously understood the nature of prayer, the system was a part of a training regimen based on the assumption that people are creatures of habit.

Did Pauahi develop the habit of prayer? Her journal indicates that she did and, since prayer and church attendance seem compatible, we may assume that she carried the habit into her later years. Besides, this habit was also consistent with her overall spiritual character as a Hawaiian. Traditionally, prayerfulness was common to all classes of Hawaiians and occupied a prominent place in their intensely religious and ritualistic life. As Kamakau states, "*Ka po'e kahiko* [the people of old] prayed constantly— in the morning, at midday, in the evening, in the middle of the night."[17] So, being culturally conditioned to the value of prayer, Pauahi, along with her fellow students, did not have much difficulty in understanding its place in the Christian context. Of course, we will never know how she prayed or with what fervor.

Another dimension of Pauahi's religious training was her participation in the choir. Pauahi not only sang in the choir but she also led it. At a Sunday evening service held in the drawing room of the King's Palace, for example, we are told by Mrs. Judd: "The pupils of the Royal School attend and constitute a choir, as they have fine voices. One of the young ladies [Bernice] leads the singing with the melodeon."[18]

Interestingly, as Pauahi records in her journal, she also attended meetings of the Temperance League, which prohibited its members from drinking alcohol and from smoking tobacco. Prohibition was popular in the early 1840s as King Kamehameha III and many of the chiefs supported the temperance movement and its so-called "cold water army."[19]

Unfortunately, while church attendance, prayer, and other activities tell us something about Pauahi's outward devotion to Christianity, they do not reveal what was happening in her *na'au* (literally, intestines) or her heart. Did she allow herself to become, as the Cookes had hoped, a believer in whom "Christ is formed?" In the absence of Pauahi's own testimony, we must look at the judgment of the Cookes, and their verdict was no. Writing in August, 1844, Juliette Cooke stated: "The most discouraging feature of our labor is that *no one* [italics ours] of our scholars is seeking the right way. I am afraid that their high stations will cheat them yet of heaven. We have daily evidences that they are depraved — *totally depraved*."[20] In March, 1845, she wrote: "Our scholars are improving, they greatly need the

Spirit's influence. Oh if they were only Christians how it would cheer us on in our labors! ... They seem more like New England hardened hearers of the word. They pant for the pleasures of earth such as the civilized world choose as delightful. They would gladly if permitted attend the dancing school and join the balls which are more numerous here than anywhere in New England."[21] We should note that, while Pauahi is not mentioned specifically, she was very fond of dancing and after her marriage attended many a lively ball. A few months later, Mr. Cooke wrote: "Perhaps I ought not to make remarks about the people, for I am quite low-spirited this evening, in consequence of some mischief among our scholars. They are like 'a wild ass' colt' ... deceitful above all things and desperately wicked."[22] In November, 1847, he remarked in another letter to his mother: "Not one of our number [referring to the students] has yet been savingly benefited by our instruction."[23] And finally, in January 1848, Mrs. Cooke concluded: "There does not seem to be any peculiar solemnity in the minds of any our scholars."[24] Again, while these statements do not single out Pauahi, they do not exclude her either. She is lumped together with everybody else. As shown by this sampling covering several years, the Cookes' feelings follow a consistent pattern. A final judgment of Pauahi's religiosity came from Mr. Cooke, who on the eve of her marriage observed: "Miss B. is not pious but has other qualifications for a good wife."[25]

In sum, by the time she left the school, Pauahi had largely formed her Christian commitment. She was deeply spiritual, but not fanatical; a believer in the wisdom of the church, but not a doctrinaire fundamentalist; a woman of faith, but not of blind, unquestioning, and unreasoning conformity. She seems to have reserved enough space in her world-view for those things in her traditional Hawaiian belief system that she deemed of abiding importance. One of those things was her belief in her identity as an ali'i-born with the obligation of honoring and perpetuating the name and glory of her forebearers. If Pauahi had a Christian commitment, she had no less a commitment to her destiny as an ali'i, with all of its mythological implications. Those two commitments existed side by side as long as she lived.

The Stance of a Scholar

Pauahi and her peers also had to adjust to being "scholars," as they were then called. Certainly, the students adjusted more easily and successfully to being scholars than to being paragons of Christian morality and faith. Indeed, if one examines closely the overall accomplishment of the Royal School, what stands out is the amount of learning that took place and the

effort that the students put into the process. We see this in the results: The
students on the whole developed a remarkable command of English, a
more than passing acquaintance with a wide variety of subjects, and a level
of sophistication about the world and people that seemed to transcend
their limited education.

The factors that determine academic achievement are myriad and
complex, but one of the most important is the attitudes and traditions
about learning that the students bring to the task. If they bring a long,
firmly embedded tradition of reverence for knowledge — with clear
rewards for achievement and equally clear sanctions for lack of achievement, and the encouragement of family and the community—the chances
are much better that students will be more highly motivated and perform
to higher standards. To be sure, students must have some natural ability
and adequate teachers, facilities, books, and equipment. But in the end,
the personal and communal values about learning that students bring to
the classroom make all the difference.

Pauahi and her classmates brought to the royal classroom a set of
attitudes and traditions that enshrined the value of learning and conditioned them to do well. The traditional value of learning derived from the
Hawaiian philosophy holds that knowledge is essentially sacred. Knowledge is sacred because it makes life possible, and life is a manifestation of
mana. If knowledge is sacred, then the process of learning is also sacred. So
are those who teach, which is why the teacher who had mastered his
subject and craft was honored and respected. Accordingly, the place where
teaching and learning take place is sacred, too, which is why the site of a
hālau (or school) was always consecrated. The "school" thus becomes a
"temple of learning," watched over by the gods who are the keepers of
knowledge and the ancestral spirits (*'aumākua*) who help and guide the
participants and the process. It should now be clear why traditional
Hawaiians equated knowledge with power — *mana*.

Another important dimension of the traditional attitude toward education or any other field of endeavor was what Mary Kawena Pūku'i calls
"achieved perfection."[26] That is to say, the standards of achievement were
so high that anything less than perfection was unacceptable. Perfection did
not mean measuring up to impossible standards, for the Hawaiian was too
practical to have such a foolish expectation. Rather, it meant achieving
what one sets out to do, being able to perform without any mistakes when
measured against predetermined standards. What is significant about this
attitude is the psychology underlying it. If a person knows that only a
flawless performance or product will be acceptable, then he will strive to

perform at a high level, perhaps, surpassing his own apparent limitations in the process. In other words, if a person believes he can be perfect, he will rise to the level of his self-perception. Conversely, if he assumes that he is flawed and imperfect, his performance will more than likely reflect that self-image. To use a modern illustration, if a student is taught to accept a "C" grade, it is not likely that he will expect much more of himself. The same psychology also acts as a great spur to the person striving for perfection, since he knows that perfection will only be achieved through hard, constant, accurate work. The traditional Hawaiian attitude toward "achieved perfection" allowed a margin of error for the student or apprentice in the process of learning. However, once the student achieved a status anywhere near being a *kumu* or master, making a mistake was fraught with dire consequences, including, in some cases, death. So, while the rewards of added *mana* and stature were clear, so were the penalties of loss of *mana:* prestige and even life itself.

While the young students may not have had a complete knowledge of this vital part of their traditional culture, their parents and some of their *kahu* could still remember or have an understanding and appreciation of it. Even when individual memories dim, the collective memory of the community tends to linger on. In the 1830s, memory of the traditional past was still alive. The value attached to learning was certainly evident in the great literacy movement of the twenties when Hawaiians flocked to the schools. To repeat Kamakau's observation: "educated people were like chiefs ... because the chiefs treated them as chiefs." In effect, Kamakau equates an educated person with a chief, even if the person is a commoner, showing the value placed on the *mana* of those who were educated.

In short, the young student chiefs were heirs to centuries of tradition and values that elevated knowledge, its acquisition and use, to a pedestal of life-giving importance. They must have been told in one way or another by their parents, family and *kahu* that they were expected to perform, to live up to their family names and their past. The eyes of their people were upon them for in their hands rested the fate of the nation. Given these high expectations, and the influence of ages past confirming the importance of education, it is not surprising that the students did as well as they did.

In trying to assess the performance of the students, Mr. Cooke, writing in a letter dated April 8, 1843, states: "In summing up what our scholars had done during the past year, I was surprised at their advancement. I cannot account for it but in the fact of their constant attendance at school."[27] He seems to have overlooked the intangible at work — the motivation embodied in an age-old set of attitudes and traditions about learning. Besides, the students' advancement may have been due in part to the sheer excitement of learning and the desire to satisfy their natural, and in Pauahi's case very large, curiosity.

Apparently, the Cookes did not issue report cards on Pauahi or any other students, so we must rely on other means of assessing her performance. There is one aspect of her academic work which can be evaluated even after 150 years and from which we can get an indication of her abilities. That is her writing. Happily, we have samples taken from her journal and school reports between 1843 and 1849 which we can compare and analyze to show how she developed into a competent writer.

But first, we need to recognize the magnitude of the challenge she faced in learning how to write. To begin with, writing is the most difficult of the four basic communication skills (the others being speaking, listening and reading) needed in order to function in a literate society. Even today, many students in our schools have great trouble mastering it. For Pauahi, the task was made doubly difficult because she had to learn to write in a foreign language, English, while learning how to read and speak it at the same time. English and Hawaiian are vastly different languages: the word order in Hawaiian is verb-subject-object, while in English it is subject-verb-object. There is no tense as such in Hawaiian, while there are three basic tenses plus their variations in English. In English verbs are inflected, but there are no inflections in Hawaiian. And so on and so forth. So for Pauahi learning English was truly a matter of learning an alien tongue.

Writing was not a part of Hawaiian culture, which was based purely on oral tradition. Hawaiians relied on the spoken word. In fact, the spoken word was invested with a power or *mana* of its own. When writing was introduced to Hawai'i, not long before the opening of the Royal School, it represented a new mode of communication and required a new way of thinking. The *mana* of the spoken word, for example, now had to be related somehow to the magic of the *palapala* or written word. Pauahi and her cohorts were pioneers, the first generation of *ali'i* children ever to be taught (and eventually to master) writing and thinking in a new and complex system of symbols. In a literate culture, it is a small step for students to go from speaking to writing, but in an oral culture it is a giant leap.

The earliest examples of Pauahi's writing in English are dated from January 1843 and are found in a journal which she was required to keep as part of her "writing school" (the journal was regularly submitted to the Cookes for correcting). Since she had already been in school for three and a half years, we can assume that she had learned some of the rudiments of writing well before the beginning of 1843. But, as the excerpts cited below indicate, she was still learning the mysteries of English orthography, punctuation, syntax, tenses and so on.

January 11, 1843

This morning I did not write my journal on the book because it is to late to write and so we had a writing school. We had a school as usal we did not got our lesson in arithmetic and this afternoon in geography we have not recied grammar. After prayer we went out to esercis...

January 12, 1843

After dinner Abigail William & I went to play in the carpenter hous we told William to go and get all his find handerchief and the bell rung for school. This noon we studied about Greece and is was very inderesting. While we were at prayers governer call on us when he was gone back we play and make a loud noise then, Mrs. Cooke came out and we asked to go round the circle.

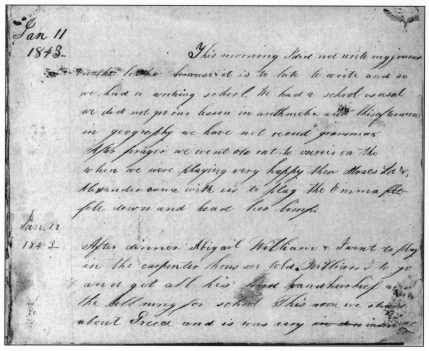

Pauahi's diary entries of January 11th and 12th, 1843, when she was eleven.
Courtesy of Bishop Museum

February 3, 1843

... We saw a crazy man sitting on the groung he was making wry
faces and laughing he new not what. We look ated and heard his bad
words some of us were vexed with him but he was poor man who lost
his reason and we aught to beer thankful that we are not crazy like
him....

The obvious faults are in spelling, punctuation and grammar. Spelling
must have been especially difficult because English sometimes seems to
defy all the rules of logic. If "ought" and "aught" can be pronounced the
same, why should one spelling be correct and the other not? Her problem
with punctuation is understandable since, as a Hawaiian, Pauahi was
unfamiliar with periods, semicolons, and exclamation marks. (Punctuation is not used in many written languages even today.) Nonetheless, she
had already learned a lot about writing, having mastered word order and
progressed beyond the elementary stage of simple sentence structure. She
also had a working understanding of tense, but not of such aspects as the
subjunctive mood, as evidenced by the fact that "if" clauses rarely, if ever,
appear in this part of her journal.

A year and a half later, however, Pauahi had made real progress, being
able to handle complex sentences with ease, use much more punctuation,
and make fewer spelling errors. To illustrate:

June 18, 1844

It is now three years since we had an examination. And the king
and most of the chiefs were present. Gov. Kekuanaoa prepared a feast
for us at the Primiers [*sic*] grass house. Capt Hudson was present at
the feast. This morning we thought of going down to Mrs. Calkin, but
she came up here before our breakfast time. She gave us the Kendall
March for our lessons ...

(The "examination" does not refer to a test, but rather a public presentation before invited guests of the skills the students have acquired in
reading, arithmetic, music and so on.)

August 5, 1844

Last Tuesday the King and chiefs arrived from Maui. Wednesday
was the 31st of July. It was the anniversary day of the Restoration of
Island, by Adimaral Thomas. About 10 o'clock there was a Temperance meeting for adults. At 3 o'clock we went to the feast ...
Thursday there was a Temperance meeting for children. We
marched about the street. The King & Queen & the Primier and
other chiefs also marched with us. We came to the meeting house.

Afterwards we sung the tune Temperance Glee. Jane played on the piano. We had a feast three days.

It was on July 31, 1843, that Admiral Thomas put an end to the five-month rule of the islands by Lord George Paulet, a commander of a British vessel, and returned independence to a grateful Hawaiian people. The magnitude of the feasting suggests the joy of the Hawaiians.

A year later, May 1845, we can see further improvement in Pauahi's writing, but, just as important, we can also observe the development of her intellectual abilities. She demonstrates, for instance, a real capacity for organizing a large amount of information and for synthesizing and presenting it in a coherent manner. The best example showing this capacity is an impressive report, of more than 10,000 words, written from notes taken during a series of lectures given by William Richards and Timothy Haalilio. The two men spoke about their experiences in the United States and Europe in 1842 when they sought recognition of Hawai'i's sovereignty from the "big powers" or major nations. The report covers a wide range of subjects and incidents, some quite complex both in their nature and in their telling. Pauahi's writing reveals her keen attention to detail, sense of humor (invariably understated) and curiosity.

Of an episode when Haalilio and Richards were observing a religious procession in Xalapa, Mexico, Pauahi wrote:

> As the possession [sic] passed by them the Englishmen and Frenchmen kneeled down & took off there hats. One of them pinched Haalilio to make him kneel down but he did not. But he stepped a little back with Mr. Richards. Afterwards they went into the house & one of the gentlemen asked Haalilio how they did at the Sandwich Island, and he said to them "We no meedle with any body that behave well," Then they all clapped their hands...

She also described an ugly incident that occurred on board the steamboat *Globe*, while the pair were on their way to New Haven, Connecticut:

> Before they sat down to breakfast Mr. Richards went to the office window to procure two tickets for breakfast. But the Captain's secretary gave him 1½. He returned the half tickets and requested two. The man told to give the half to Haalilio (his servant). Mr. Richards said to him "he is not my servant, I am his, He is an ambassador from the King of the S.I. to the President of the U.S. & has been received as such." "That does not make any difference" said the man "we do not wish any colored man to sit down at the table."

Keenly aware of the political importance of the mission, Pauahi related such matters as the following:

On Monday morning they sailed for England at 8 o'clock and landed at Dover. That was the first time their passports were examined in England and Sir George Simpson [who was traveling with Richards and Haalilio] was very much annoyed. They took a railroad and went to London. They first called on Mr. Addington and he told them to write an official letter to Lord Aberdeen. And they also told Lord Aberdeen that M. Guizot said that he had no objection to acknowledging the independence of the Hawaiian Islands. They then called on the most distinguished lawyers in London to get their opinion on various subjects of dispute at the Sandwich Island....

In a slightly different type of assignment, a short essay on electricity, she showed writing that was nearly perfect. She also demonstrated that she could deal confidently with quite abstract and highly technical subjects. She wrote:

Electricity was discovered by Belsey of Prussia about the beginning of the eighteenth century. He found by rubbing a piece of amber that it would attrect light substance and he called this attrective power electricity ... Last evening Mr. Douglass brought his electrical machine into this room and he gave us a lecture about it ... He said that substances that conduct the electric fluid *rapidly* are called good-conductor. Substances that *do not* conduct the electric fluid rapidly are called non-conductors.... Conductors is a substance which conducts electric fluid. All metals are good-conductors also the bodies of animals, all moist substances—the air is a good conductor. Dry silks are non-conductors & also substances & dry woods. We also tried experiments....

In the summer of 1846, Pauahi, along with eleven other students, accompanied by Mr. Cooke, John Iʻi, Dr. Thomas Rooke and his wife, visited the islands of Hawaiʻi, Maui and Molokaʻi. She described this experience in a fairly lengthy day-by-day account. As the account has been published and is readily available,[28] only a few brief passages are cited to show her rapid mastery of the art of writing. The following describes her descent into the crater at Kīlauea:

July 2, 1846

The next day, Thursday, we all went down into the crater, servants an all. We were about 50 in number. We were very much fatigued, at least I was. I was disappointed some with the appearance, because it looked very different from what I had seen in pictures. The lake was the most wonderful part that I saw ... The lake was not in a very vigorous state of action. In some places we saw the fire boiling, but not on a very grand scale, as it did some few years ago. A little way, from the lake, there was a furnance of a fire. The fire was very hot indeed. The smell of the sulphar was very unpleasant to us, as we were walking in some part of the crater. There were a great many fissures. In some of them I could not see the bottom it was so deep and smoke came out of them. Near the edge of the lake there was some Pele's hair. As we were going along we looked for some specimens. About 2 o'clock we ate our dinner in the crater near the spot from where we had started in the morning....

The report is filled with similar descriptions, all in some detail, with sequences of activities and times carefully delineated. Such daily reporting requires a retentive, well-ordered mind. The writer also has to be very observant and discriminating in order to paint the best possible picture with words. In addition, as anyone who has kept a daily journal knows, this kind of writing demands discipline, since you must stop and record the events of the day consistently and faithfully. Pauahi traveled by boat (which made her seasick) and by horse (e.g., she and her party rode horseback some 35 miles from the town of Hilo to the crater), so it would have been natural to get tired and to put off writing. But in spite of her weariness, which she mentioned often, she persisted and finished the report.

Pauahi showed a flair for descriptive writing in such passages as: (On the way to Haleakala, Maui) "There were a great many Alpine plants on the mount that resembled sheep lying down." Another passage reads: "There were two roads leading to Lahaina, one was long & bad, and the other was short, yet *very* bad." Or: "Kealakekua is a very stony place and very few trees excepting coacoanut trees which grow near the sea shore." In another passage telling of the generous welcome she received from the Green family in Makawao on the island of Maui, she writes: "They received us very politely...and seemed to be very much pleased to see us. Their heart was larger than their house."

In 1846 Pauahi was fourteen years of age and had already proven her prowess in writing. Perhaps, the crowning affirmation of this achievement came when Mrs. Cooke allowed Pauahi to write some letters for her to her family on the Mainland. One such letter dated November 2, 1847 reads:

Dear Miss Montague:

There is a ship to sail for the United States to-morrow, and your sister, Mrs. Cooke, has given me permission to write to you, being unable to do so herself, owing to cares, etc. It is with great pleasure that I avail myself of this opportunity to commence a correspondence with you. Your sister has so frequent and full letters that I feel confident that I shall have an answer — quite as much so as the milkmaid did of her green dress.

I hardly know how to write to you, but I suppose that if I write anything about Mrs. Cooke and her family it will not come amiss. Mr. Cooke has been confined to his room with an abscess on his knee accompanied with fever and headache so that he has not been able to teach school as usual. He is better now, but not entirely recovered. He has just come in limping from school, is reclining on the sofa near me. He looks as if he had been sick for a fortnight. Boils have been common for the last few months and everybody had them. Mrs. Cooke is about starting for Punahou with Alexander for a beau. We have a very gentle horse and sometimes he comes into the court, and did we not shut the doors he would enter into some of our rooms. On one occasion he passed through the sitting room into the yeard occupied by our teacher....

(Pauahi goes on for another paragraph, but Mrs. Cooke finished the letter because, as she explains, "She has written in haste — the bell has rung and she has gone to school so I close it.")

There is almost no comparison between her earlier writings of 1843 and this letter of 1847. Pauahi could now write almost flawlessly and effortlessly. In a matter of eight years, she had learned a skill that few Hawaiians, particularly ali'i, had ever mastered. Though she may have been gifted linguistically, it was still a major accomplishment and a testimony to her motivation, discipline and intellect.

If Pauahi was adept at writing, she was equally adept at reading. Mr. Cooke comments in a letter dated September 18, 1847: "J—[Mrs. Cooke] succeeds in getting some of the scholars to read to her about two hours daily, *especially Bernice who has become a very good reader.*"[29] (italics ours) About the same time, Mrs. Cooke echoed her husband's judgment when she wrote: "She [Pauahi] reads to me every day an hour. She is now reading 'Coelebs in Search of a Wife.' She has just finished the History of Egypt — is very fond of reading...."[30] In recognition of her fondness for books as well as her sense of responsibility, Mr. Cooke appointed Pauahi librarian.[31]

It should be noted that all of the students were "fond of reading" and that as a result they wasted "little of their time."[32] The students read a variety of material, all in English, of varying degrees of difficulty, none written especially for them. That is to say, the texts were standard ones used in English or American schools. At the lower end of the scale, the books included *Parley's History,* Part I, *Webster Spelling Book,* the *Worchester*

Readers, *Mitchell's Geography*, and the *Rollo* books, a series based on the exploits of a nine-year-old boy. At the upper end, the older students read *Olmstead's Rudiments of Natural Philosophy and Astronomy*, *Gallaudet's Youth Theology*, and *Olney's Geography*. The Bible was, of course, required reading. They read or were read to widely, in subjects ranging from history[33] to botany, algebra, geometry and "moral science." The Cookes suggest that the students would have read more, but there was always a lack of suitable books.

Besides writing and reading English, Pauahi also became fluent in speaking English. From her first days in school she had to set aside the language of her childhood for English. All instruction at the school was conducted in English. So much stress was placed on English that by 1843 Mr. Cooke could report that the students spoke it predominantly, even among themselves in everyday exchanges. He wrote:

> ...All their studies have been and are still in the English language. Hitherto they would have learned more if their studies had been pursued in native, but from this time forward they will learn a great deal faster for having the English language. They now use very little native even among themselves in common conversation.[34]

But Pauahi and her cohorts had not abandoned the Hawaiian language. They continued to speak and to be spoken to in Hawaiian by their *kahu*, their parents, family, relatives and other such visitors. These conversations in Hawaiian occurred often enough, in spite of the Cookes' attempts to insulate the students from the Hawaiian community. Pauahi herself told of an amusing incident in which she spoke in "native" one evening to a ship's captain visiting with the Cookes:

> Tuesday, November 14, 1843
>
> That captain is not intoxicate(d) ... and he made us funny and I think he do not know what he is talking about. And he taught us in French Spanish and Chillian [Chilean] languish [*sic*] and we do not understand so Mrs. Hooper told us that we might talk in native languish so we did and he could not understand us and we all laugh....

Actually, the Cookes did not entirely forbid the use of Hawaiian. Even they themselves slipped in a word or even a sentence or two of Hawaiian now and then, because both were fluent in the language, particularly Mrs. Cooke. Mr. Cooke was fluent enough to give sermons in Hawaiian and to write articles for the missionary paper, *Ka 'Elele Hawai'i*. In fact, he even had some of the students translate articles from English into Hawaiian for the paper. He wrote on June 12, 1848, "This morning I gave some pieces

in the Penny Gazette to Lot, Alexander, William & Bernice to translate for
the *'Elele Hawaii*." Like other missionaries, the Cookes wanted to preserve
the language which they rightly viewed as an integral part of the preservation of Hawaiian sovereignty.

By now Pauahi was truly bilingual, enjoying the benefits that only the
mastery of languages can bring. Hawaiian was the language of her sacred
past preserved in the *mele* (chants) of her culture, and of her people. But
English was the language of the world beyond, of commerce, government,
religion, and scholarship. It opened the windows of her universe to
science and technology; Euclid and Newton; the great civilizations of
Egypt, Greece, Rome and China; the geography of the earth and the
cosmos; and so on. For Pauahi and her fellow students knowledge of
English was like a magic key that unlocked the door to otherwise inaccessi-
ble treasures and pleasures.

The power of language—the Hawaiian understood this very well. For it
is out of the symbols we use that the world is made and is known. Pauahi
understood this, too, as she understood the *mana* of knowledge and those
who possess it, the standards of achievement and diligence that her
traditions exemplified—and that she demonstrated.

The Eclectic Personna

Pauahi was not only a bright and serious student; she had multiple
talents and a wide range of extracurricular interests. Mrs. Cooke extolled
her virtues: "She is a most lovely girl — lovely in feature, form, and
disposition—plays and sings well, paints prettily, works worsted, makes
her own dresses, is now studying chemistry and Euclid."[35] She might have
added that Pauahi played the piano and accordion, led the singing, rode
horses, cooked and baked, and kept house — not everybody's image of
what a princess is supposed to do, but one consistent with Mrs. Cooke's
image of the ideal woman. Since these activities formed such an important
part of her character and life, we turn our attention to them.

Like so many Hawaiians — *ali'i* and *maka'āinana* — Pauahi had a
musical soul. When, where or how it was first stirred — whether by the
traditional sounds and rhythms or by the melodies and harmonies of the
hīmeni or new Christian hymns — we shall never know, but her love of
music blossomed during her years at the Royal School. Her Western music
education most likely began with her learning to sing songs familiar to the
Cookes, either hymns or secular melodies and ditties. While much of this
activity took place at the School, some of it also took place in the singing
school at the nearby chapel. Singing schools were a popular institution

established by Hiram Bingham and other missionaries in the 1820s, and scores of them were scattered throughout the islands. Most, if not all, of the singing schools were attended by Hawaiians, and the hymnals used were printed in Hawaiian (such as the *Hīmeni Kamali'i* or "Hymns for Young People").[36] Pauahi and the other older students probably sang mostly in Hawaiian rather than English. The students went to the singing school for most of the time they were enrolled in the Royal School.[37]

Pauahi and the other students reportedly had fine voices and as a group sang "excellently." They often entertained themselves, as well as visitors to the school, by singing. Occasionally, they also performed for the King and his court, for example, as mentioned earlier when Pauahi led and accompanied the group with the melodeon. Pauahi also enjoyed listening to good singing, and even enjoyed listening, as she put it, to the "beautiful voices" of the birds in Nu'uanu.

She may have been a better pianist than a singer. She appears to have started taking piano lessons sometime prior to 1841, studying with Mrs. Hooper for several years. According to Pauahi's journal, she and Jane, her roommate and "bosom" friend, would go to Mrs. Hooper's before school began in the morning (or sometimes in the afternoon) for one or several hours at a time. They once stayed so long that, when they returned late to school, Mr. Cooke was "very much displeas(ed) with us."[38] She seemed to be as diligent about the piano as she was about her studies, practicing in the parlor on the School's instrument sometimes as many as "five times a day."[39] She played for her parents, but more often for guests, including once for sea Captain John Clavell who heard "Yankeed Doodale" and "God Save the King."[40] By 1846, she was good enough to surprise a visiting pianist from Germany. Amos Cooke relates the event: "This evening a celebrated German pianist called ... Miss Bernice played some and the German expressed great surprise at her skill." He was also impressed with the way she handled the "Aeolian attachment" (a contrivance attached to a piano to prolong and increase the volume of sound by forcing a stream of air upon the strings).[41] Before too long, she was teaching piano to the younger students at the school.

Characteristically, she seemed to delight in listening to others play, but with a discriminating ear. She was impressed with the playing of Mrs. Calkin, for a short time a teacher of hers, and two visiting "Danish gentlemen." One time she even heard a private performance by Admiral Thomas himself. She neglected to record her reaction, although she added that when he asked her to play a tune, "I ran away."[42]

Pauahi also learned to play the accordion, and she started taking lessons in 1844 from a Dr. Smith.[43] Given her eclectic tastes, she may have taken up other instruments such as the guitar or flute, both of which were quite popular in Hawai'i at the time. (Moses was quite an exceptional flutist.) We do not know whether she learned to use or perform on the *pahu* (drum), *ipu* (gourd drum) or other traditional Hawaiian instruments, but she would not have had much encouragement or opportunity to do so during her years under the Cookes. Such instruments were intimately associated with the *hula* which the Cookes and other missionaries had consigned to a cultural purgatory.

Unlike her sister Lydia or Lili'u, who was younger by several years, Pauahi did not seem to show any bent for composing music. She could sight-read when playing the piano and teach the basics, but, so far as we know, she neither composed nor arranged music. In contrast, Lili'u had near perfect pitch and led the students by singing the notes. She wrote, "To compose was as natural to me as to breathe...."[44] It may be that since Lili'u along with her natural siblings, David Kalākaua, Leleiōhoku, and Likelike, were all distinguished composers, the talent of composing songs was distributed more generously among the members of the Kalākaua dynasty than that of the Kamehamehas. Be that as it may, Pauahi had other gifts to leave her people.

Was Pauahi also a budding artist? Mrs. Cooke, her art teacher, commented that she "painted prettily," something she said of no other student. Since drawing was a part of the curriculum and an activity that Pauahi mentioned frequently in her journal, she no doubt learned the rudiments of art. While Mrs. Cooke was not an artist herself, she taught well enough to convey the basic skills and, even more importantly, to increase her student's awareness, perception and sensitivity. Pauahi seems to have had some natural talent, because without it no amount of teaching could have enabled her to paint "prettily." Mrs. Cooke seems to have meant that Pauahi was aware and sensitive enough to see more than the surface beauty of an object and to express its essence on canvas with charm and grace. The term suggests dexterity and delicate care rather than the imposing strength and force which come from years of maturity and experience. If she had continued painting into her married life, as she did music, Pauahi might have blossomed as an artist. She undoubtedly began to cultivate her longlasting appreciation for European art here at the school.

Pauahi's enjoyment of piano playing and painting, which are Western forms of art, should not be taken to mean that she did not appreciate traditional Hawaiian art forms. But she was at the Royal School to learn how to appreciate the things of the West; she did not need to go to school to learn how to appreciate the art of her own culture. Appreciation of traditional art could not be separated from her being as an *ali'i*. As we shall see, she was to inherit traditional art of the highest quality, created by the most skillful of Hawaiian artists and craftsmen, objects not only of artistic but sacred beauty. She would cherish and protect these objects which would eventually form the nucleus of the collection at the Bishop Museum, established in her name and honor. Her appreciation of Western art did not lessen appreciation of her own art. Perhaps an understanding of both made her aware of the universality of the principles of what is fine and beautiful, whatever the particular form.

Pauahi did more than play the piano, sing for royal audiences or paint "prettily." She also cleaned and tidied the premises and washed and sewed her own clothes. On July 24, 1844, for example, she recorded, "After breakfast Jane and I went out in Mrs. Cooke's yard to wash our dresses."[45] On another day she wrote, "I cleanse the parlor and we move the piano on the other side of the room." On still another occasion she stated, "Girls spend most of the afternoon in sewing." And again, "After dinner I went in my room to sew my dress."[46] She also learned how to cook because the Cookes tell us that on December 5, 1846, she baked a "Christmas cake."

At first glance, the picture of a princess occupied in domestic chores may seem a bit incongruous — a Cinderella in reverse. In ordinary circumstances, a chiefess would not deign to wash her own garments, clean house, or do other seemingly menial chores. Her *kahu* would have attended to such matters. Yet Pauahi as well as the other student princesses consented to learn and then do these tasks not for a day but for years. And do them willingly. There is no hint of complaining in Pauahi's journal.

To begin with, these were obviously not ordinary circumstances. Within its walls the Royal School had a life and rhythm of its own. It was life patterned after many of the customs and values of the Cookes. They did not come from aristocratic backgrounds where maids might have done the chores. Washing clothes, sweeping the floors, sewing a dress or shirt, cooking, baking, and so on, were tasks they had done themselves as an essential part of self-reliant lives. Such tasks were neither menial nor demeaning. In fact they were socially acceptable, economically necessary, and, perhaps even more important, morally right, for in the Calvinist ethic of New England, there is dignity in all work. This ethic trumpeted the virtue of work, hard work, self-reliance, dignity and equality, all principles that the Cookes wanted to impart.

Neither Pauahi, her fellow students nor their *ali'i* parents took offense at these values. Contrary to what some of the missionaries and other *haole* observers said about the work habits of Hawaiians at the time, hard work, self-reliance, dignity, discipline and the like were always important elements of the traditional value system. No civilization as sophisticated and complex as Hawaiian society could have been created and maintained without such a system. The problem of the Hawaiians was not their values but the changing cultural and technological context. Pauahi was not afraid of manual work. She could easily have had her *kahu* do her sewing. Instead, as she described the scene in her journal, she and Jane one morning after breakfast cut the sleeves of her green silk dress, then carried the dress and other materials to "my servants" and stayed there to sew all day. Later she wrote, "This noon we went to our servants place for my pattern sleeves [*sic*]," and there she and Jane continued the work.[47] The same willingness to work seems to be shown in everything else she either wanted or had to do.

Another reason Pauahi and the others seemed so ready to follow the Cookes' lead was that the sewing, the cleaning, the washing, and so on, came with the technology of the West. That is, these seemingly menial chores provided an education in understanding, utilizing and maintaining a new material culture in the form of new fabrics, utensils, foods and their preparation, furniture, machinery, amusements, building materials, frame housing, and so on. For example, there would be no point in having a Western-style house if you did not know how to care for and keep it. The same would apply to clothes or furniture or a piano. By the 1850s Honolulu was becoming an international port and a technological enclave of the West. New things and ideas were constantly being introduced, and they had to be learned about and adapted to the Hawaiian setting. Who better to know about this new world than its future leaders? Traditionally it was the *ali'i*, more often than not, who approved or initiated technological change, a role epitomized by Kamehameha I. In short, Pauahi's attitude to these so-called chores was that they were new learning experiences, hence exciting, useful and self-rewarding. This view helps to explain her uncomplaining, good-natured approach to such tasks.

Finally, there is the obvious reason for Pauahi's acceptance and acquisition of these practical skills. It is that they represented the values and practices of being a model wife and mother. Mrs. Cooke was her model. She sewed, washed, cleaned, cooked, baked, taught school, nursed and raised her own children, and countless other tasks — and did all of this while still managing to maintain her composure and some semblance of her sanity under some trying conditions. After ten years of living with Mrs. Cooke, being brought into her confidence and being the object of her special care, Pauahi had developed profound respect and affection for her. Mrs. Cooke was worth emulating in many ways, not the least of which was knowing how to keep a proper home.

If there is a need to develop the mind and spirit, there is no less a need to develop the body. The Cookes clearly subscribed to this dictum, as physical exercise, besides a wholesome diet, formed an integral part of their program. The exercises included, in Cooke's words, "riding in the wagon, on horse back, walking early in the morning and just at evening, playing ball, rolling hoops, bathing and swimming weekly and innocent plays to keep them from sleeping during the day."[48] At one point Mr. Cooke bragged that the students had never exercised so much until they came to the school.[49] He expressed special pride in the fact that the regimen had helped to keep his charges healthy, which was perhaps justified because in spite of the spiraling death rate of Hawaiians none of the students died while at the School. Pauahi, for example, enjoyed good health throughout except for one brief illness.

This emphasis on physical development and Pauahi's own natural vigor and stamina help to account for the energetic life she led. In one of her earliest journal entries she lets us know that she and her companions "played hard" until it hurt.[50] She seems to have played hard, sometimes to the discomfort of the Cookes, at everything from "sissors" and swings to kite-flying. One afternoon, for example, she tells of making a kite for the Cookes' children and then going out to fly it.[51] Since kites were popular with the Hawaiians long before the arrival of the missionaries, Pauahi probably learned how to make and fly the *lupe* at home, as did Lot and the other children who also enjoyed the sport.

Of all the physical activities she seems to have spent the most time horseback riding and presumably enjoyed this most. She wrote, "We arose early this morning and went to ride as usual."[52] "As usual" meant several times a month, and sometimes consecutive days in a week, throughout a great part of her sojourn at the school. She invariably wore a riding dress, always with a bonnet, and rode sidesaddle, and she may have well had her own horse or at least several to chose from. The shorter rides took her to the house of the king or the governor (Kekūanaō'a), the harbor or downtown, and the longer rides to Punahou School, Punchbowl and Nu'uanu. Since the latter rides were several miles to and from, even if they were fun, they were also strenuous. Pauahi doesn't tell us, but perhaps she liked to ride because it offered her a sense of freedom, taking her away from the confines

of the school and giving her a chance to be among her people. The ride to
Nu'uanu appears to have been a favorite, perhaps because of the mountain
air and the cooling winds that gave her temporary relief from the sometimes oppressive heat of the plain of Honolulu. Pauahi may have especially
relished the scent of the flowers and trees or the sight of the taro patches
ascending up the valley or the feel of the rain that blessed the vegetation.
She had a Hawaiian sense for rain as, after a downpour, she once looked
out and wrote: "we rejoice with the tree and the grass."[53] And, finally,
maybe she just enjoyed the feel of power and strength that a galloping steed
gives to its rider. Whatever her reasons, riding was an important dimension of her total personality.

Intellectually, spiritually, artistically, emotionally, and physically
active, Pauahi was the image of a well-rounded person. But she was still a
school-girl princess, barely eighteen years of age at the end of her days at
the Royal School. Well-rounded model students sometimes do not fulfill
their potential in later life, but Pauahi would yet achieve her full promise—
that which Kekūanaō'a and other chiefs saw in her ten years before.

Winding Down

By the fall of 1848 the Chiefs' Children's School was drawing to an end.
The Cookes wanted a change, especially Mrs. Cooke, who was suffering
from sheer physical and emotional fatigue.[54] The senior students were
getting too old and too big to restrain. Mrs. Cooke noted that Alexander
was not yet fifteen but was almost six feet tall and weighed 160 pounds, and
Lot, two years older, was no smaller. In contrast, Mr. Cooke was only a
little taller than five feet and weighed less than 110 pounds. Several
students had already left: Moses, who was expelled in February 1847;
Abigail, who left about the same time to get married; and Jane, who left in
September of the same year for the same reason. Other students, according
to contemporary observer Laura Fish Judd, were "growing restive and
impatient to break their bonds and act for themselves. Some of them have
outgrown the institution."[55] In early 1849 Alexander and Lot departed to
work for a short time as clerks, before leaving for Europe with Dr. Judd on
their historic diplomatic mission. More serious than this attrition of
students was the fact that there were no other ali'i children to replace them.
The only two children who had been expected to enter the School were two
little girls who died during the epidemics of 1848.[56]

Attempts were made to dissuade the Cookes from resigning, but in the
end it was decided gradually to wind down the School's activities. In May
1849 some of the students were transferred to Mr. Fuller's School, and a few

months later, some of the youngest were returned to their parents' supervision. The rest, Elizabeth, Victoria, Polly, John Pitt, Lili'u and Pauahi, continued to live under the Cookes' care until June 1850, when Pauahi married Charles Reed Bishop.

Beyond question, the Royal School, the Cookes and her fellow students had an immeasurable influence on Pauahi's growth and development. Intellectually, ten years of schooling (1) provided her with some factual knowledge of the natural world and the world beyond Hawai'i, (2) honed her ability to reason and to think, and (3) reinforced some old while adding some new values. The mastery of English as a second language was her single most important accomplishment, not only because it opened the way to new knowledge for her, but also because it helped her to bridge the traditional and modern worlds. Spiritually during these years she drew closer to her Christian faith, yet she never became the fanatical convert blind to other truths, such as the integrity of her *ali'i*-hood. Artistically, through music and art she enlarged her aesthetic appreciation of the cosmopolitan world which was increasingly becoming a part of her life, and she also developed talents that would add delight to her own life and the lives of others. Physically, she set the pattern for leading a vigorous and, most importantly, a healthy life. This enabled her to live beyond the limited years of the average *ali'i* of the time, so that she could accomplish her life's purpose.

In one respect, the Royal School did not prepare Pauahi or any of the other students as well as its founders may have hoped. The students were ill-prepared to function in the arena of politics and government, at home and abroad, as modern *ali'i*. The Cookes were not able to train them properly in the art of leadership, political science and philosophy, comparative government, constitutional law and government, public administration, economics, and similar subjects that a sophisticated ruling class had to understand to meet the needs of the time. The Cookes did expose the students to some ideas and practices of parliamentary government using, ironically in view of their own anti-monarchical bias, the British model. They were sincerely dedicated to preserving Hawaiian sovereignty, although this was in part due to their desire to further their own evangelical purposes through having some influence over a strong self-governing monarchy. Nonetheless, in the final analysis, the Cookes could not give the future rulers the kind of training for leadership that the Hawaiian populace needed. Had they been able to fortify these students with such training, some of Pauahi's later decisions might have been different.

In another respect, the School did fulfill an important objective of its chiefly founders. It brought together in one place the scions of the leading families of high chiefs and welded them into a peaceful group, thus continuing the unifying efforts of Kamehameha I. As Mr. Cooke once put it, the students began "to feel and act like brothers and sisters."[57] Pauahi played an important role in this process because of her maturity and the respect she gained from her fellow-students. One should not underestimate the importance to her future life of her friendships with her fellow-*ali'i*, five of whom would eventually become monarchs.

Finally, in summing up Pauahi's formative years, this period of her life may be likened to a river that begins as a little stream at its source, and then, as it accumulates more water from its tributaries, grows in volume and momentum, flowing relentlessly toward the open sea. Though the river may wend its way through strange terrain, collecting water from many different tributaries, and constantly growing in size and power, its essential nature remains the same. So it was with Pauahi, as she moved from her sacred birth into the years of childhood, shaped and molded by her Queen Mother Kīna'u—the "second Kamehameha"—through the brief transition with her natural parents Konia and Pākī, and then into maturing womanhood at the Royal School. The events, people, ideas, and activities that Pauahi encountered helped her to grow in stature and understanding, to enlarge her vision of the world and of herself. But, like the water of the moving river, her essential nature remained the same. Pauahi did not come to think of herself as less Hawaiian or as more *haole* because of the Royal School's preoccupation with Western ideas and values. If anything, as we have tried to demonstrate, she became even more Hawaiian, reinforced in her essential nature. An understanding of this idea is critical to an understanding of her legacy, for Pauahi's formative years were the well-spring of her future development and destiny.

3

FROM COURTSHIP TO MARRIAGE

Next to her royal lineage, no other aspect of Pauahi's life was as important to her fulfillment as a woman — and as the founder of the Kamehameha Schools — as her marriage to Charles Reed Bishop. He brought her the love and esteem she needed as a woman and the organizational and financial acumen she needed to ensure the successful founding of her estate. But Pauahi's pathway to marriage was blocked at first—by a betrothal she had no part in making to a "brother" she wanted no part of as a husband, and by a tradition and society allied against her independence. Her decision to reject not only Lot but her parents and the *ali'i* Establishment was the first part of her baptism in personal crisis. The second part was her decision and determination to marry one not of her kind, a *haole* commoner, in the face of opposition from her parents, many *ali'i*, missionaries, foreigners and her own people. This was the first major crisis of her life and may well have been the most traumatic.

The story is one of high drama, the stuff of which exciting theater is made. Pauahi arrived at her decision to reject first the presumption of Kīna'u, who made the betrothal, and then Lot's own proposal. She had met Charles and their courtship took place at the Royal School. Their marriage was shunned by her friends and people but was made possible by the connivance and support of the Cookes. She was alienated from Konia and Pākī but was later reconciled with them. Then she and Charles began the first years of marital compatibility that set a pattern for one of the most successful intermarriages among Hawai'i's nobility. If it is high drama, it is also a profile of high courage. An eighteen-year-old girl, standing nearly alone, in all her vulnerability, prepared to make the most important decision of her life against the uncommon opposition of so many disparate groups — and against the weight of tradition.

It is also a story of the love of a "knight" from New York for a princess. For her he would swear allegiance to a new land and later give up a fortune. It was a love reciprocated in full, the reason for his enduring marriage and his service to her people.

The Oncoming Crisis

Pauahi's first crisis might seem to have entered her life like a thief in the night — unannounced, uninvited and unwanted. Yet, given the circumstances of her formative years, her own standards, and the high stakes involved, it was not entirely unexpected. The trauma and drama of it all lay in its predictable inevitability.

In Hawai'i it was customary in traditional times, especially among the *ali'i* to betroth children, sometimes even before birth. This practice of promising one's child in marriage *(ho'opalau)* was normally done between distinguished families to assure that their offspring would be marrying others of equal rank, in order to maintain genealogical purity, to effect a political alliance or to strengthen inter-family ties. Royal children did not have the freedom commoners did to select their own mates based largely on their own personal evaluation.[1] And once betrothed, *ali'i* children were pretty well bound to go through with the marriage, since breaking a promise was considered a serious offense. So when Kīna'u promised Pauahi in marriage at an early age, she was merely following established custom. It was not unusual for *ali'i* siblings to marry each other.

We do not know exactly when Kīna'u arranged the marriage, but it was clearly done by the time Pauahi was eight, since Kīna'u died before then. I'i suggests that it was done quietly and that Kekāuluohi or Auhea (Kīna'u's sister) was the person Kīna'u had told,[2] but more likely Kīna'u told others as well. Royal betrothals were not the kind of news to keep secret, and Auhea would likely have done the same. Konia and Pākī must have known, if not before then after Kīna'u's death. Since it was such an ideal match in their minds, they would have spoken to their daughter more than once about it during her years at the School. Pauahi and Lot were very likely aware of their childhood engagement, or at least of the expectations of their future union, a long time before 1850.[3]

Even the Cookes were aware of the possible marriage of Pauahi and Lot. Mr. Cooke, writing in September 1847, said: "Jane and Bernice were and are as much attached to each other as sisters could well be. We laugh at the latter [Bernice] and say that she must be married next. We greatly hope that Lot will so conduct himself, as to render himself worthy of her."[4] Did he? While the Cookes may have uttered some hope, it was mixed with misgivings about Lot's moral conduct and perhaps his intellectual capabilities. His list of demerits almost rivaled that of Moses: leaving the school premises at night, visiting the dance halls and bars, drinking and smoking, and illicit sex. Intellectually, they rated Lot much lower than Alexander,[5] although both seemed to have attained almost equal proficiency in the English language and in other subjects. The Cookes betrayed their real attitude toward Lot later, when they readily encouraged Pauahi's romance with Charles.

In the meantime, Pauahi was making up her own mind about Lot. She had had ample time to do so since she grew up with him for part of her childhood when they had shared the same mother (Kīna'u), and had spent nearly every day with him as a boarding student for all the years of the Royal School. As naturally observant and perceptive as Pauahi was, she would have been even more so with Lot, realizing that he might one day become her husband. On countless occasions she had every kind of opportunity to see him at his best or at his worst and, of course, Lot had the same opportunity to observe her.

Pauahi had many opportunities to compare Lot with other men, including foreigners who seemed to be in a constant parade near her. An anonymous writer, describing members of the Hawaiian royalty in May 1845, wrote: "Of the young female chiefs Miss Bernice Pauahi, scarce 16, is a sweet girl, of good education, fine features, approaching the Grecian, light complection and very lady-like manners. She attracts admirers everywhere, but is very retiring...."[6] A year later, another foreign visitor described her as being "pretty and more bright in complexion than the other ones" and "absolutely full grown."[7] It is no wonder that she attracted so much male attention even though she was still a teenager. In fact, when Pauahi was only twelve, Mr. Cooke suspected that she was being eyed as a possible wife by Gorham Gilman, a business agent and friend of both Kīna'u and Konia, when he briefly served as assistant teacher at the Royal School.[8]

In the 1800s social, economic and cultural conditions dictated that most girls would marry in their teens, rather than getting an education and finding a job. This pattern was certainly true of the *ali'i* and of Pauahi's own classmates. Abigail, for example, had gotten married in January 1847 at age seventeen, and her half sister Jane had done the same in September at age eighteen.[9] Pauahi was a bridesmaid at her best friend's marriage, and Jane's example might have increased her anxiety a bit.

After years of interaction with Lot, at some point Pauahi collected all of her impressions and found him wanting. She was no doubt fond of him and perhaps admired some of his qualities, but her fondness for him was that of a sister for a brother. She probably understood him better than anyone else and could judge him fairly and sympathetically. We will never know on what grounds she based her judgment. She may have sensed intuitively a basic instability in his character, as later manifested in his bouts with alcohol. Or she might have felt he could never come to terms both with his traditional beliefs and with Christianity, as seemed to be indicated by his later adult behavior.[10] Whatever the case, she concluded that even at his best Lot could never be the man she would marry and live happily with.

Pauahi undoubtedly agonized over this process because she realized that she would hurt Lot's feelings. There is no question that Lot cared for her, admired her qualities, perhaps even loved her and would have taken her even at her worst. Pauahi knew she could handle Lot. What she probably dreaded more was incurring the wrath of her parents and the displeasure of the King and his court, as well as many of her *kahu* and her own people. She may even have trembled at the thought of ignoring the wishes of her foster mother Kīna'u, and of bringing shame upon herself for elevating herself above others. But Pauahi had her own needs and desires, a sense of her own self-worth, and a feeling for her own destiny. All of this she felt deeply enough to be willing to confront the worst. The worst was to come, but not before she met Charles.

Charles' Emotional Storm

Charles arrived in Honolulu on October 12, 1846, with his closest friend, William Little Lee, on their way to the Oregon territory. Charles had been born on January 25, 1822 in Glens Falls, New York. He was still a young man, restless, eager to depart the slow-paced confines of Sandy Hill, a small town not far from his birthplace. Charles had worked there as a store clerk. Lee, who was a few years older, had worked there as a lawyer, having received a Harvard education.[11]

Oregon, like California, was attracting a steady stream of American settlers; in fact, 2,000 had entered the territory in the month of October alone.[12] Apart from its vast land and ocean resources, its mild climate was particularly attractive, especially to Lee, who was suffering from tuberculosis.[13] Oregon was also appealing because it was on the verge of being admitted as a territorial government within the United States.

Their little ship, the *Henry*, had just made the longest, and one of the roughest voyages between New York and Honolulu at the time. After eight months on board, Charles and Lee were happy to step ashore. There to greet them warmly were the Reverend Samuel C. Damon, Chaplain of the

Seamen's Chapel, and Gorham O. Gilman. Both were to become lifelong friends of Charles and Lee.[14] The *Henry* had taken such a battering that it had to remain in Hawai'i for several weeks for repairs. Charles and Lee had the option of remaining or risking the winter passage to the northwest. Upon the urging of their new-found friends, they decided to stay. This decision was made easy by the hospitable welcome they had received. It is doubtful they would have stayed because of Honolulu's attractiveness. Henry M. Lyman described what he saw in 1846:

The landing-place at Honolulu presented no attraction for passengers from the sea; a slaughter-house and meat-market projected over the muddy water of the harbor, while on the opposite side of the way a long row of filthy shanties defiled the air with odors of decaying vegetables and dead fish. No one yet dreamed of the fine stone buildings that were to rise around the port; the majority of the dwellings were grass huts reared by the aborigines, or structures of *adobe,* put up by natives and foreigners who brought their model from the Mexican coast. The narrow crooked streets were deep with dust, and few trees but the scrubby hibiscus and an occasional algaroba could maintain life in the thirsty soil, where all the water was pumped by hand or by windmill from shallow wells sunk in the coral rock. Here and there, belonging to the "quality," was a wooden house of two stories surmounted by an odd-looking platform, a "lookout," copied from the perch of some retired sea-captain in Nantucket, where one must betake himself to the housetop in order to get sight of the sea and the ships laden with oil, coming on "camels" over the bar in the palmy days of whale-fishery. A large part of the sea-front was obstructed by the fort, a square enclosure surrounded by high walls of coral rock on which were mounted a number of wheezy old cannon, some of them ancient brass-pieces bearing inscriptions in strange tongues, sold to the savages years ago for ten times their weight in sandal-wood. The only place where prosperity seemed to abide was a stone building, a little apart from the street, approached through an arched gateway over which glittered a crown like that over the stern of the royal yacht. This was the new Post-office, Custom-house, Treasury, and Government offices, all in one. Farther east, toward the mission premises was the Palace, a large stone mansion shaded with wide verandas, and surrounded by an enclosure filled with trees, above which floated the gorgeous royal banner of Hawaii. But the unlighted streets of the city were destitute of pavement and sidewalks; the shops were low, dark, and repulsive. An attractive retail store, a hotel, or any place of refreshment better than a grog-shop for drunken sailors, did not exist.

Such was Honolulu in the year 1846; one of the least inviting spots on the face of the earth.[15]

It is easy to sympathize with those foreign residents who urged the two young men to stay: both were well-mannered, intelligent, and educated (Lee was especially well-educated), and they had skills that were badly needed. Lee was persuaded by both Damon and Dr. Judd who felt that his legal skills were badly needed to fill an important vacuum in the Kingdom's judicial system, which was just being reorganized. Within two months of his arrival Lee was appointed as an appellate judge. In Kuykendall's opinion, Lee's appointment "marks the beginning of a new era in the history of the Hawaiian judiciary."[16] Charles' start was not as auspicious. He was given a government job to help straighten out the records of Ladd and Company. This was the first sugar company in the Islands and it had gone bankrupt in 1844 and been taken over by the government. Ladd and Company was then in constant litigation involving its owners, creditors and the government. Charles made his first forays to Kauaʻi, where the company had its sugar operation at Kōloa. His interest in future investments in the islands may first have been piqued during these visits. Before the company was foreclosed, at the end of 1847, Charles accepted an offer to serve as clerk of the U.S. Consulate in Honolulu.[17]

Pauahi and Charles probably met during the early half of 1847, perhaps for the first time on February 25 at a party hosted by the Cookes. While it is reasonable to assume that Pauahi and other students were present, no specific reference is made to that possibility.[18] In any case, Charles tended to visit on a rather regular basis after this time. For example, he spent the evening of March 18 at the Cookes; on April 23, he called with his friend Lee; and on June 28, he called again with Lee and John Jasper,[19] a young *haole* resident. Although no explanation is given for his visits, they might have been prompted by the "young man's fancy." He may have been taking his cue from Jasper, who had been calling on Jane and was about to marry her. Or he may merely have been looking over the field, without any particular interest in anyone. Lee had no ulterior purpose when accompanying his friend Charles, because he already had a sweetheart in New York who he hoped would eventually join him in the islands.[20]

The first public function when Charles and Pauahi were reported as being together was on September 4, 1847, at the wedding of Jane and Jasper. The event drew quite a distinguished crowd: the king and queen, all members of the Privy Council, officials in the foreign community, missionaries, students and others, seventy-five people all told. Beside Jasper and Jane, the wedding party was comprised of Lot, Pauahi, Charles and Elizabeth Judd (the daughter of Dr. Gerrit and Laura Fish Judd). We know that Pauahi and Elizabeth were the bridesmaids, and it appears that Lot and Charles were the groom's bestmen. As the Reverend Armstrong performed the nuptial ceremony, the four stood on the same raised platform with the bride and groom, with Charles towering over Pauahi.[21] We can only guess what thoughts were in the minds of Lot, Charles, and Pauahi at this moment.

While it is possible that a budding attraction existed at this time between Charles and Pauahi, the Cookes apparently did not think so. As indicated earlier, Mr. Cooke wrote to his sister two weeks later that they still had great hopes that Lot would "conduct" himself so as to be "worthy" of Pauahi. He also added that, if Lot did not do so, then Alexander might be a worthy match for Pauahi, although he was two years younger. The Cookes did not think it too early to talk about the possibility of Pauahi's marrying someone, though that someone was not Charles.

During the next twelve months Charles continued to call on the Cookes, once or twice alone, but mostly in the company of others.[22] Neither Amos nor Juliette Cooke commented in their journals as to the purpose for Charles' visits. It may be suggested that Pauahi was already the object of his interest, for he had no other close ties to the Cookes, even in his later years in Hawai'i. While he was not afforded any private moments with Pauahi, just being near her may have been enough. Besides, they could still communicate however silently in the way only two persons who are attracted to each other can communicate.

An intriguing entry in Mr. Cooke's journal, dated September 2, 1848, reads: "Yesterday afternoon Mr. Bishop called to see Mrs. C. and she answered his inquiry in the negative." What did she say no to? Whatever it was, Charles wanted it to be kept quiet, for two days later, Mr. Cooke records in his journal that Charles had sent a note to Mrs. C. "requesting that nothing might be said."[23] Was it a message regarding his relationship with Pauahi? If it was, was he requesting permission to see her more often or alone? And did she say no because she thought Pauahi was too young or that he was not worthy of her? Or did she feel still that there was a chance that Pauahi would marry Lot or Alexander? We do not know, but it is interesting to note that Charles kept calling on the Cookes at the School.[24]

About four months later, Charles made an uncharacteristic move that seemed to surprise his friends, including William Lee. He joined eight others in taking out an advertisement in the January 6th issue of the

Polynesian, a local paper, announcing that they were leaving the islands. The advertisement read: "The subscribers hereby give notice of their intention to depart from this kingdom, and request all persons having demands against them to present them immediately."[25] At the time, anyone leaving Hawai'i was required to give public notice or to get a passport from the government. Yet, within two months of the announcement, Charles made a complete reversal, for instead of departing, he took up a new position and became a citizen of the Kingdom.

Why? Did Charles really plan to leave Hawai'i and Pauahi? This is an important question because, had he left, the course of Pauahi's life, and of Hawaiian history, might have been very different. In answering the question we may discover more of his underlying character and the possibility that he, too, was going through a personal crisis hand-in-hand with Pauahi.

At first glance, it seems plausible that Charles' "original restlessness" was aroused by the excitement of the California Gold Rush. Perhaps, like many other able-bodied men in the islands, he wanted to join the race to Sutter Creek.[26] But it seems strange that he waited until a year after the rush started. For a man who made timing a fundamental part of his business credo, this wait seems out of character. Besides, he was no doubt aware that some disillusioned islanders had already returned from California. Charles Brewer II, for example, came back "a wiser and doubtless, a sadder man."[27] Charles' character was not that of a gambler or rough-neck eager to mix with the unruly mobs that stampeded to the gold mines. Of course, he may have intended just to stop in California to explore the prospects for business and then to continue on to Oregon. But why would he have done so in the middle of winter?

Possibly, Charles was disillusioned with his chances for success in the kingdom and so decided to move on. He no doubt thought about his friend's rapid rise as a judge heading towards fame and power as the first chief justice of Hawai'i's supreme court; while he tarried behind clerking for the small U.S. Consulate. Charles admired the integrity and ability of William Lee too much to feel any petty jealousy, however. For a young man driven by the masculine *animus* to move forward, two years in "uninviting" Honolulu may have seemed like two centuries. But in the light of what happened two short months later, when he was made Collector of Customs and then made his first business investments, the opportunities seemed there for the asking or taking. Charles was, after all, a born entrepreneur with a golden touch, who created his own opportunities. It is unlikely that he planned to leave out of disillusionment with Hawai'i's potential, for he must have known it was there.

What is most baffling about his behavior at this point is his failure to consult with his closest friend about leaving.[28] Here was a friend with whom he had charted his life's course and whom he deeply respected—his only true friend—and yet he ignored him in making this decision. For a man who placed mutual trust and loyalty at the top of his value system, this seems to be quite inconsistent. We are told that, when Lee learned about the advertisement, he immediately sought Charles out and persuaded him to change his mind.[29] Apparently, Charles did not require much persuading, but Lee must have been surprised by the situation. Perhaps Charles was even a little embarrassed at his own treatment of Lee.

How then should we account for Charles' rather sudden decision and somewhat contradictory behavior in view of subsequent events? His decision to leave was most likely an impetuous act caused in large part by frustration with his inability to resolve his feelings for Pauahi and to gain control over a situation fraught with social and political complications. All the signs indicate that he was falling in love with Pauahi. Consider his circumstances: a young, virile, and very eligible bachelor moving in the highest circles of Hawaiian society and looking for female companionship. His field was limited by the aristocratic nature of the society, by his own character and standards, and by the fact that Honolulu was a small town. Pauahi—young but "absolutely full grown," pretty, intelligent, articulate, talented, affectionate, modest, high-born and available — must have appeared to him as an image of fortune. There was no one like her, certainly not in Honolulu or perhaps even in Sandy Hill. If he was going to settle down in Hawai'i, whom better to do it with than a princess? No doubt these rational considerations ran through his mind, but they were fueled by his own emotions and yearnings. After nearly two years of visits to the Cookes, open and public meetings with Pauahi, casting slightly surreptitious glances at each other, exchanging a thousand and one nonverbal signals, yet all the while not being able even to hold her, Charles had understandably worked himself into a state of frustrated passion. When Mrs. Cooke turned down what must have been his first serious initiative toward Pauahi, he felt even worse for having been rejected by a third party. He slowly realized that his feelings for Pauahi would not be approved by her parents, the king, and many others in both the Hawaiian and foreign communities. Indeed, his relationship would complicate and even jeopardize her standing among her people, and he was in no position to help her or himself.

When these highly combustible elements were mixed together, it took but a little spark to cause a fire. Charles must have been caught in this highly charged atmosphere when he made his decision to leave, which showed an impulsiveness unlike his usual deliberateness. This interpretation also helps to account for his somewhat selfish attitude toward his lifelong friend, in not confiding in him. Finally, it helps to explain his apparent readiness to give up a land that held so much promise for him. Passion accounts for many otherwise contradictory departures from normality.

If our analysis is right, Charles had just gone through his first emotional storm. It is clear that he experienced it alone, and that his formal exterior may have hidden his inner turmoil from everyone, even Lee. Furthermore, it is unlikely that he would or could have talked to Pauahi about his decision or feelings. And the first time she learned about his intended departure was probably on the 6th, along with everyone else. We can only surmise what she might have felt then.

With this perspective, we can better fathom the aftermath of the storm. Charles seems to have abandoned his plans to leave as suddenly as he had announced them. On February 23, Dr. Gerrit P. Judd, then Minister of Finance, proposed Charles' appointment as Collector of Customs, a very important position since government generated a large portion of its revenues from customs duties rather than taxes. Four days later, Charles swore allegiance to the King and the Kingdom and became a Hawaiian citizen. On March 1, he was confirmed as Collector of Customs. He seemed primed to move with a commitment that he had never mustered before.[30]

On March 14, he called on the Cookes and presumably Pauahi, although her name is not mentioned. In his journal entry for that day Mr. Cooke stated that "Mrs. C. questioned Pauahi about Lot and Alexander and she said no."[31] Could she have asked Pauahi about whether she was interested in either Lot or Alexander? If she did, a "no" from Pauahi would have been the expected answer. That would have cleared the way, then, for Charles' return on the evening of March 30, when "he had a long talk with Bernice" alone.

We do not know what they talked about, but it was obviously serious talk or else the Cookes would not have permitted it. Significantly, the fact that they did indicated that they would now be supportive of a relationship between Charles and Pauahi. It seems only logical that he would have talked of his affection for her. Perhaps he confessed the pangs he had suffered about his abortive decision to leave and his anxieties about his acceptance by her parents and others. He would have also mentioned their possible marriage, which would have been even more on his mind since he had witnessed his best friend's marriage just two weeks before off Diamond Head. As for Pauahi, she would have revealed her own sentiments and maybe her concerns for her parents' opposition to any contemplated marriage. Since this was the very first time they had to share privately, it is not difficult to imagine the outpouring of emotions and words that filled their hearts and minds.

In the meantime, Charles had a rival of sorts, Brother Samuel G. Dwight, a 35-year-old bachelor missionary, who had been calling on the Cookes to see Pauahi as early as January. At one point he was told that he could not stay with the Cookes because "people talked so much about him and Bernice."[32] Five days after Charles' rendezvous with Pauahi, Mrs. Cooke "had a long talk with Brother Dwight" and evidently squelched his further pursuing of Pauahi.[33] (Brother Dwight, when he was head of a girls' school in Moloka'i several years later, married one of the Hawaiian girls, Anna Mahoe.) It is highly unlikely that Brother Dwight was anything more than a mild distraction to Pauahi. Her sights had always been set on her knight from New York.

As far as Charles was concerned, the matter of his marriage to Pauahi was settled on August 16. That is when he spelled out his intentions to the Cookes. Mr. Cooke described the event as follows: "Mrs. C. received a note from Mr. C. R. Bishop respecting B(ernice) & today she replied to it. It will probably lead to the union of those two."[34] Mr. Cooke's tentative tone was not so much indicative of Charles' commitment as it was of the obstacles that lay in the path of his marriage to Pauahi.

A Test of Love and Courage

Once Charles had committed his proposal of marriage to writing, this seemed to signal the beginning of the battle of Pauahi, and to a large extent the Cookes, arrayed against Pauahi's parents and the others opposing the match. It is a familiar story. In its retelling here, the story is important for what it says about the love and courage displayed by Charles and by Pauahi, in particular.

Pauahi took the lead, for in a real sense it was her fight, not Charles'. On August 30, she went to see Governor Kekūanaō'a, her *hānai* (foster) father, about his desire to have her marry Lot. "She told him she did not like Lot," the Cookes' journal states. And it adds: "It made her quite unhappy all day & she went to bed early with a headache."[35] Pauahi was distraught because, in rejecting Lot, she was compounding his hurt, Kekūanaō'a also being Lot's father. Furthermore, Kekūanaōʻa may have reminded her that it was the wish of Kīnaʻu, his late wife and her foster mother, that Pauahi marry Lot. She was dishonoring that wish and to that extent Kīnaʻu's memory as well. These were painful realities, and Pauahi's love for Charles could not have taken away all the pain.

The encounter with Kekūanaōʻa must have placed her under considerable stress for she and Charles talked about it and other matters at great length. The Cookes reported, for example, that on September 4, "Mr. B. & B. did not return til 11-1/2 'clk" which kept them up, like worried parents, until near midnight.[36] The pressure building seemed too much for Pauahi to handle for the moment, and she and Charles decided to "suspend matters for six months or so."[37]

This hardly eased her situation. Two days later, she had to confront Kekūanaōʻa again, along with her natural parents, Konia and Pākī. Lot was about to leave for San Francisco with Dr. Judd on his way to France. They wanted Pauahi to be engaged to Lot so that they could be married on his return. In fact, as the Cookes recorded it, "[T]hey wish her to decide at once without seeing him and without his saying to her whether or not he loves her."[38] Since the Cookes were not there, it is obvious that Pauahi went home, related what transpired, and then discussed her options with them. The Cookes were entirely on her side, for which she was very grateful.

Pauahi was facing unflinching opposition from parents who had long set their hearts on her marrying Lot and who would not accept anything less. Protestations by Pauahi of her lack of affection for Lot and her love for Charles were not going to change their minds one iota. Plainly from their viewpoint, how Pauahi felt about Lot did not really matter. Indeed, they did not care what either Pauahi or Lot might feel for each other. Traditionally, marriages were arranged by the parents without consulting their children. The presumption was that the parents knew better, that the interests of the family and politics transcended any individual feelings, and that two reasonable people could in time grow to love or at least tolerate one another. However, Hawaiian tradition was never as blind to love and romance as the attitudes of Pauahi's parents might suggest. The legends of old tell of acts of love on a heroic scale. Such love was shown by the young chief Makakehau who "laid his love in a grave prepared by his own hands" and by Kaʻaialiʻi for Kaāla, who died as Kamehameha the Great himself watched. But beyond the drama of the stories, there was, as Kawena Pūkuʻi reminds us, "real love" in the quiet lives of many Hawaiians.[39]

Pauahi was not breaking tradition because she loved, but because she challenged parental authority.

Confronted with her parents' ultimatum, Pauahi devised a two-part strategy. The first part entailed a face-to-face meeting with Lot. She sent a note to Lot asking him to meet her, which he did. The Cookes' journal explains what happened: "She told him the wishes of her parents and said she would consent in accordance with their commands, but she knew it would make her always unhappy for he did not love her, nor did she him."[40] While Lot probably already knew that she did not love him, hearing her say it directly to him, perhaps for the first time, was something else. But was she totally accurate when she said that he did not love her? Or did she say that more out of her own need for self-justification? She may have been right, but there is no question that Lot admired her deeply. If what the Cookes reported is really all that she told Lot, she didn't tell him everything she would do if she were forced to marry him. She knew that there was a limit to tampering with his pride and sensitivity.

The second part of the strategy involved Pauahi's writing a letter to Kekūanaōʻa spelling out the dreadful consequences of forcing her to marry Lot. To quote the journal: "She wrote to the Governor and said if they [the Governor, Pākī and Konia] wished her buried in a coffin, she would submit to their authority. That she would as soon have them bury her as to promise to marry Lot."[41] We must seriously ask what she meant by her statement. On the one hand, she might have meant it in the way that a person might say, "I'd rather be dead than married to him." We don't take the meaning of this statement literally because it is only a harmless figure of everyday speech. Pauahi's statement might have been the kind of melodramatic gesture that children sometimes resort to when they do not get their way. That is to say, she may have been posturing with an empty threat. On the other hand, Pauahi might have meant exactly what she said. First, neither she nor her parents were playing games; too much was at stake for that. Second, she was addressing very formidable authority figures whom she could challenge but not defy. She did say that she would submit to their authority. Third, and most importantly, she could not make an idle threat because her Hawaiianness would not let her. *"I ka ʻōlelo ke ola, a i ka ʻōlelo, ka make."* "In the word there is life, and in the word there is death."[42] Pauahi was too much of a Hawaiian not to believe in the power of her words, certainly not to bandy them about in Hawaiian (the letter was no doubt written in Hawaiian instead of English) in front of her elders. She was certainly not suicidal, but she was saying that in a forced marriage with a person she did not love she would be so unhappy as to wish herself dead. The pain of melancholia would, in effect, kill her slowly but surely. This was not unlike the "death wish" phenomenon that accounted for the demise of many Hawaiians in the first half of the nineteenth century. They simply wished themselves dead because of sadness and despair. In short, Pauahi was saying to her parents that she was willing to conform to their authority, but she and they would have to pay a high price.

According to the Cookes, Governor Kekūanaō'a shot back a terse reply saying that "she was deceiving herself."[43] Did he mean that her seeming threat was a form of romantic self-deception? Or was he referring to the way she approached the whole prospect of marriage? Since he was still very much a traditionalist, he probably took what she said at its face value. That was obviously a risk he was willing to take, but in all likelihood he did not believe that her life with his son Lot would be that unhappy. After all, Kekūanaō'a knew many *ali'i* women who had been betrothed and married to men whom they had not known and yet managed to live with them. His own wife, Kīna'u, had been so given to Liholiho at an early age, and yet she survived it all. In his mind, it was wrong for Pauahi to think that a marriage based on love was more important than a marriage based on family priorities, on maintaining genealogical purity, or on reinforcing political bonds—she was meant to marry Lot.

Lot, in the meantime, was shown the letter Pauahi had written to his father. What he did next was to be the turning point in this entire drama of immovable wills. He immediately wrote a note to her, as the Cookes indicated, in which "he exonerated her from all her promises in her youth, that he would not be the means of rendering her unhappy, that he knew *he* was unworthy of her, but that there was one who was worthy, even the one she loved, and he hoped she would be happy with him."[44] It was a magnanimous gesture by one who had been rejected just moments before. His message was very clear and it undercut everything her parents were trying to do to Pauahi. Lot's reference to "all her promises in her youth" pertains to the betrothal imposed upon them by Kīna'u, unless as a child Pauahi had really made promises to Lot. When he disclaimed any association with anything that would make her unhappy, he really negated the validity of his possible marriage to her. He underscored that point by admitting that he was unworthy of her, a view the Cookes had probably influenced along the way. And he brought out in the open the issue of Charles, which to this point seems to have been studiously avoided in Pauahi's encounters with her parents. Lot quickly did away with the issue by assuring her that he thinks Charles is the best choice and the one she would be happy with. If there is any question about Lot's affection and admiration for Pauahi, the contents of this note should remove any doubts. Many years later Lot would again demonstrate the same feelings for Pauahi. But for now, Lot, according to the Cookes, had made Pauahi feel "more lighthearted."[45]

Though Lot had virtually derailed the arguments of Pauahi's parents, they were still adamantly opposed to her marriage to anyone else. They became rather bitter towards the Cookes, blaming them for Pauahi's talking "so plainly to Lot"[46] and for allowing Charles to call on Pauahi and "steal her heart" away.[47] Pākī tried to marshall official support for his opposition to the marriage and to Charles as well. For example, he wrote a letter to Robert C. Wyllie, the Minister of Foreign Relations, about Charles, probably complaining about his worthiness. Mr. Cooke told what happened next. Mr. Wyllie "came to talk with Bernice & was so pleased with her maturity etc—that (he) went & told Mr. B. that he had made a fine choice." Wyllie went back to his office and, we are told, "called together some of the Ministers of State & Chiefs & talked over the affair." While there was some opposition, Cooke felt that "they will not oppose strenuously the match."[48] Apparently, the marriage had become a political affair not because of Charles' involvement as a foreigner (although he was already a Hawaiian citizen), but because Pauahi had been and was nominally still a student at the Royal School and therefore a responsibility of the government. This was also the case with Jane Loeau, who had to get the government's blessings for her marriage to Jasper.

Opposition to the marriage was coming from various quarters, but, strangely enough, according to Mr. Cooke, "It comes mostly from Mrs. Judd & her family."[49] Perhaps Mrs. Judd's close ties with Kīnaʻu led her to prefer Lot. Or perhaps her opposition was related to the uneasy feelings that existed between her and the Cookes, whose conduct of the school she had openly criticized several years before. Thus, the Judds' opposition may not have been directed personally against either Pauahi or Charles.

The ensuing tension was, to say the least, very unsettling for Pauahi. On November 14, without any prompting from the Cookes, she wrote a note to Charles releasing him "if he wished" from their mutual ties.[50] She sympathized with Charles, perhaps, as the innocent victim of unwarranted attacks for which she felt partly to blame. He had done nothing except to fall in love with her and that could hardly be held against him. There was another issue that, while it did not surface in the recorded journal entries of the Cookes, was not far below the surface: his race. Some who opposed their marriage would have objected on that ground alone, no matter what

Charles' virtues were. The King had expressed his view on the subject
when, a few years before, Mrs. Cooke had asked his opinion about "the
girls taking up with foreigners for husbands." He answered, at the time
"Aole pono" (not right).[51] Yet, no one had objected to Jane's marrying
Jasper because of his race. While some prejudice existed, by and large
Hawaiian society was still rather open and tolerant, especially toward the
haole. But, besides Pauahi's sense of guilt, maybe her gesture to release
Charles was merely a reaching out for his reassurance that he would love
her come what may. If that is what she wanted, he quickly set her mind at
ease by calling on her that evening and then the next and by writing her a
note. In truth, Pauahi did not need to feel apologetic about the situation
because, if the opposition had hoped to split them apart, it did just the
opposite: it drove them into each other's arms even more and strengthened
rather than weakened their resolve.

By December the worst of the opposition seems to have dissipated and
things began to quiet down for Pauahi and Charles. They had apparently
forgotten about their agreement made early in September "to suspend
matters" for a while, because Charles called frequently during this Christmas month. On the 10th, for instance, he spent the evening there and
Pauahi "played for him and sang for him." That romantic interlude was
followed by another visit to celebrate her birthday on the 19th, then
another visit two days later, and another on Christmas Eve.[52]

His visits in January seem to have been curtailed somewhat, not by any
diminution of ardor but by Pauahi's having to take over some household
duties, due to Mrs. Cooke's illness. Imagine a pretty eighteen-year-old
princess, minus her *kahu*, cooking, washing, sweeping, sewing, tidying up,
nursing Mrs. Cooke, taking care of her children and newest baby, Charles
(appointed many years later as one of the first trustees of Pauahi's estate).
She also did other household chores, while at the same time trying to take
care of her own needs, which included spending time with Charles. Some
of her own people surely would have said that it was beneath her dignity as
an *ali'i* to work like a servant, but that did not bother her, and it never
would. In fact, she felt it was the least she could do for Mrs. Cooke, who in
the last ten years had acted as her surrogate mother, teacher, friend, and
now the champion of her marriage. If aloha and *kūpa'a* (loyalty) meant
anything to her, this was an opportunity to dignify those values by
example. In a sense, she had to earn her keep as well, because the Cookes
continued to keep the school open, long after classes had ended, mainly so
that Pauahi would have a place to live until she could have a home of her

own.[53] It was a godsend for Pauahi since, under the circumstances, she could not have returned to 'Aikupika to live with Konia and Pākī.

The contrast between January 1850, and the same time a year ago was startling. Then, Charles was on the verge of giving Pauahi up and leaving for Sutter Creek. Now he was comfortably seated in the Cookes' parlor reading passages from the "Life of Hannah More" to Juliette and Pauahi. Or he was being serenaded by Pauahi as she sang while accompanying herself on the Aeolian attachment. Or they were exchanging affectionate and Platonic glances.[54] Here was the Collector of Customs courting an obliging chiefess under the watchful eyes of a pair of New England missionaries. Actually, his pursuit was all but over, as they had begun to make wedding plans. Mr. Cooke's letter to his sister of January 28, 1850 seems to summarize Pauahi's mood: "It is very apparent that her thoughts and affections are centering in him, and well they may, for he is in every way worthy of her heart and hand. I hope and pray that it may turn out to be a match made in heaven, and that heaven's blessing may ever attend them, both in this world and in that which is to come."[55]

The match was still to be made on earth, however, where Pauahi and Charles were still encountering obstacles. In late March, Charles attempted to get a marriage license, but was told by a clerk that he could not obtain one unless he consulted with Pākī.[56] It is plain that Pākī had well-placed friends and that he was still intent on blocking the marriage. We do not know what action Charles took then, but apparently Pauahi took matters into her own hands the next morning. She herself went to speak with her father and asked for his cooperation. It must have been a warm meeting, because he not only gave his permission for them to be married, but also asked that they be married at his home, if they could wait the two or three months for it to be completed.[57] It is difficult to account for such a dramatic reversal in Pākī's hostile attitude. Perhaps, he was overjoyed that Pauahi had come home to talk with him personally. Just two weeks before, when Pākī had asked her and Lili'u to come and see him on his sickbed, she had refused.[58] He must have still loved her dearly as a daughter, despite their present *pilikia* (trouble). Whatever the reasons, Pauahi undoubtedly left feeling relieved at her father's seeming change of heart.

Pauahi and Charles proceeded to make plans, and they decided to have "a very little wedding."[59] They may have had little choice in the matter in view of the opposition to their marriage. They also decided that no foreigners would be invited, save of course the Cookes. Not even Lee was to

be invited, although Charles had been the bestman at his marriage the
year before. But, as it turned out, almost no Hawaiians were invited either.

By May 25th nearly two months had passed since Pākī had offered to
hold the wedding at his home. He had said that it would take two or three
months to complete the house, so there was still time for his offer to be
accepted. Charles and Pauahi apparently decided to set the date for June
4th. Charles told Pākī that they intended to be married on that Tuesday
evening and asked whether his house would be ready. Pākī said it would
not be and told him that, if he wished to be married so soon, it would be
just as well to hold the wedding at the Cookes'.[60] Why Charles insisted on
giving him ten-days notice is not clear, unless he was trying to accommodate the Cookes, who were eager to move out of the school. But this seemed
to be an opportune time to effect a reconciliation with Pākī, who had made
the first overture. Anyway, this reconciliation was not to be.

A few days later, Mr. Cooke seems to have taken it upon himself to see
and personally invite Konia and Pākī to the wedding. He described what
happened: "The latter manifested a good deal of opposition & asked 'what
wedding?' & why we had helped their daughter against them, etc. I drew
up my artillery & we kept at it till ten o'clock."[61] It must have been quite a
duel, waged between the huge six-foot four-inch Pākī and the smallish
Cooke, firing salvos at each other in Hawaiian. Pākī clearly put most of the
blame for the alienation of their daughter on the Cookes. This was unfair
because the Cookes were only symbols of the sweeping changes taking
place on the psychological and social landscape of the Hawaiian people.
Pauahi did not turn against her parents. If anything did, it was the times.

At any rate, Mr. Cooke's duel and its aftermath got him into trouble
both with his wife and Pauahi. As he told it, "The next day when Bernice
& Mrs. C. found out what I had said, they felt very bad, especially when
they read notes from each, declining to come to the wedding & saying she
must look to us, Mr. and Mrs. C., for all her *pono*."[62] Pauahi was even more
disappointed with this turn of events since she felt that she had come so
close to smoothing over the hard feelings. What must have shocked her
was the statement that she would have to look to the Cookes for "all her
pono," which meant everything — her food, shelter, clothing, and her
spiritual, physical and material welfare. She was being cut off by her
natural parents. Though this step seemed to follow the logic of the course
of events over the past year, still, for a Hawaiian, parental and family
rejection was an awful burden to bear. And this rejection came only five
days before what she knew would be the most important event of her
young life. This was, indeed, a bittersweet moment.

A very private, quiet wedding was held on the evening of Tuesday, June 4, 1850, in the parlor of the Royal School — a fitting place in view of Pauahi's past and future. The Reverend Richard Armstrong, who held the position of Minister of Public Instruction, performed the ceremony, in spite of Pākī's efforts to persuade him not to do it.[63] Besides the Cookes, Mrs. Armstrong and a few witnesses, including schoolmate Elizabeth Kekaaniau but not Jane, were present. As Elizabeth later recalled, Pauahi wore a gown of white muslin and a wreath of jasmine.[64] The *lei* was a typical Pauahi touch. After the ceremony, according to Mr. Cooke, "they sat down to tea & at 9 o'clock they went in a wagon to Judge Andrews' where they are to board."[65] That was it. In one hour the entire affair was finished, culminating more than two years of personal turmoil and crisis. It was all so exquisitely quick and simple. What a contrast to Jane's wedding, a gala event attended by the King, members of the Privy Council and other dignitaries, with easily ten times as many guests present. If Pauahi had looked back to that time and felt a twinge of disappointment that her wedding was not what it could have been, no one could blame her for that. But, on this night, when she and Charles left the Cookes, she took with her everything she ever wanted to possess. And so did Charles.

Reconciliation

The next day Pauahi and Charles boarded the interisland boat *Kalama* and sailed for Kōloa, Kaua'i, where they would be "tasting the sweets of their honeymoon," as the Reverend Daniel Dole, minister of the local church put it. Charles was familiar with the Kōloa area because of his work with the Ladd Company and knew some of the people, including Dr. James W. Smith, a missionary-physician, at whose home they may have stayed. Dr. Smith sent a letter to Amos Cooke saying "they were much pleased with Bernice."[66] It is possible that the couple chose Kaua'i because Pauahi had apparently visited all the other islands but this one. The port-settlement was near several thousand acres of land that Charles had invested in the year before, in a partnership with Henry A. Peirce and William Lee which would later grow into the Līhu'e Plantation.[67] It is quite likely that Charles wanted to combine business with pleasure. After three weeks they returned to Honolulu on July 2 and Pauahi, who apparently could not wait, reported to Mrs. Cooke that same day.[68]

Some have said that Charles and Pauahi "fled" to Kaua'i to escape the wrath of Pākī and Konia.[69] This seems unlikely given the reasons for their visit, suggested above. Besides, neither Charles nor Pauahi was of the mind or character to run away from a problem, especially one as important as the *pilikia* with her parents. Pauahi had come as close to being disinherited as anyone could, and she felt the hurt keenly not only for herself and Charles, but for her parents as well. Setting things right or * hoʻoponopono* was an urgent matter; their marriage would not be allowed to fester in ill feelings.

For the first few months of their marriage, Pauahi and Charles dwelled in the friendly confines of Judge Lorrin Andrews, first for a short while in his downtown residence, and later in a cottage he owned in upper Nuʻuanu Valley.[70] It was important for the newlyweds, especially Pauahi, to be among friends during this always delicate initial period of married life, particularly in view of the uproar in the community over their union. Andrews was a friend. In fact, for several weeks he, Charles and others were in the process of establishing the Royal Hawaiian Agricultural Society, which was to play an important part in the Kingdom's development.[71] He was also an important friend, for he was then serving with John Iʻi as an associate justice on the Supreme Court, over which William Lee presided. Andrews was good for Pauahi, too, because of his deep and sympathetic understanding of the Hawaiian culture and community. This understanding had begun during his days as the first principal of Lahainaluna High School on the island of Maui and would lead to his authorship of the first important Hawaiian-English dictionary. Pākī was still showing his pique by refusing to pay Pauahi's bill at the Royal School,[72] but he could not question Andrews' credentials.

Pauahi and Charles spent most of this period in a home that Andrews had just completed opposite the site of the present Royal Mausoleum. Like many Hawaiian homes of the time, this one had a name, Wānanakoa, for the grove of *koa* trees in the yard.[73] It was one of several homes in the far end of the valley which included the home of Dr. T. C. B. Rooke, the *hānai* father of Emma, and the summer residence of King Kamehameha III.[74] Overlooking the stream, the taro patches, the fragrant *maile* vines she used to pick and the paths she once rode up on horseback, it was a pleasant place for her to be, but only temporarily until their own home was completed.

Their new home was being built on a piece of property Charles had purchased on the diamond head *ma uka* (toward the mountains) corner of Hotel and Alakea Streets in the heart of Honolulu. It was kitty-corner from the site of the home of David L. Gregg, the U.S. Commissioner.[75] Their home was very modest, since they apparently did not dine or entertain there, but took their meals at the nearby home of John Ladd.[76] While this practice was not unusual for families then, the situation probably reflected the size of Charles' pocketbook. He had not yet amassed his fortune. Yet, in the four years since his arrival he had been able to accumulate enough cash to buy property, invest in a partnership in Līhu'e, and now build a cottage of his own. This spoke well for his drive and thrift. We do not know when the new home was completed, but Charles probably carried his bride over its threshold either in late 1850 or early 1851.

However modest their dwelling it must have been a thrill for Pauahi finally to be in her own home, away from the peering eyes and eavesdropping ears of teachers, roommates and parental figures. Now, in the security and privacy of her own little "palace," she could practice at least some of the "domestic science" she had acquired in school and from the Cookes. She may not have had any alternative, since there were probably few, if any, servants at her disposal. But that would have been a small price to pay for the bliss of living alone with Charles.

Meanwhile, Pākī had completed the construction of his new residence on the site of his original home.[77] By the standards of the day, it was a splendid structure that was probably the equal of any of the better homes and gardens in town. It was a large two-story stone-and-frame building with *lānai* (porches), supported by pillars on both first and second floors, extending around at least three sides of the house. Its extensive gardens combined shrubbery, flowers and trees and included the special tamarind tree planted at Pauahi's birth. The name Pākī gave his new home has been translated as "House of the Sun" or Haleakalā, but he probably meant it to be Hale'ākala or the "Pink House," after the color of the stone used in its construction.[78]

This, of course, is the house that Pākī had offered to let Pauahi use as the site for her wedding. The house had not been completed by June 4th, the wedding date the couple chose. Had they waited, assuming that Pākī was sincere in his offer, Charles and Pauahi would have been married at Hale'ākala and perhaps in the presence of a much larger number of guests. Then, it is quite likely, Pākī would have invited the pair to stay in his household. This scenario seems to be what Pākī had in mind, as suggested by what happened next.

It is said that Pākī, under the relentless coaxing of Princess Victoria Kamāmalu, who was then only twelve years old, broke down one day and called on Pauahi.[79] As he examined her humble home with its rather simple appointments, he seemed to feel embarrassed, believing, perhaps, that a woman of her *ali'i* status should be living in greater splendor. Mrs. Mary S. Rice, who was close to Pauahi at the time, recalled Pākī saying to his daughter, "Had you remained with me, I would have given you a fine, large house."[80] This remark seems to indicate Pākī's view that the couple should have been married at Hale'ākala. The differences between the young couple and her parents could then have been smoothed over, Pākī would have invited them to stay, and he would eventually have given the house to Pauahi.

Pākī probably built the house with the intention of giving it to Pauahi. Clarice B. Taylor stated that he really built the house "hoping Pauahi would marry Prince Lot and make her home with her parents."[81] This interpretation is consistent with Pākī's anxiety and frustration in his efforts to get Pauahi married to Lot. It also explains why he built such a large and splendid home, one he would not have needed just for himself and Konia. 'Aikupika would have been adequate. The cost of the structure must have been heavy, in view of the fact that Pākī, who was a member of the House of Nobles at the time, was not necessarily a wealthy man. As a matter of fact, he had sold his lands at Mākaha to raise the money for its construction. If he was bitter, even heartbroken, over Pauahi's marriage to Charles, it was partly because of the personal investment he had made in a home for her and for his posterity.

In any event, after he left Pauahi, he had a huge rococo mirror delivered to her house. It was too big to fit easily anywhere, but it was also too important not to be fit somewhere. The mirror went into a front room where it reached from the floor to the ceiling[82] — its outlandish size reflecting, perhaps, the magnitude of Pākī's wish to be reconciled with his daughter.

Another version of the reconciliation involves only Pākī and Charles. According to this account, the Reverend Richard Armstrong was visiting Pākī one day when Charles came to call. "Armstrong placed Bishop's hand in that of Pākī and left. That was the start of the reconciliation between Bernice's parents and the young people."[83] Kent, who related this story, said that it came from Ellen Armstrong Weaver, who had "heard the story from Bishop himself years later."[84] In this version the beginning of the reconciliation is not Kamāmalu's coaxing of Pākī, which Amos Starr Cooke saw as critical.[85] But the two accounts are not necessarily incompatible. The important point is that a first step had been taken to heal past wounds.

In time, Konia and Pākī came around to accepting fully the fact of Pauahi's marriage. It would have been hard for them not to. By all accounts, Pauahi was well-adjusted, entirely capable of managing her home, socially poised and confident whatever the nature of the company, well-liked and admired — and serenely happy. As for Charles, he was industrious and honest, hospitable and generous, admitted into the highest circles of society, and transparent in his love and care for Pauahi. The marriage was off to a wonderful beginning, close to fulfilling Mr. Cooke's wish for "a match made in heaven."

Besides, Charles was rapidly making an indelible mark on the community, and his fortune as well. In April 1853, he resigned his post as Collector of Customs to form a partnership with William Arthur Aldrich.[86] They opened a general merchandise store and then expanded to buy and sell local produce, to act as agent for the Līhuʻe Plantation, and to advance cash for drafts on mainland firms. By early 1855, Charles' business was prospering. Lee wrote to Joel Turrill, who had been the U.S. Consul when Charles worked as secretary at the consulate: "Bishop is as usual in a flourishing condition, and he and Aldrich, next to Capt. Spencer, are said to be making more money than anyone else in town. Bishop is the cautious one, financial member of the firm, and Aldrich the selling member. Bishop grows every day in public esteem."[87]

Pākī, from his vantage point in the government, knew full well what his son-in-law was accomplishing, if not the details of his profits and investments. He had no cause to worry about whether Pauahi would be adequately provided for materially. Nor from what he had seen of their personal life, could he have any reason to doubt that Charles would provide his daughter with the love she needed. By the time he died on June 13, 1855, still a comparatively young man, he must have been favorably impressed with Charles.

Acting on impulse, Pākī had once come close to disinheriting Pauahi. Upon his death, however, he affirmed his aloha for her by giving her everything he owned. First, he left her his lands, about 5,780 acres, mostly in Heʻeia and Waiʻalaeiki on Oʻahu, plus a few small plots in downtown Honolulu.[88] Had he not sold his lands at Mākaha or ʻEwa, he might have left her a few thousand acres more. This inheritance was the beginning of Pauahi's estate and made her at the age of 24 a landlord with the responsibility of managing her own lands.

Then, Pākī left Pauahi what he had always intended to give her: Haleʻākala. His one regret may have been that she and Charles had not shared the house with him before he died. But, following Pākī's demise, Pauahi and Charles moved and lived with Konia until her death, two years later. With this, the circle of *ho ʻoponopono* was completed and, in a sense, so was the marriage of Charles and Pauahi—all things had been set aright.

In sum, the details of the story of Pauahi's courtship and marriage underscore the fact that Pauahi and Charles loved each other deeply. The ordeal of their courtship tested the quality and magnitude of that love by showing the lengths they would go to in proving themselves. Charles gave up his plans to go to Oregon and then California, and became a citizen of the Kingdom; Pauahi challenged her parents and came close to being disinherited, and braved the disapproval of the *ali'i* and her own people. Had she been made of lesser mettle, she might have married Lot; won the plaudits of Pākī, Konia, the King and her people; enjoyed a royal wedding; and eventually become a queen. That she did not and instead chose a life with Charles led ultimately to the founding of her estate and the Kamehameha Schools. And the source of her estate and the Schools was in the love that Pauahi and Charles shared with each other, a love that never seemed to dim even in their twilight years. This love is really the key to understanding some of the major decisions Pauahi and Charles made later in their lives.

4

LIFE AT HALE'ĀKALA

The move to Hale'ākala signaled the beginning of a decade of new directions and personal growth for Pauahi. Living with her family, which included her younger sister Lili'u and the usual retinue of *kahu* or retainers, offered Pauahi a way back to a more traditional *ali'i* lifestyle. The move brought mother and daughter to live together in the same house for the first time since the days of Pauahi's "*kapu* birth." Their time together was cut short, however, because Konia died in 1857. She left Pauahi her lands, two times more than what she had received from Pākī. This meant that at age twenty-five, Pauahi had a sizable estate to manage. Her administration of these lands would be an important part of her life and gives us a window to understanding her attitude toward land and nature.

While Pauahi developed as a landlord, she developed even more grandly as one of Honolulu's most hospitable and respected hostesses. It was Hale'ākala's space and splendor that enabled Pauahi to do this. In this role we see clearly the varied facets of her personality: her warmth, charm, generosity, and fun-loving nature. We also see how she used the skills and knowledge she acquired at school to develop a *savoir faire* and cosmopolitanism that would stand her, as well as Charles, in good stead throughout their lives.

In his business career Charles headed off in new directions that marked the real start of his fortune-building. From running a store he turned to founding Hawai'i's first bank, an institution which would play a vital part in the agricultural and industrial development of the islands. His spectacular success helped to elevate him to the highest seats in the Hawaiian Government. However, his success was not a solo act—Pauahi contributed significantly to his overall stature through her own character, skills, and social and political position in Hawai'i.

Yet, hanging over this period of personal growth and financial success was a pall of sadness that would linger in their married life to the very end. It was a sadness caused by their inability to have what Pauahi may have

wanted above all things: children of their own. It was not only a matter
of fulfilling her womanhood, but of renewing the bloodline of the
Kamehamehas. Sadder still was the fact that, even when she resorted to
adopting children, she was somehow unable to keep them for long. Some
Hawaiians have suggested that she was the victim of a sacred curse or
"*kapu* lap" that destined her never to bear any children of her own, yet to
care for everybody else's.

Return to the 'Ohana (Family)

Although Konia was Pauahi's mother, in a way they were still strangers.
Mother and daughter had never lived together except for those first few
days at 'Aikupika. They had seen each other occasionally as Pauahi grew
up with Kīna'u and then with the Cookes at the School, but these visits
were no substitute for living under the same roof and sharing daily
experiences. Pauahi knew Kīna'u and Juliette Cooke far better than she
knew her own mother. Of course, the rift over her marriage with Charles
did not help, and though they had since been reunited, there may still have
been a bit of tension left.

In the move to Hale'ākala, Pauahi had to make the larger adjustment,
both physically and psychologically. Giving up her home meant that she
surrendered much of her privacy, freedom to go about as she pleased, and
the intimacy she shared with Charles. But, however important these
values were to her, she must have felt an overriding concern for taking care
of a widowed mother. "*E mālama i ka makua, o mālama auane'i i ka ha'i
'elemakule,*" as every Hawaiian was admonished: "Take care of your parent, before you take care of someone else's oldster."[1] It would have been
easier to remain at her home near the corner of Alakea and Hotel Streets,
but she chose the alternative—being true to her '*ohana*.

Charles acquiesced in this move. We shall never know whether he had
any qualms about living with a Hawaiian mother-in-law in a home that
was not his own, but if he had any doubts, he got over them. From now
until Pauahi's passing in 1884, he never lived in a home that he had built or
owned himself. Pauahi was always his landlord, too.

Actually, Pauahi assumed care not only for Konia but for Lili'u, too.
Lili'u, at this time seventeen years of age, had been living with her *hānai*
mother since leaving the Royal School. In addition, Pauahi took responsibility for the household servants and retainers who lived on the premises in
separate quarters. We do not know how much of their upkeep was
provided by the legacies of Konia and Pākī, but it seems likely that much of

this burden would have fallen on Charles and Pauahi. Added to the cost of maintaining such a large house and the gardens, the financial burden was probably significant.

We have no information about how Konia and Pauahi got along in the short time they lived together, but there is every indication that Konia loved her only natural child and shared Pākī's pride in Pauahi's beauty and accomplishments. While they were of two different generations, they still had important things in common. Both were descendants of Kamehameha and of great chiefesses. Both were Christians, members of Kawaiaha'o Church, and regularly attended its services.[2] Both were deeply committed to the preservation of the monarchy and Hawaiian sovereignty. Both could not help but share many of the same traditional and even some modern values. Finally, they were very much alike in their personal warmth, hospitality, generosity and evidences of aloha. So there is good reason to suppose that their reunion was quite compatible.

It is not hard to imagine Pauahi and Konia having long conversations between themselves, or with Lili'u, all, of course, in their mother tongue. Since Konia was not very fluent in English, reading to each other, except from the *Paipala* or Bible, would not have been a big part of their time spent together. Talking, as it had always been among the people of old, was the way to share thoughts about themselves and their worlds. Charles, after ten years in the islands, probably knew enough Hawaiian to participate in these conversations.[3]

Lili'u's good relationship with Pauahi and Charles certainly helped make the reunion a happy one. Lili'u had admired her older sister from their years at the Royal School, although we do not know how she felt about Pauahi's marriage. The only hint she gives is found in this statement: "She was betrothed to Prince Lot ... but when Mr. Charles R. Bishop pressed his suit, my sister smiled on him, and they were married."[4] Of Pauahi and Charles she wrote: "Mr. Bishop was a popular and hospitable man, and his wife was as good as she was beautiful."[5]

Unfortunately, Konia did not live long enough to see how the life of Hale'ākala would eventually be transformed. Her health deteriorated during 1856, and Lili'u dutifully accompanied her on a restorative trip to the islands of Hawai'i and Maui. They returned to Honolulu in May 1857, but without any real improvement having taken place in Konia's condition.[6] Konia passed away on July 2nd, and for the second time in a little over two years, the sounds of *uwē helu*, or wailing, reverberated through the halls of Hale'ākala.

As had her husband, Konia left Pauahi her entire estate, about 10,231 acres of land located in Kona on the island of Hawai'i, on O'ahu, and on Kaua'i. She bequeathed to Pauahi the most important legacy she could give: The *'āina*, the lands of her *kūpuna* (ancestors).

On Becoming a Landed Ali'i

Combining the acres she inherited from Pākī and from Konia, Pauahi now owned 16,042 acres of land. These lands formed the beginnings of her estate and so should be identified in detail. From Pākī she received the *ahupua'a* of He'eia or 4,172 acres which included the 89-acre fishpond (an *ahupua'a* was a division which usually extended from the uplands to the sea).[7] She also received 1,608.20 acres in Wai'alaeiki which included 6,700 feet, or more than a mile of beach frontage.[8] In addition, she obtained the following fourteen parcels of land in Honolulu:

Punchbowl	0.84 acre
Pualoalo, Nu'uanu	1.24 acres
Kapohuluhulu	2.40 acres
Kalawahine	0.43 acre
King Street (the Hale'ākala site)	2.11 acres
Richards Street	0.75 acre
Hotel & Fort Streets	0.10 acre
Queen & Punchbowl Streets	0.98 acre
Kaumakapili	0.26 acre
Alakea & Queen Streets	0.55 acre
Corner of Nu'uanu & King Streets	0.55 acre
Laimi	6.15 acres
Laimi	12.63 acres
Beretania & Nu'uanu Streets	2.65 acres

These parcels amount to 31.64 acres,[9] but though small in size, their strategic location made them valuable pieces of property. The exact acreage she received from her father was 5,811.84 acres.

From Konia she received the entire *ahupua'a* of Lumaha'i in the Halele'a District of Kaua'i, about 3,150 acres; the *ahupua'a* of Ke'ei in South Kona, Hawai'i, about 5,478 acres; and Kaonohi in 'Ewa, O'ahu, about 1,603 acres. This amounted to a total of 10,231 acres.[10]

The total amount of land received from her parents was 16,042.84 acres. In 1857, this made Pauahi, at twenty-five years of age, one of the largest landowners among Hawaiian chiefesses.[11]

For the most part, these lands were productive and populated areas. Take He'eia, for example. The *ahupua'a* consisted of an extensive area of terraced taro patches along with an irrigation system. Besides taro, other crops ranging from sugar cane to rice were grown there. There were also the large fishing grounds near the beach and beyond into Kāne'ohe Bay. And there was the great fishpond, with its 5,000-foot wall, stocked with mullet. Census figures indicate that as many as 500 people lived there in the 1830s.[12]

As for Wai'alaeiki, the Hawaiian newspaper *Ku'oko'a* gave this description of what it was like then: "Many people lived along the shores and they worked at farming and fishing. Plants grew. There were taro patches, tobacco, sweet potatoes, bananas and sugar cane."[13] In Lumaha'i, Kaua'i, by the mid-1800s, there was a population of about 120 people involved in farming.[14] And in Ke'ei, several hundred people worked the land and fished in the nearby waters.

Before Pauahi received these lands, they were cared for in the traditional way by *konohiki* or land managers. For instance, Pākī himself had served as *konohiki* of Ke'ei from 1832 to 1848. He had also appointed agents who lived on the land to do some of the day-to-day management chores.[15] We are told that Pākī was "responsible for settling people on land" and that his agent, Uhuuhu, "saw to it that those who were already there made their lands productive."[16] In order to make the lands productive, the *konohiki* saw that the irrigation system was well maintained, the *'auwai* or channels cleaned, and the water parceled out to each farmer efficiently. If any disputes occurred among the planters, it was the job of the *konohiki* to resolve them. The *konohiki* also had other responsibilities, not the least of which would be looking after the general welfare of the producers and their families and collecting the rent.

Like the resources of the land, those of the sea required the services of a *konohiki* as well. Thus, in Wai'alaeiki we are told by the same *Ku'oko'a* informant that "there were many konohikis" such as Kamāmalu who was Wai'alaeiki's *konohiki* of fishing. And in neighboring Wai'alaenui, the *konohiki* of fishing was Pākī.[17] The fishing *konohiki* had an important responsibility, because the fishing grounds near the beach of the *ahupua'a* were reserved for the use of the landlord or tenants.

The *konohiki*'s management was particularly necessary for fishponds, which required a great deal of maintenance of walls and gates, cleaning, stocking, feeding of the fish and then catching and distributing them. For a large pond such as He'eia with its nearly mile-long wall, upkeep required many, many man-hours of labor that had to be planned, organized and supervised.

After these lands were given to Pauahi, she took on the responsibility of managing them. While the record is sketchy on exactly how she went about doing this, there is no question about the fact that she did. For example, in 1858, a year after Pākī's death, she signed an agreement to lease Heʻeia to ninety-seven individuals, presumably tenants who had been living in the *ahupuaʻa* for awhile. In later years, she arranged to lease the area to other parties. She signed the last lease for the area in 1883 with the Heeia Sugar Plantation Company.[18] Mrs. Krout informs us that Pauahi visited her estates "frequently, sometimes remaining for weeks," and that one of these was Heʻeia.[19] We read that on these visits she was "accustomed to invite parties of her friends" where she would entertain them in her "delightfully informal manner."[20] Obviously, she combined business with pleasure on visits to her estates. We do not know if she made any such trips to distant places like Lumahaʻi or Keʻei.

Though she relied on *konohiki* or agents, as landlord she had the ultimate responsibility for management. She had some assistance from Charles; in fact, all leases of her lands were signed by both she and Charles. But, since he was busily engaged in his own commercial undertakings, especially after 1857, she carried the main burden herself. After all, she was far more familiar with her lands and people and the *konohiki* system than he was. Pauahi may have learned something about estate management from Pākī and Konia. If not, she gradually learned the art by trial and error and through contact with experienced *konohiki* and, of course, with fellow landlords such as her cousin Ruth Keʻelikōlani. Attention to management was required by her own sense of obligation to the lands and tenants. Another incentive was the income, either in kind or gold (the medium of exchange at the time), that she would obtain. By the end of the next ten years, Pauahi would be well on her way to becoming an experienced *haku ʻāina* or landlord.

She was no ordinary landlord, certainly not in today's terms. As a Hawaiian and an *aliʻi* in the mid-1800s, she had a distinctive perspective about land and her relationship to it. In the first place, though she now owned the land, ownership in the Western sense was still somewhat foreign to her, as it was to other Hawaiians. The new concept of ownership and property rights had been introduced and put into laws known as the *Māhele*[21] less than ten years before. The *Māhele* caused a revolutionary change in the traditional land system because it sought to alter in a very fundamental way the mythological, philosophical and socio-economic values upon which Hawaiian society was predicated. These values and their underlying concepts formed a major part of Pauahi's frame of reference.

Prior to 1848, no one, not even the *aliʻi*, had the right to own land as real property. A Hawaiian had rights to use the land but not possession by mere title. Use rights were constantly transferred to this or that person or chief, but this had nothing to do with changing the essential nature of the land. The notion that land was a commodity that you could possess, exploit and then dispose of at your personal pleasure was inconceivable to the Hawaiian of old. Land was never something that could belong to you; on the contrary, you belonged to the land.

One reason why Pauahi's forebearers could not think of land as disposable property stems from their natural philosophy and mythology. Based on their systematic observations and reasoning, they believed that the *'āina* as part of nature is not an inert, lifeless object. Rather, the *'āina* lives and breathes because *honua* or earth is like a living organism. It has a life-force or *mauli*, with its own organic system, its rhythm, and even its own kind of consciousness.[22] This naturalistic view dovetails with Hawaiian mythology, which explained the origins and nature of life through the *mo'olelo* (myth) of Papa and Wākea, the gods who symbolized Mother Earth and Father Sky respectively. Their union, that is, the coming together of Earth and Sky, was the source of life. Therefore, life was inherent in all of nature. That was why so many elements of nature, from plants to animals and other phenomena, had their spiritual counterparts who were perceived as conscious entities. In the Hawaiian world, everything was in a state of dynamic motion, a kind of perpetual dance — the very symbol of being alive.

Given this point of view, how could the Hawaiians conceive of land as something inanimate, as a lifeless commodity? How could you possibly own something that has its own *mauli* and then regard it as disposable? Surely, these were some of the questions that Hawaiians — and Pauahi along with other *ali'i*—had to wrestle with in order to come to terms with the new land laws of the *Māhele*.

Another reason why Western assumptions about property were so difficult for Hawaiians to comprehend was that they undermined and ignored the sacred relationship between the gods, *ali'i*, and the *'āina*. That relationship was based on the idea that as agents of the gods, the *ali'i* received the lands in trust. They functioned as divine custodians of the *'āina* with the authority to grant rights of use but never of ownership. Their responsibility was to make the land productive through proper management and to care for the security and well-being of the *maka'āinana* (commoners) who lived on the land. In return, of course, they would receive a portion of the labor and productivity of those who worked the land and the protection of the gods. Although in practice this sacred relationship was abused by both chiefs and commoners, the concept remained valid.

Finally, there is one more factor that cannot be overlooked in understanding Pauahi's attitude toward her lands. The lands she inherited were
the legacies of her progenitors, the Kamehamehas and the Pākīs (Pākī's
lands, or at least He'eia, were given to him by Kamehameha III
because, as a member of the Hulumanu, he was one of the king's favorites).[23] Some of these lands, particularly in Ke'ei where Kamehameha
once roamed, may have been ancestral lands. These were special places
because of their connection with family history and genealogy. Ancestral
lands had a kind of organic relationship with the living because these lands
embodied the memories and deeds of kūpuna, those who were born or had
lived and died there. They became the homeland, in the truest sense of the
word, where the Hawaiians had a place to stand. Ancestral lands were the
most precious because they were the source of the Hawaiians' roots, that is,
their identity with their primordial past.[24]

Drawn in broad and rapid strokes, this is a composite picture of the
traditional concepts and values about the 'āina familiar to Pauahi when she
inherited her estates. We cannot say for sure how much of this she believed
in. For it is entirely possible that some of her native sensitivity and
understanding may have been dulled by exposure to Western scientific
rationalism and Anglo-American concepts of property rights. Also, she
may have been influenced by the day-to-day actions of many of her foreign
friends, who not only favored and promoted the new land laws but in fact
instigated some of them.

Nevertheless, many of these traditional values and ideas were too deeply
embedded in her psyche to have been so quickly forgotten or so easily
compromised. Throughout her life, Pauahi would demonstrate her appreciation of Hawaiian beliefs about land time and time again in many ways.
In short, she was too much an ali'i not to respect the traditional basis of
her obligations to the 'āina and her people, and too much a Kamehameha
not to honor the memories and deeds of her kūpuna, entombed in the lands
entrusted to her care and keeping.

The Consummate Gardener

When Pauahi took over control of Konia's estates, she also became
owner and mistress of Hale'ākala and, by all accounts, readily assumed
management of the home and gardens. It was not an extraordinarily
large house, though it was one of the largest homes in the city. In addition,
there were two low buildings on each side of the house which "were divided
into rooms and occupied by numerous families," i.e., her retainers or
kahu.[25] These facilities stood on a parcel of land about two acres in size

which contained a large garden and a tennis court. Pauahi managed the property well enough to make Hale'ākala a showcase in the middle of Honolulu.

The gardens captured her interest and a great deal of her time. The Reverend Henry H. Parker, an intimate acquaintance, wrote: "In this garden she passed many a spare hour during the year caring for the wants of her plants. I've seen her there with protecting sunbonnet, or hat, and trowel in hand directing her helpers in pruning, planting and the general cultivation of the grounds."[26] Similarly, Mrs. Krout wrote: "Her love of flowers, almost a passion with the Hawaiians, was gratified in the large fine gardens of Haleakala ... Although she had well-trained gardeners, those who dropped in on mornings informally often found her not only directing them, but working herself, with trowel and pruning shears, in the beds and borders."[27] Obviously, Pauahi was not afraid of getting her hands dirty or of physical labor. She enjoyed touching and handling the soil, plants and flowers.

Pauahi was the consummate gardener, possessing "a growing hand" or *ka lima ulu.* She handled drooping plants and shrubs with such "intelligence and loving care" that she could coax them into "luxuriant leaf and blossom."[28] Another observer remarked that she "loved the garden, and it responded generously to her careful tillage."[29] Evidently, she had that peculiar extra sense, with which certain people are endowed that makes them unusually attuned to plants and that plants somehow seem to respond to. Perhaps she felt that she could communicate with them — maybe even talk with them as, no doubt, many a Hawaiian planter did with his plants. Pauahi regarded her time among the flowers and plants as a form of communion with them or with their spiritual counterparts. We remember her youthful observation that the trees "rejoiced" when the rain fell upon them.

Pauahi's affinity for gardening was a small but important part of her larger love of nature. Rev. Parker said of her: "Mrs. Bishop was very fond of the out door life. Nature in its visible forms appealed to her. The out-of-door world, created things, animal and plant life interested her vastly."[30] This love for the outdoors and nature was nurtured early in her life. At the Royal School she took a keen interest in botany, one of the few academic subjects she discussed in her journal and she enjoyed horseback rides in Nu'uanu among the *maile* and taro, the forest and streams. This love of nature was evident in her first years of marriage, when she lived deep in the valley, "mowed her own lawn, trimmed the flowers and did most of the yard work."[31] The tender care and respect with which she managed her lands no doubt came in part from this life-long interest in the natural world.

Domestic Management

For Pauahi, managing the plants and flowers was far less challenging than managing the servants and their families, whom she inherited along with the house. The exact number is unknown, but there were probably at least thirty or more people in her household corps. It was customary for *ali'i* of high rank to have large numbers of servants. We recall, for example, that at least thirty retainers accompanied young Alexander to the Royal School. The frugal Pauahi may have wondered about the economy of keeping so many, but they had served her parents for their entire lives and some may even have been present at her birth. Such lifetime service was not uncommon partly because Hawaiians viewed working for a high chief as a prestigious and comfortable life, although it had its hazards. Sometimes retainers were relatives or *ali'i* themselves, though of a lower rank. In some cases, certain posts were retained by the same families from one generation to the next. Over time, very close ties based on loyalty and mutual support developed between servants and chiefs who formed a kind of extended family. But if the retainers were like those Lot had inherited from Kekūanaō'a, not all were very productive or diligent.[32] In any case, Pauahi was obligated to ensure their welfare.

At this point Pauahi had to bring into play all of her resources and management skills, for ensuring the welfare of her retainers meant clothing, sheltering, and feeding thirty or more live-in servants and their families. We can appreciate the size of this burden by looking at just one aspect: supplying the food such a "family" would consume. Take *poi*, which was still the staple of the Hawaiian diet. If each person ate an average of two pounds a day (a conservative estimate), some 66 pounds (33 persons x 2 pounds)[33] would have to be supplied each day. If we add the *poi* consumed by the guests that Pauahi constantly entertained, we can conclude that she would have needed a ton of *poi* every month. When we include the hundreds of pounds of other foodstuffs such as fish, pork, fruits and vegetables, to round out the diet, we may wonder at the size of her food budget alone.

But more than economics was involved here. The logistics of regularly supplying this mountain of food must have been formidable. In the 1850s the economy of the islands was in part still self-subsistent. Honolulu had a small number of stores retailing foodstuffs and so on, but many Hawaiians produced a good deal of their own food. Pauahi naturally had to rely on her estates, tenants and *konohiki* in He'eia and Wai'alaeiki for some part of her provisions. Fresh mullet, for example, came from the fishpond at He'eia; other seafoods from Kāne'ohe Bay or Wai'alaeiki; taro and *poi* along with bananas and other fruits from He'eia; and from her gardens at Hale'ākala, perhaps, some vegetables and fruits. It was then necessary to transport the food from the fields to Hale'ākala. Pauahi could have used her own runners, porters, or horsemen to deliver the produce. And, to complete the process, the food would then have had to be prepared and cooked and finally served with the appropriate ceremony.

Overseeing this entire operation was Pauahi herself. Like a good manager, she delegated a great deal of authority, particularly to her *konohiki,* but when it came to running Hale'ākala, she took nearly full control. It was reported that "There was no detail of her housekeeping which she did not personally supervise."[34] And the Rev. Parker wrote that she presided "over the conduct of her own household" like a "queen." With *ke ali'i* Pauahi, there was no question as to who was in charge.

What kind of leader was she? We get some insight about her style from Emma M. Nakuina, who knew Pauahi from the 1860s on.[35] She recalled that Pauahi was "very strict and stern to her own immediate retainers for carelessness in work." The Hawaiian term for being careless or sloppy is *kāpulu.* In admonishing her retainers not to be *kāpulu,* she was being vintage Hawaiian, for this is something that Hawaiians still say today. Very few things disturbed the Hawaiians of old more than *kāpulu* work, because it violated one of their most important ideals: the flawless or perfect performance. For example, the hula dancer, chanter, canoe-maker, and ritual priest were all held to such a standard, its importance reinforced by the severity of the penalty for failing to attain it. Since doing less than perfect work was such an anathema to Hawaiians of old, Pauahi was being perfectly consistent with her cultural ideals.

Pauahi was also hard on her staff for "being late in arriving" and preached the value of "promptitude." Today we would praise managers who insist on people being prompt and getting their work done on time and would consider them to be responsible, efficient, well-organized, diligent or economical people. All these attributes could easily be applied to Pauahi as well. What is especially interesting about this is that promptness is normally perceived as a Western rather than Hawaiian value. Pauahi's penchant for being on time reveals her adaptability in accepting a *haole* value. She understood that Western economic and industrial culture is organized on the basis of time, that is, time as told by the clock. She was anxious about her people not being able to deal with time in the Western sense and falling irretrievably behind. She felt it important to teach Hawaiians about the practical relevance of being prompt.

A good leader is a good teacher, and Pauahi seemed always to be teaching her staff and other Hawaiians both by precept and example. She gave lectures on practical values such as diligence and economy and on practical subjects such as sewing and homemaking. For example, she "taught sewing to her servants," but only after improving her school knowledge by a stint as an apprentice to "Mrs. Nellist's dressmaking shop which was located near her home."[36] In Pauahi's teaching of sewing, "The cutting of material was most exact and the seams were basted together first, then overcast or backstitched as the case might be. No snipping of ends from careless bastings was permitted and every bit of basting thread drawn out was carefully rolled on empty spools or wads of paper to be used over and over again."[37] This practice of saving thread was an object lesson in frugality, in not wasting your resources. It was a lesson that Hawaiians always taught, but one that was reinforced by her experiences with the Cookes and with Charles, who had a reputation for economy. The frugality shown by Pauahi and Charles should not be confused with stinginess, however, for their lives were the antithesis of being *pīpine*.

Though it is often difficult to distinguish a leader's counseling from teaching, it can be said that Pauahi spent much time dispensing good counsel. One of the most vivid images we have is of Pauahi seated under her favorite tree counseling retainers and other people. This image comes from Mrs. W. F. Allen, Charles' niece, who first visited Hale'ākala in 1864. She wrote: "I was always interested to see her seated out under a large tamarind tree, surrounded by her people many of whom had come in from the country to advise with her. She would sit for hours with the utmost patience listening to them."[38] The tree was thirty-three years old, having stood there since Pauahi's birth as if waiting all the time for its mistress' return. It bore witness to the counsel she gave to all who came to sit under its shade.

A good counselor should listen well, and Pauahi must have been a fine listener. Able to sit for hours at a stretch listening to different people speak about their problems, she was blessed with concentration, patience, and understanding. Active as opposed to passive listening demands a retentive and supple mind that can receive a message from the speaker, analyze it and prepare an intelligent response, while simultaneously listening to what is being said. Listening well is a fine art that few people ever develop fully, but Pauahi seems to have perfected the art.

Being "surrounded by her people" meant that Pauahi was surrounded not only by her retainers but also by people from the country or *kua'āina*.[39] Many of these may well have been tenants and members of their families who sought their *ali'i* on their own or at her invitation. Holding court like this was something she undoubtedly enjoyed, although in time it may have taken a physical and emotional toll. But it was an effective means of keeping informed about events and problems in her realm and of staying in touch with the grassroots. In traditional times this constant and almost indiscriminate contact with *maka'āinana* would rarely, if ever, have occurred.

Pauahi was an approachable chiefess for a number of reasons. Accustomed by now to American democratic ideas, she accepted a more egalitarian, less elitist relationship between royalty and commoners. Given this view, she and her audience felt more at ease. This did not mean that the *maka'āinana* came to her feeling any less deferential. Pauahi's willingness to meet with them face-to-face may have made an even greater impression. Pauahi was probably one of the very few among her royal contemporaries who was willing and able to play that role. She was approachable also because of her own character, in which there was little if any room for arrogance, but a great deal of room for humility or *ha'aha'a*. The Hawaiian term literally means being low, as "among the clumps of grasses" *(ke ōpū weuweu)*. It was the ideal *ali'i* who could be humble, but not abject or timid so as to compromise self-respect or authority. As a counselor, Pauahi could be accommodating and charitable, but she could also be stern and blunt, setting a person straight or speaking plainly whenever necessary. Her basic humility gave her the ability to achieve rapport with the common people and the willingness to listen to their joys and sorrows.

The hallmark of the ideal *ali'i* was his or her capacity to give generously. From her school days, this was instinctive in Pauahi who gave of her time, talent and aloha whether in teaching the younger children or in caring for the ill Mrs. Cooke. Beyond her instinctive sense of giving, though, generosity was part of the role she was expected to play as an *ali'i*. We recall what she learned as a child under the wing of Kīna'u: *E ōpū ali'i* or "Be as kind and as generous as a chief should be." As previously mentioned, being generous was part of the chiefs' economic function since those who controlled the resources were in the best position to redistribute them. Pauahi followed this dictum whether in dividing up the surplus production among her *konohiki*, or in making improvements on her lands to better the living conditions of the tenants, or in feeding and clothing her retainers. Being

generous or *lokomaika'i* also had a psychological function. The more
generous the chiefs, the more likely they would be praised and supported
by their people. This was partly a matter of satisfying the human ego, a
need that Pauahi was not immune to. But, more importantly, the praise
and support of one's people meant added honor and prestige—or *mana*.
In a real sense, increased *mana* was the final payment for every chiefly act
of generosity. It was for Pauahi, too, because it constantly reinforced her
feelings of leadership and *ali'i*-hood.

Extracurricular Leadership

Pauahi took part in various civic and cultural organizations as both a
leader and an active member. One of the first organizations she joined was
the Stranger's Friend Society, established in July 1852, to aid the sick and
destitute traveler. It was organized by Julia Mills Damon, perhaps with
the assistance of her husband, the Rev. Samuel C. Damon. He was
chaplain of the Bethel Church that catered to the spiritual and moral
needs of foreigners and visitors, particularly seamen. Mrs. Damon was the
Society's first president and Pauahi its vice-president.[40] Pauahi may have
been induced to take part because of her long friendship with the Damons,
whose home she had frequented while at the Royal School. Charles may
have prodded her because of his own experience with having been welcomed upon his arrival by Rev. Damon. But apart from this, Pauahi was
genuinely interested in seeing that the troubled traveler was helped and, in
keeping with the Hawaiian spirit of *ho'okipa* (hospitality), in making sure
that the *malihini* or guests were properly received. Although Julia Damon
was several years older than Pauahi, they worked together for many years
as a compatible and effective team. After the move to Hale'ākala, Pauahi
held many of the Society's meetings there, with "the ladies spending the
afternoon, bringing their sewing" and "the gentlemen coming after business hours for supper, remaining for the evening."[41] Such lengthy agendas
may have been due more to the leisurely pace of the day than to the
magnitude of business, though the proper care of visitors was an important concern not only of the Society but of the Government, which
depended heavily at the time on traders and whalers for its revenues.

Pauahi was also active in sewing, as were so many women of that era.
Though by the 1860s she could have bought almost any dress her heart
desired, she did not have a high opinion of the ready-made wear which had
come into fashion and preferred to sew many of her own things. What
appealed to her most about the craft was its practicality and economy,
though she also saw its social value. She joined the Women's Sewing

Society which was supposed to do sewing for the poor, but its meetings turned out to be primarily social gatherings.[42] The Sewing Society met once every two weeks, beginning at two o'clock, at the house of one of the members, and these events were well-attended. Pauahi often had the group meet at her home and these meetings usually "resembled gay parties" with innocent games and musicales, but no dancing.[43]

Pauahi considered sewing's values of such importance that she insisted on Hawaiian women learning the art. Sometime prior to or shortly after 1860 a sewing society for Hawaiian women was organized. Pauahi may or may not have organized it, but she became its president. It was mainly for young ladies some of whom, like Emma Nakuina, she herself recruited to join. Some of Pauahi's female servants also took part. Since they met in the basement of the Kawaiaha'o Church, the meetings were far more somber than the gay affairs of the larger sewing group. Pauahi not only directed this society but also taught sewing techniques along with many practical lessons about life. Nakuina remembered her as being "always very kind and affable" but always in command. "She was my chiefess...and I stood in the greatest awe of her."[44]

Not surprisingly, Pauahi was also engrossed in musical activities as a performer, teacher, organizer and home-grown impressario. From accounts of her days at the Royal School, we know of her talent for playing the piano, but we now learn that she had "a very sweet and well-trained contralto voice."[45] Sanford Dole recalled "Mrs. Bishop's beautiful contralto in solo."[46] She sang with the Amateur Musical Society or with other groups, often at recitals in her own home. As a teacher, she continued giving piano lessons after moving to Hale'ākala. One of the few students she taught described her experiences with Pauahi as follows: "A friend and myself always took our lessons on Saturday morning and she then kept us to luncheon. We were always highly gratified at this, and she took as much pains to entertain us as though we had been grown."[47] Pauahi enjoyed teaching piano but shortly had to stop because of other pressing duties.

She was an active member of Honolulu's Amateur Musical Society and served on its executive committee for several years. It was largely a *haole* organization since most of its members also belonged to the Sewing Society.[48] Its main purpose was to promote and conduct musical performances of all kinds, from vocal to instrumental offerings. It also had a definite social function, as its monthly meetings usually turned into parties with "a few waltzes" thrown in. According to Madame Louise De Varigny, who played a major role in the Society between 1855 and 1868, there was "no lack of lovely voices" but "they hardly ever ventured any choral singing beyond English and American glees, with above all an abundance of parlor ballads. A duet between a tenor and a soprano was an event...."[49] Apparently, the quality and variety of the Society's fare began to change in 1861 when Eugen Hasslocher trained the chorus to perform excerpts from "Il Trovatore" and "Martha."[50] The next year, he and a recent arrival from Europe, Mr. Waldau, transformed the Society by organizing a regular concert series, systematic rehearsals and a schedule of compensation for the musicians.[51] Recruiting "anybody who had the faintest claim to any vocal ability," the Society performed Haydn's oratorio "The Creation."[52] Operettas and oratorios; Verdi, von Flotow, and Haydn; orchestras, ensembles, and choral groups — these were Western imports, but such was the nature of the Musical Society.

Pauahi and her Royal School classmates had all been trained in, and felt at home with, Western musical forms. Though they appreciated the traditional *mele*, they had not been so well trained in Hawaiian musical forms. Not only Pauahi, but Alexander, Lot, Lili'u, David Kalākaua and others were active participants in and supporters of Western musical culture. Modern Hawaiian music, with its classical compositions, had not fully emerged by the 1850s or early 1860s. Lele'iōhoku, Likelike, and Lili'u and other Hawaiian composers began to have an impact on the musical scene only in the next decade and later on.[53] As with economics and technology, the rise of Western music was just another manifestation of the dominating influence of the outside world on Hawai'i at the time.

In reviewing Pauahi's leadership of social activities, it is clear that she did not sit back as a royal spectator. She was only twenty-five in 1856 but, despite her relatively young age and comparative inexperience, she asserted her leadership in whatever she was involved in. It didn't seem to matter whether her audience was Hawaiian or *haole;* Pauahi moved freely and confidently back and forth, from her traditional culture to the Anglo-American-European and the emergent hybrid culture of the monarchy. The adjustment process she had begun many years ago was not complete, but she showed remarkable *lōkahi* or an ability to bring things into harmony. She would show even more in her role as the hostess of Hale'ākala.

The Hostess of Hale'ākala

Hale'ākala was the ideal place for Pauahi to play one of her most important roles, that of royal hostess. Pākī's house had the proper architecture and space, landscaping, servants, aura of splendor and sense of history. It was a credit to his foresight, as much as it was to his ambition for his daughter, that his home was turned into a place of significance. A vital ingredient which only Pauahi could supply in full was *ho'okipa* or hospitality.

For traditional Hawaiians, *ho'okipa* was more than a quaint custom: it was akin to a moral obligation. According to David Malo, "any breach of the duties of hospitality" was viewed with such scorn that the guilty party became the object of public ridicule. The consequences for any *ali'i* who refused to make a genuine show of *ho'okipa* were even greater, for much more was expected from the wealthy and the powerful. The greater the chief, the more lavish the hospitality. Such was the expectation. The *ali'i* who failed, for whatever reason, risked shame, loss of face and pride, and becoming the laughing stock of the *maka'āinana*, not to mention other chiefs. This ridicule would eventually diminish one's status and *mana*. The high social price that was exacted for inhospitableness only emphasizes the great priority given to *ho'okipa* by the Hawaiians of Pauahi's time.[54]

In Pauahi's various and countless acts of *ho'okipa*, she was responding to a deeply internalized value that had not been materially affected by the changes taking place in her environment. While being hospitable may have been a natural and instinctive part of her character, she was behaving in a form dictated by a traditional *ali'i* code. The lively parties and entertainment she lavished on guests were not a royal extravagance or elitist self-indulgence. To view these acts as insincere or superficial would be an unfair and inaccurate reading of Pauahi's Hawaiian-ness.

By all accounts, Pauahi was a model of *ho'okipa*. Sanford B. Dole, a contemporary of the Bishops, regarded Hale'ākala as "one of the most hospitable homes in the town."[55] William T. Brigham, a young scientist and a recipient of the Bishops' hospitality, wrote that the house was "the greatest centre of hospitality in Honolulu."[56] And Mary Krout added that Hale'ākala was "the centre of all that was best in the social life of the Islands. She made the stranger welcome. The fame of her grace and dignity as a hostess... spread far and wide."[57] Charles was noted for his hospitableness, too.

To make the stranger welcome is the quintessence of being *ho'okipa* (hospitable). Pauahi and Charles welcomed a seemingly endless parade of guests, including foreign naval officers, emissaries, members of royalty, merchants, intellectuals, and scientists. For example, as Honolulu was a regular port of call (and the Kingdom almost as regular a pawn among the Great Powers), American, British, and German naval officers were frequent guests. In her memoirs of Sanford Dole, Ethel Damon tells of these officers who "could be seen from the McGrew's fence, where young Kate and her brother Tarn would climb up to watch the trim Navy men playing tennis with Honolulu girls in hats and long, full skirts."[58] We do not know whether Pauahi ever played tennis, but she did play croquet with them on the adjacent grassy ground. Croquet was a fashionable game then and Pauahi was reportedly "quite an expert."[59] High-spirited Pauahi, who had been accustomed to acting as the hostess for naval personnel since her days at the Royal School, enjoyed the exercise out-of-doors and the company of young men and women.

One of the first and most interesting groups of foreign diplomats hosted by the Bishops[60] was the first Japanese mission sent by the Shogunate to Washington, D.C. in early 1860. The group's unplanned arrival in Honolulu in mid-February was caused by stormy seas which forced their ship to port for repairs and re-coaling. The group of more than seventy persons plus their American escorts created quite a stir, for they probably appeared as strange to the Hawaiians as the Hawaiians did to them. One of the members of the mission recorded his impressions as follows: "The people of this island have a black and yellow skin, with eyes large and keen. The lower class people walk about bare-footed and they resemble painted demons. The higher class men wear shoes and clothes with tight fitting sleeves and trousers. The higher class women wear a piece of white cloth wrapped around them reaching from the waist to the ankle ... A white cloth is wrapped around their breast ... They wear a garland of flowers around their heads. Around their necks they wear a string of beads made of red berries. This seemed so strange to us...."[61]

The group stayed at the Dudoit Hotel[62] in Honolulu for nearly a week before they were formally received by King Kamehameha IV and Queen Emma, although the King had acknowledged their presence by sending them gifts of mullet every day. Apparently, the delay was caused by the need to make preparations for their audience at the palace and for a special public celebration. At the palace reception, there were some twenty ladies-in-waiting along with other officials. Charles might well have been in the group, because the King had just made him a lifetime Noble. As the Japanese returned to their hotel from the palace, "there were crowds of people lining both sides of the street. In the evening all the shops closed, and the people held a festival in honor of the safe arrival of the Japanese, it was said. There was much dancing to the accompaniment of the flute, drum, and Hawaiian guitar. They call this noisy sound music." So wrote Mr. Yanagawa of the mission.[63]

Pauahi probably entertained the members of the mission with a dinner or reception at Hale'ākala. Whatever she did impressed the Japanese, for on their departure they remembered her with a little *o-miyage* (gift).[64] We have no reports of what she thought about her guests from the Land of the Rising Sun. As for Charles, the Japanese would figure importantly in his future. As Foreign Minister and a banker interested in developing the sugar industry, he would see the need to use immigrant labor.

Among other foreign visitors, Pauahi entertained Lady Jane Franklin. Lady Franklin came to Hawai'i in 1861 in search of her husband, Sir John Franklin, the Arctic explorer who was lost on an expedition in 1855. The evening's fare included an after-dinner concert by a choral group, with Pauahi charming her guests with a "beautiful contralto" solo.[65] She no doubt offered many such programs for a variety of guests over the years.

For other guests, especially her own people, the fare may have been a little different and less formal. For example, Lili'u described many frolicking evenings that involved Alexander: "The king, Kamehameha IV, Alexander Liholiho, would often appear informally at our doors with some of his friends, the evening would be passed in improvised dances, and the company always grew larger when it became known that we were thus enjoying ourselves; sometimes we would all adjourn to the house of some friend or neighbor from whom we had reason to expect like hospitality, and the night would be half gone ere we noticed the flight of time."[66] It would seem natural for the musical fare to include strumming guitars and perhaps some of the more popular ballads and early Hawaiian-type melodies. When Hawaiians get together to entertain themselves, they have a festive time. It was probably no different then, and Pauahi may have been as lively as any of her peers.

In September 1862, Hale'ākala was the scene of the wedding of Lili'u and John Owen Dominis. Pauahi and Charles both approved of John. It was "a small and quiet wedding" with the honored guests including King Kamehameha IV, who had once advised against Lili'u's marrying Prince William Lunalilo.[67] Not present was Lili'u's new mother-in-law, who let it be known that she did not approve of her son's marriage to a Hawaiian.[68] With Lili'u gone, only Pauahi and Charles were left in the big house.

In 1864 the Bishops entertained two young scientists, Dr. William T. Brigham, who was later to become the first director of the Bernice Pauahi Bishop Museum, and Horace Mann, the botanist son of the famed educator. The pair stayed in the islands a year to carry out their scientific investigations, and they spent many evenings and days with Pauahi and Charles. Brigham recalled their first dinner at which Pauahi served Hawaiian food, including fish from her pond in He'eia. "Mrs. Bishop explained the many new and native dishes as I sat by her side, while the little kahilis waved over our heads...."[69] The *kāhili* were royal standards made of feathers. Large *kāhili* were held by four retainers, one standing at each corner of the table. Other servants waved smaller *kāhili* or used them to whisk away insects. Having men to care for and bear her royal regalia was a ceremonial affirmation of Pauahi's *aliʻi* status.

The young Brigham described some of the good times he had at the Bishops': "More than once, dropping in for a call after dinner, Mrs. Bishop suggested charades, and while we youngsters went up stairs to dress and make up our parts, the many retainers of the Bishop family were sent over the little town to ask friends to an informal entertainment and by the time the players were ready the parlors were full of friends, and any shortcomings of the acting were overlooked by the amused company; then came the cakes, jellies and lemonade (there was no ice in the town then), and by ten o'clock all were scattered to their homes and the streets were dark unless the moon lighted them. When the moon was full we had our horseback rides, or the king's boat and often the governor's also were put at our disposal and with Mrs. Bishop, Liliuokalani and other Alii, with songs accompanied by guitars, we were rowed about the harbor. In all these amusements Mr. Bishop seemed pleased."[70]

Pauahi's hospitality was based on symmetry. She sought a constant balance in music, dining, games, people, and ideas. While her calendar was filled with delightful entertainments, it also had a place for more serious and intellectual activities. She and Charles formed a reading club which met regularly at Haleʻākala. The sessions attracted a variety of people including Alexander and Emma. Brigham, who attended many of these sessions, said, "... we did not hesitate to dive into Shakespeare, Schiller, Milton."[71] These lively meetings involved both reading and critical discussions of the passages read. On nights like these, Haleʻākala served as a salon for intellectual conversation rather than as a parlor for charades.

There was no arrogance or pretentiousness in Pauahi's approach to such intellectual activity. Both she and Charles genuinely enjoyed reading, and their home was filled with books. Apart from personal pleasure and enlightenment, reading and involvement in related discussions had an important social benefit for Pauahi. One of the requisites of being the complete hostess is to be able to conduct a stimulating conversation. Since she was in constant contact with a wide range of accomplished people in many diverse fields, it was prudent for Pauahi to be as well informed as possible. Just as no water ever flows from a dry spring, nothing of import ever comes from an empty mind. In her respect for the human intellect and the power of knowledge, Pauahi was following a traditional Hawaiian value.

In July 1869, Pauahi helped to fete the Duke of Edinburgh.[72] Liliʻu considered his twelve-day stay "one of the grandest occasions in the history of those days."[73] Lot, who was then Kamehameha V, having succeeded Alexander a few years before, spared no effort to entertain a representative of what was then one of the most powerful monarchies in the world. Like other *aliʻi*, Lot felt a close kinship with the English royal family who he felt understood well the virtues of a monarchical system. He had asked Pauahi and Liliʻu to hold separate functions. Liliʻu gave a grand *lūʻau* at Hamohamo, her Waikīkī residence. Lot and everyone else of high title seemed to be there, wearing their symbols of authority. The Queen Dowager Kalama, for instance, came with her state carriage, with the drivers and footmen wearing *kīpuka,* royal feather shoulder capes. Other chiefesses wore their own *kīpuka,* along with a feather lei *(lei hulu manu)* or a *palaoa,* the highly prized hook-shaped pendant. There were the *kāhili* bearers standing tall, the ladies-in-waiting, the retainers, and others in the retinue of the court. The hospitality of the moment seemed like a pretext to show the waning splendor of the Hawaiian monarchy. The *aliʻi* from *Beretania* (Britain) was grateful enough, if not impressed.

Several other dinners and *lūʻau* were given for the Duke, including one given by Pauahi and Charles. Evidently, the Duke enjoyed the Hawaiian dishes because we are informed that he was "pleased" with the *lūʻau.*[74] At the end of the Duke's stay, Lot, ever appreciative of Pauahi, thanked her with a special silver tea service.

To sum up, with her beauty, talent, intelligence and grace, Pauahi seemed ideal for her role as hostess of Haleʻākala. Perhaps, just as some people are born to be great singers, dancers or athletes, so was she born to be the consummate hostess. Still she had to prepare herself, as shown in her reading and musical training, in order to perfect her skills. In a word, she worked at it. Apart from her intrinsic desire to be the best she could be, part of her motivation lay in the premium placed by Hawaiian society on *aliʻi* hospitality. And perhaps an equally important part of her motivation came from her concern for Charles' happiness and success: the better she carried out her duties as mistress of the house, the better he could do at his business and other areas of endeavor. It was a natural division of labor, and Charles no doubt was happy and at ease in his own mind to see her do so well. Hospitality on the scale they practiced was bound to be costly, but Charles did not begrudge the money, time or energy it absorbed. He himself enjoyed his role as the genial host, and undoubtedly gave Pauahi

what she needed most: his own personal and emotional support for the
style of life she was determined to create at Hale'ākala.

Partnerships

While Pauahi learned about managing her estates and directing and
organizing the domestic and social affairs of Hale'ākala, Charles was
pouring his considerable energies into business and government. Between
1855 and the end of the next decade he established the foundation for a
financial kingdom that would nearly save the Hawaiian Kingdom. Yet, for
all his entrepreneurial drive and know-how, he depended heavily on
partners. If Charles followed an organizing principle in his life, it was that
of forming good partnerships — with William Lee, William Aldrich,
Samuel Damon, and especially Pauahi.

When the Bishops moved into Hale'ākala in 1855, Charles' partnership
with William A. Aldrich, established only two years before, was flourishing. There were a few setbacks, but nothing serious enough to prevent
them from dividing up a healthy profit two years later.[75] The year 1857 was
a happy one for business. It was also a sad year for Charles as his original
partner, William Lee, died of tuberculosis, the cause for his leaving New
York. Kōnia died that same year. In their grief Charles and Pauahi had
reason to console each other, and perhaps to depend upon each other as
they had never quite done before.

Though Aldrich & Bishop was doing well, Charles, the typical
entrepreneur, looked for even better and bigger challenges. Five years
before, Robert C. Wyllie had presented a plan for establishing a bank to
the Royal Agricultural Society. It seemed to be a good idea on paper at
least, for two years later a bank was organized. But it closed after a short
time and Hawai'i was without a bank.[76] Though the need was waiting to
be filled, Charles was a cautious risk-taker. He must have studied the local
demand for banking services, investigated the potential problems, projected his expenses and profits, and talked with a few people who could
influence his success: a few key customers, government leaders and, of
course, Pauahi.

However deep Pauahi's faith in Charles, her prudent nature may have
led her to view his decision as a daring, if not foolhardy step. He was
ending a thriving business in order to launch a venture with no guarantee
of success. If Pauahi had such fears, they were understandable, because
she now had to worry about the expenses of her new home and the care of
Lili'u, not to mention the welfare of the retainers and their families. If
only to lessen her anxiety, Charles would have consulted with her. But he

would have wanted to discuss his new undertaking with her in any case, given her status in the community, particularly her close ties with the ruling *ali'i*, and her intelligence and good judgment. After all, he had a very important partnership with her, too.

In any event, Charles and Aldrich dissolved their successful store and reorganized their partnership. On August 17, 1858, they opened for business in a small office, twelve by sixteen feet, in downtown Honolulu. Charles, the leading partner in the new bank, assumed most of the duties, from taking care of customers to keeping the books. He hired one person, William Kaluna, as a porter.[77] Such were the humble beginnings of Bishop & Company, known today as the First Hawaiian Bank, the oldest financial institution of its kind in the State of Hawai'i.

In describing its origins, Edward Joesting, author of the official history of First Hawaiian Bank, writes: "The reputations of the partners were the only assurances of safety customers of the bank had. The memory of the closing of Page, Bacon certainly was a worry to many in the community. Bishop and Aldrich, however, had each been in the Islands for many years and their reputations were established by their business success and the woman each had married."[78] This statement recognizes the contribution Pauahi made to the bank's successful start. Since all business is transacted on the basis of trust between two or more people, every business stands or falls on the reputation or creditability of the proprietors. Especially in the banking business, ultimately nothing is more critical to success than public trust and confidence. If anyone connected with the bank's ownership had had less than an unimpeachable reputation, that would have jeopardized its standing and prospects for success. Charles must have been pleased with the fact that his wife had an impeccable reputation that he could draw upon in establishing the bank's initial credibility. He may have been able eventually to achieve credibility on the basis of his own very solid image in the community, but Pauahi's status and *mana*, as it were, must have helped, although it is impossible to tell how much.

If Pauahi had the gardener's touch, Charles had the golden touch. His bank made money from the beginning. In less than five months, he paid back in full a $5,000 startup loan, and after the first year, each partner received as his share of the profits "the very substantial sum of $3,900."[79] Charles was on his way to making the fortune that would one day endow some of the best schools in Hawai'i, including that founded by Pauahi.

Charles hardly had time to adjust to his new career as a banker before he was harnessed into government service. In January 1859, King Kamehameha IV made him a member of the Privy Council which evolved out of the former Council of Chiefs.[80] In effect, Charles had been granted the office of a chief. A year later, he was named a life member of the House of Nobles. Charles was thus made an *ali'i* in all but name and blood. Though Charles was greatly admired for his own merits, would he have been so honored if he had not married a chiefess of Pauahi's standing? This is not to suggest that Pauahi connived with Alexander to have Charles raised to the peerage, so to speak. Charles would not have condoned such a gesture, however well intended. But in the highly status-conscious, close-knit society of the *ali'i*, Pauahi would probably have encouraged any effort to give Charles his due as the consort of a Kamehameha.

The state of the bank was a fairly good barometer of the state of the Hawaiian economy. Thanks to the whaling industry, the 1850s were profitable years and the bank's initial success reflected that fact. The 1860s, however, were a different story: whaling was dying. The number of ships that called on island ports decreased drastically, purchasing of provisions from local merchants dwindled, and spending by seamen and other visitors dropped sharply. All of this affected government revenues. The industry's decline was gradual and predictable so that some steps could be taken to develop other viable economic alternatives. Agriculture, particularly sugar, loomed as the best hope. Charles and his partners had anticipated this turn of events, as evidenced by their early investments in Līhu'e Plantation. Sugar, in fact, had become Charles' "chief business specialty" aside from banking.[81] The bank was primed to take advantage of the shift to an agricultural economy based on the export of sugar.

The shift was reflected in the production figures. In 1860 island sugar growers produced only 750 tons, but in 1865 they produced 5,000 tons.[82] In the summer of 1865, the *Hawaiian Gazette* had already placed its bets on sugar's future: "But a new era has dawned upon the Islands—the era of sugar — and the cultivation of cane overshadows by far all other agricultural enterprises...it is considered beyond a doubt that sugar is to be, in the future, as it already is at present, the staple product of our Islands."[83]

Sugar was becoming king and Charles was one of the king-makers. He helped to finance the growth of the industry in its adolescent and mature years. He had saved the industry from early collapse a few years before by coming to the rescue of the largest sugar agency, Walker, Allen & Company, then on the verge of bankruptcy.[84] Charles was not strictly a banker, but more a financial entrepreneur providing the range of money services needed in the freewheeling system of the times. Even more, he helped to provide a steadying influence. The early stages of any new industry are always fraught with great trauma and require a steady hand, not to mention deep pockets, if events are to be kept under control.

Yet, while sugar may have sweetened his balance sheet, growth of the industry would have bitter consequences for the Hawaiian body politic. It would cause deep cleavages in the economic and political life of the people, including Pauahi and Charles.

The Unfulfilled

With the bank successfully launched and Charles securely emplaced in a position of *ali'i* status, Pauahi had practically everything she had ever dreamed of: a loving, upright, dynamic and prosperous husband; a splendid home with all of the trappings of chiefly position; friends among the rich and famous as well as the poor and unknown; the hope of health and longevity — everything, that is, except children of her own.

After more than ten years of marriage, the expectations Pauahi and Charles had of having a family were still unfulfilled. We have no clues about the cause of the problem, whether infertility or impotence or some other health reason. There were certainly not any psycho-cultural reasons, because, as we have seen in her experiences and attitudes from childhood on, Pauahi loved and wanted children. Aside from fulfilling her own maternal instincts, for a Hawaiian chiefess procreation was also a sacred responsibility.

It was no comfort if Pauahi knew that her condition was common among the *ali'i* and the Kamehamehas in particular. Ka'ahumanu had no children and Kalama, the wife of Kamehameha III, had either one or two children who died at birth. As we shall see, neither Alexander, Lot nor Lunalilo would leave any heirs. Nor would the Kalākauas, that is, Lili'u or David. For a society that based its existence on the preservation and continuity of *ali'i* with genealogical and genetic purity, the lack of royal children was a grave concern. And for the Kamehamehas, whose dynastic succession was at stake, the problem was even more critical.

This is why there was immense joy, if not relief, in the Kingdom when Emma gave birth to a son in May 1858. It was the first time in many decades that a reigning queen had given birth. By the same token, there was an equal amount of sorrow when, four years later, the "Prince of Hawai'i" died. Pauahi was particularly moved, as she was at the bedside of the dying child along with Emma and Alexander on that fatal morning of August 27.[85] Emma would never give birth to another child.

Having many reasons for wanting a child, Pauahi decided to adopt one — not any child but a Kamehameha. At the time there was only one possible source, her magnificent cousin, Princess Ruth Ke'elikōlani, the daughter of her aunt and namesake, through whose veins coursed the same blood. In 1856, Keʻelikōlani had married Isaac Young Davis. He was the son of George Davis Huʻeu, whose father was the famed Isaac Davis, one of Kamehameha I's closest advisers along with John Young.[86] By the middle of the summer of 1862, Ruth had become pregnant. Around that time Pauahi approached Ruth and asked for her next child. Since they were close and had enormous respect and aloha for each other, they must easily have reached an agreement.

The adoption, however, was to be greatly complicated by Lot's interference. The story is related to us by Liliʻu. It was February 1863, and Ruth was about to give birth. Liliʻu was in Hilo on a tour with Lot. Kalaikuaiwa, one of Ruth's people, was about to leave for Honolulu to attend the birth. Kalaikuaiwa inquired of Lot if he had any message for Ruth regarding the child. He told her to charge his sister (Lot and Ruth had the same father, Kekūanaōʻa) that on no account should she give the child away. To this Kalaikuaiwa said that "it had been already promised to Mrs. Pauahi Bishop." Lot insisted again saying, "You must go back and tell my sister that on no account is she to give that child to another. I am an adopted child myself, deprived of the love of my mother, and yet I was a stranger in the house of my adoption."[87]

But there was more to it than this, for after the death of the "Prince of Hawaiʻi," Lot became heir apparent to the throne, and he was a bachelor without an heir. There was no other Kamehameha except an acknowledged natural son of Kamehameha III, Prince Albert Kunuiakea. Thus, when Lot learned of Ruth's pregnancy, he saw an opportunity. Though he had no idea at that time that he would be the King of Hawaiʻi within another year, he evidently realized that Ruth's child would be a possible heir to the throne.[88] In effect, he wanted the child available just in case.

Lot returned to Honolulu in time for the birth and was summoned to Ruth's home for the event, along with Emma, Pauahi and others. While he waited on the *lānai*, Emma and Pauahi attended to the delivery inside. The baby was delivered at about three o'clock in the afternoon, but Lot was not told until about half-past five. Then Emma appeared and asked him if he had heard from Ruth, to which he replied that he had not. According to Liliʻu, Emma "expressed much surprise, and told him that the newly born infant had been taken away as her own by Mrs. Bishop over an hour ago." When Lot heard this "extremely unpleasant" news, he was furious and "at once declared that he would never have anything to do with that child."[89]

Lili'u's account is instructive both for what it says and does not say about Pauahi's relationship with Ruth. First, it should be clear that there was some conspiracy among Ruth and Pauahi and the women in attendance. This explains the fact that Pauahi slipped out of the house with the child without Lot's knowledge. It also explains why Ruth and Emma allowed Lot to wait for two and a half hours before he was informed of the birth. Normally, such glad tidings would have been transmitted immediately. But the apparent deception was probably the best way to handle the situation, to prevent an ugly scene between Pauahi and Lot. Neither she nor Ruth would have wanted that.

Ruth had promised the child to Pauahi and was not about to break her promise. She knew the child would be well cared for by Pauahi and Charles, and the gift of the child symbolized her aloha for Pauahi. Besides, Ruth was not about to risk the punishment associated with *hua'ōlelo*, a broken promise. She was too much a Hawaiian to take that risk, and Lot should have known that. Whatever Ruth's feelings for Lot, his actions had forced her to make a choice between him and Pauahi, and for Ruth there was really no choice.

At last Pauahi had her child and heir, part English and part Hawaiian, a son named Keolaokalani or "The Life of the Heavenly One." We can only wonder at how Pauahi might have allowed her feelings to engulf the child like an endless rising tide generated by currents of maternal affection from deep within. She was, after all, releasing feelings she had been reserving and accumulating inside for thirty-three years, or what would be more than half of her life. If she now became so engrossed in caring for and holding the child as to neglect Charles a little, he would not have begrudged her these fulfilling moments. For now Hale'ākala was full and so was Pauahi's life.

But six months was all the time she would have with her son. He died on August 29, 1863. We don't know the circumstances, but we know how Pauahi must have grieved. It is said that "All Hawai'i grieved with the stricken chiefess" although no one knew then that Keolaokalani would be the last baby born into the Kamehameha line.[90]

Many years later Pauahi tried to adopt another child, only to have the child's mother refuse her request. Some Hawaiians feel that she was destined never to have any children to raise or adopt because of *'ūhā kapu* or *kapu* lap. This belief stems from the idea of the sacredness of *ali'i* women. Such a woman was considered so sacred that a child should not be held on her lap unless the *ali'i* chiefess took the child herself. Or if the child accidentally wet the chiefess, that child would automatically become the adopted child of the *ali'i*. Even more extreme, if the child were of lesser rank, unfit to be adopted by an *ali'i*, it could be killed. For this reason, Hawaiians supposedly kept their babies away from such *ali'i* women. It is averred that Pauahi had had this *kapu* laid upon her by the gods long before she was born.[91]

Did she believe it? We will never know. Whatever her belief, during her lifetime she would have no children of her own. The heirs she would have would be the children of Hawai'i-nei.

5

A CAPTIVE OF
THE POLITICS OF FATE

Eventually all of us are touched by politics, but there are those few who become deeply entangled either of their own volition or through circumstance. In Pauahi's case, entanglement in the politics of the day was more a matter of birth and marriage than of choice. She was not a politician, yet she spent her entire life near the centers of power. She did not openly seek influence, yet she was in so many ways a source of it. When she sought to disengage herself from political events, she was nearly engulfed in their wake. In a sense, she was a captive of the politics of fate.

The focus of this chapter of her life is a series of events that converged in the early 1870s. The first is the famous episode when the dying King Kamehameha V (Lot) offered Pauahi the throne, and she refused it. Although this poignant moment has been dutifully described by nearly every writer of modern Hawaiian history, these accounts give us little insight into Pauahi's possible reasons. These reasons have to do with a complex of early experiences, attitudes and values that help to explain an otherwise baffling event. We need not speculate on what would have happened had she accepted Lot's offer. But in examining the factors involved in still another rejection of Lot, we can come to an understanding of Pauahi's own politics.

The second is less an event as such than a clash of principles between Pauahi and Charles over the economics and politics of sugar. It was one of the few disagreements that marred their relationship, but their positions and reasons mirrored what was happening in Hawaiian society as a whole. The specific issue was whether the Reciprocity Treaty was worth the cost of turning the lands of Pu'uloa or Pearl Harbor over to the United States. This very complex problem involved not only Charles' bank, but the livelihoods of thousands of Hawaiians as well as their ultimate political future. Circumstances intervened to resolve the issue for Charles and Pauahi and for everyone else.

The third event is Pauahi's final opportunity to weigh and then to reject a chance at ruling the Kingdom. It involves the succession of Lunalilo, the "Citizens' King," who died in 1874, after a reign of only little more than a year. The story of the battle for succession between David Kalākaua and Emma the Dowager Queen has been well-documented, but far less has been known about Pauahi's involvement. In some revealing letters written to her cousin Peter at Kalaupapa, we are treated to rare glimpses of Emma's suspicions of Pauahi's deeds and words.

These episodes show that Pauahi was much more than the dutiful Christian wife tending to her domestic chores or obligations, rather oblivious to the political fray going on around her. Pauahi was caught inevitably in the cross-currents of Hawaiian politics, yet managed never to be swept away.

The Kingdom in 1870

If the 1830s were "troubled times," the 1870s were hardly less troubled. The period is one of the most critical for modern Hawaiians.[1] For one thing, important developments were taking place in the size and composition of the Kingdom's population. In 1831, the native (full and part-Hawaiian) population was about 124,500. In 1872, it was 51,500. In her lifetime Pauahi witnessed more than a 59 percent decline in the number of her people. The population of the Kingdom as a whole, both Hawaiian and foreign, reached its nadir between 1875 and 1876, and then began to climb. But the decline of the Hawaiians and part-Hawaiians continued for many more years. Death was no respector of persons, and the ali'i and maka'āinana were dying together. As the Hawaiian population decreased, the foreigner population increased slowly and then by dramatic leaps. In 1853, for example, there were 1,828 foreigners, including 364 Chinese, most of whom had arrived the year before as contract laborers for the plantations. By 1872, the number of foreigners was 5,366, climbing to 36,446 in 1884. Although Pauahi did not live to see it, she understood the trend; six years later the foreign population had reached 49,368, more than the entire ethnic Hawaiian population.[2] It was the first time since the arrival from Hawai'iki of the islands' original settlers that there were more outsiders than native Hawaiians. Hawaiians had become not merely a displaced but a dying race. As we shall see, this change would become a basic factor in Pauahi's later determination of what her legacy should be.

The increase in foreigners, of course, was caused by the demands of sugar planters for additional labor to meet higher production levels. There were simply not enough Hawaiians willing to endure the drudgery and toil of plantation life in preference to their own way of life. It was not that Hawaiians were lazy. Kuykendall states: "Hawaiians did work on sugar plantations in fairly large numbers. In the decades when the sugar industry was getting its start, they performed nearly all of the labor on plantations...As late as 1869 some plantations employed Hawaiian labor exclusively. There were many planters who considered such labor the best obtainable. A writer in 1870 made this comment: 'Whilst the population has largely diminished, there are probably as many or more Hawaiians working upon plantations to-day than ever before, and doing it cheerfully, of their own free will....' "[3] Only after the Reciprocity Treaty was signed in 1875, opening up the huge U.S. market and the raising of productivity levels by many millions of tons, were the floodgates of immigrant labor opened wide.

Many Hawaiians looked upon these demographic and economic changes with deep foreboding. As more Hawaiians died, more of their lands were bought up by others. As more immigrants arrived, more Hawaiians were displaced or forced to compete against ever mounting odds. And as sugar and other foreign economic interests gained more and more control, Hawaiians lost more and more of their economic and political power.

One of the ugly consequences of this spiral of gloom was the rise of racial conflict. Once free of any racial prejudice, Hawaiians gradually aimed their resentment at foreigners of any stripe. By 1870, for example, anti-Chinese sentiment was rife in certain quarters. One newspaper observed: "There is already quite enough bad feeling existing among the natives against the coolies."[4] Several petitions were introduced in the 1870 legislature opposing any further introduction of Chinese. This feeling increased in the 1880s as Chinese, after leaving the plantations, began to take over farming (including taro) and retailing activities once dominated by Hawaiians. One bitter Hawaiian spokesman said: "They have demoralized, debased and decimated our people."[5]

A good deal of native pique was reserved for *haole* Americans who had long since gained economic control over Hawai'i. From the 1850s on, the Americans repeatedly threatened to gain political domination by having Hawai'i annexed to the U.S. mainland. King Kamehameha V (Lot) greatly feared American interests, including the missionaries, who would "lead to the overthrow of the monarchy, annexation to the United States, and ultimate extinction of the Hawaiian race."[6] Lot was adamant in his opposition to annexation, labeling those who advocated it as "hellish conspirators."[7] His pro-Hawaiian policies took on an increasing anti-

American tone as Hawaiians everywhere voiced their hostility against the *haole* who were forever conspiring to hand the Kingdom over to Washington. Verbal battles in the legislature between Hawaiian and *haole* members sometimes ended in fist fights, symptomatic of the growing split between the races.[8]

The hostess of Hale'ākala was under no illusions about what was going on in the sugar or taro fields, bank offices or legislative halls. The merry parties, charades, croquet games, moonlight boat rides, the pomp and circumstance, none of these could muffle the wailing for the dead, or conceal the growing antagonism among the races, or suppress the economic disparities between the few and the many. Her intelligence network at the grassroots level and at the decision-making levels let her know all that was important for her to know about the state of the Kingdom. If the Kingdom was troubled, so was Pauahi.

Prudence in the Face of Glory

It was Lot's birthday, Wednesday, the 11th of December 1872. In the early morning, preparations were under way for its usual celebration as a national holiday. Sanford Dole, who was present, described the scene: "Flags fluttered from the government and private masts and shipping in the harbor. Business houses and shops were closed, and working men of all classes rested from labor. Parties of townspeople were starting out into the country to enjoy the holiday in rural festivities, while a scattered army of natives on their half-trained horses galloped gaily into town over the various roads, from all parts of the island, men, women, and children, and even the horses crowned and garlanded with flowing wreaths of the fragrant *maile*, all eager to join in whatever merry making or excitement the city had to offer."[9]

In the meantime, a tragic scene was unfolding in the King's private quarters: Lot was dying. Acknowledging the supreme irony of the moment, he is reported to have said, "It is hard to die on my birthday, but God's will be done."[10] One of the physicians who called in the morning, Dr. George Trousseau, gave him no hope. He advised that if Lot had "any business to settle he had better do it at once, as he would not live through the day." But Lot already knew his time had come.

He had been seriously ill for several months with "dropsy on the chest" (a form of pleurisy) but had managed to conceal the severity of his condition from the public, partly by issuing regular bulletins that declared he was "in excellent health."[11] However, the King's absence from all state occasions and drives in the city for the past two months had led to many rumors about his true condition. The truth caused anxiety among high government officials who were deeply concerned about his succession.

Lot's condition had deteriorated the night before, and a number of officials, chiefs and trusted friends had been hastily summoned to his apartment. Among them were Lili'u and her husband, Governor John Dominis, but apparently neither Pauahi nor Charles were there during the night. Lili'u and the others spent the entire night near Lot's bedside "watching in silence" as he lay in a stupor.[12]

Sometime very early the next morning, a palace messenger informed Pauahi of Lot's condition and of his request that she be with him. Why she had not been told the evening before is not known. She hurried to his side. When she got there, Lot, who was weak but conscious by then, indicated he wanted her to sit next to him. She may instinctively have taken his hand in hers, as she did with the sick she often visited.

The room was filled with a royal audience. They included Lili'u, Judge Kamakau and Colonel Prendergast who were standing at the head of the bed; Mrs. Brickwood and Kamaipuupaa who were opposite Pauahi; the attorney general Stephen Philips who stood in the *ma uka* door near to the bed; and Ruth, who was seated on the floor some distance from the bed, on the *ma kai* side (toward the sea). The governor of Maui, Nahaolelua, a close friend of the King, was kneeling beside the bed at the King's head. Governor Dominis, who, at the King's request, was taking notes of his last words and acts, was standing next to Pauahi. Standing near the *ma kai* door were Lunalilo, Kalākaua, and others.

It was no accident that the candidates for the throne and the attorney general were present. Lot had not named a successor, despite the pleas of his advisers during the preceding months to do so. Neither had he drawn up a will. In fact, for a few moments after sunrise Philips had tried to draft a will for him to execute and had urged him to name a successor then and there. Irritated by Philips' insistence, Lot told him "he wanted time to consider so important a subject and that he had been taken by surprise at the statement of the physicians, and was naturally nervous and under a great state of excitement."[13] But, with death only moments away, the naming of a successor could not be put off. So, at this eleventh hour, he set out to select his successor.

Lot began in a strange way by asking Nahaolelua to name his successor. At first Nahaolelua would not answer. He was put in an awful position and finally declined, saying that they were all his *ali'i*. Perhaps this was Lot's own prelude to what he really wanted to do.

Lot turned to Pauahi at his side and declared, "I wish you to take my place, to be my successor."[14]

Pauahi was taken aback. She replied: "No, no, not me; don't think of me, I do not need it." If any of the others in earshot of Lot's weakened voice were also surprised by his declaration, we do not know.

The King, who was about to press the issue, interrupted himself by inquiring suddenly why the room was so dark. Looking towards the *ma kai* door he asked, "What are all those people doing in there?" The "people" were Lunalilo and Kalākaua, among others. Pauahi then motioned them to go away and they left.

Lot continued, "I do not wish you to think I do this from motives of friendship, but I think it best for my people and my nation." Lot was alluding to his own personal friendship to Pauahi since the calling off of their betrothal, and he wanted to assure her as well as others that his choice was based on objective and rational grounds.

Pauahi, still unnerved by his request, said, "Oh, no, do not think of me, there are others; there is your sister, it is hers by right." Pauahi was referring to Lot's half-sister, Ruth, her own cousin. Lot quickly answered, "She is not fitted for the position."

"But," Pauahi insisted, "we will all help her; I, my husband, your ministers; we will all *kōkua* (help) and advise her."

Lot replied, "No, she would not answer." That is, she would not be suitable as his successor. We do not know whether Ruth heard his remark, and if so how she reacted to Lot's opinion. But no doubt she would have been touched by Pauahi's loyalty to her.

After seeing that the King had rejected her first suggestion, Pauahi offered another. "There is the Queen, Emma; she has been a Queen once, and is therefore fitted for the position."

Lot answered, "She was merely Queen by courtesy, having been the wife of a King." It was probably just as well that Emma was not present to hear these words.

Either out of resignation or weariness or both, the King stopped the exchange. Governor Dominis wrote, "The King wishing at this time to get out of his bed, we all left the room, and after that he never alluded to the subject of a successor or expressed any further wishes." About an hour later he died, undoubtedly disappointed at his failure to name a successor and at having misread the motives of the woman he admired above all.

A little before half-past ten, the cannon, on the crest of Pūowaina (Punchbowl crater) overlooking the city, once primed to herald the celebration of the King's birthday, "began to thunder forth in mournful minute guns, the announcement that he, whose birth the people were then commemorating, was dead." Sanford Dole continued, "... national festivities scattered over many a league were checked and hushed with the ominous warning, and the echoes of the death peal reverberating among the cliffs and crags of the mountains bore to the distant parts of the island a vague hint of the brooding of a public crisis."[15]

In failing to announce a successor, Lot left an enormous problem for the Hawaiian nation—and a string of questions for posterity. For example, why did he feel Pauahi was the best qualified to succeed him? If this was his feeling, why hadn't he made a decision earlier, so as to avoid a national crisis? Why did Pauahi defer to Ruth and then to Emma? And, most importantly, why did Pauahi so completely reject his offer? Other, even more speculative, questions arise: What would have happened if Pauahi had accepted Lot's offer? How might Hawaiian history have changed? Would the Bishop Estate and the Kamehameha Schools still have been founded?

Let us consider just the first set of questions. What were Lot's reasons for believing Pauahi to be the best qualified? When he said he was not speaking "from motives of friendship," Lot wanted to make very clear to Pauahi and everyone in the room that, whatever his personal emotions for her, he was acting responsibly and honestly. He did not want his decision to be in any way tainted by suspicions of favoritism or nepotism. He made it known that his reasons were entirely based on her merits and qualifications and the needs of the nation.

It was a courageous and magnanimous statement for a King to make on his deathbed. Lot admitted openly that in spite of the disappointments, if not humiliation, dealt him by Pauahi in the past, including the adoption of Keolaokalani, he still held her in the highest regard. Had Lot been any less a man, he might have behaved differently, but he showed no malice or hard feelings of any kind toward her. Pauahi was the one woman who would have made his life complete, the one woman whom he would have married — the one woman whom fate seemed to have placed in his way almost at birth and now at death. He seemed heroic in his attachment to Pauahi, and we can only wonder how she may have felt at the time.

Lot had been King for nine years and had had more than ample time and experience to know the personal qualities a monarch should have. He was also steeped in his culture and history and had a good understanding of those characteristics that traditionally marked the strong *ali'i*. He knew Pauahi as well as any other person except Charles. So, when he looked critically at Pauahi's qualities and compared her with the others, he was making an informed judgment. We do not know the specific qualities he stressed. But they would have included her courage, independence and determination, humility, generosity, industry, leadership and intelligence — all traits that characterized his mother Kīna'u and grandfather Kamehameha I. Lot also knew of Pauahi's aloha, tolerance, caring, frugality, patience, faith, prudence, *lōkahi* and integrity. Any defects he observed must have been overshadowed by the sum of her virtues.

Character alone does not make a leader in any political system. Lot also had to consider Pauahi's knowledge and experience. Her formal schooling under the Cookes had certainly not prepared her or any of the other students to head a government. The knowledge she had gained about administration, economics, policy-making, or international relations, among other subjects, came largely through her extensive reading, interpersonal contact, and observation. She obviously had no government experience, unlike Ruth who was Governess of the island of Hawai'i, nor any legislative experience except through her association with Charles. But she had gained a good deal of experience in practical leadership and management through her estates, including Hale'ākala, and the various organizations she belonged to.

One of Pauahi's strengths was her understanding of the *haole* world and ability to work with white people. Her English was impeccable. She had firsthand knowledge of the United States, having traveled there in 1866 and 1871, a trip which lasted for five months and took her across the country to the East Coast and to Canada as well. She knew more about the United States than any of the other candidates for the throne and comprehended better the nature of the challenge America posed to the survival of the Kingdom. As well as any of the chiefs, she understood Americans, whether they were missionaries or businessmen. Most important of all, she was well-liked and respected in the foreign community for her intelligence and understanding. The U.S. Minister, David L. Gregg, observed in a report to his superiors in Washington that Pauahi was "a well-educated, intelligent lady, moving in the best-circles of society, and worthy of the general respect she receives."[16] Lot must have seen in Pauahi what he himself lacked: a deep understanding of and rapport with America and Americans. If he realized that coming to terms with the United States politically and economically was one of the major problems facing the nation in the 1870s and beyond, then it was logical for him to see Pauahi as his successor.

More important to Lot, however, was Pauahi's philosophical position on the issues that meant the most to him, such as the preservation of the monarchy and the political independence of Hawai'i. Pauahi fully sup-

Kamehameha in Red Vest, *pencil drawing, with watercolor wash, by Louis Choris, artist with Russian explorer von Kotzebue, 1816. King Kamehameha I (c. 1758–1819) was Pauahi's great-grandfather.*

Courtesy of Bishop Museum

*High Chiefess Kanaholo Konia
(1808–1857), the mother of Pauahi.
Konia was the daughter of Kaʻōleiokū,
the first son of Kamehameha I.*

Courtesy of Bishop Museum

*Abner Kaʻehu Pākī (1818–1855), Pauahi's
father. A high chief from Maui, he was
noted as having an imposing physique
and a light complexion.*

Courtesy of Bishop Museum

Kahoʻanoku Kīnaʻu (1807–1839), returning from church services. The hānai *mother of Pauahi, Kīnaʻu was the eldest daughter of Kamehameha I and prime minister of Hawaiʻi when she adopted the infant Pauahi.*

Courtesy of Bishop Museum

High Chief Mataio Kekūanaōʻa (1791–1868), hānai *father of Pauahi and husband of Kīnaʻu. Kekūanaōʻa was the father of Kamehameha IV, Kamehameha V, and Victoria Kamāmalu.*

Courtesy of Bishop Museum

KA NONANONA.

"E ka mea hiamoe, e hele oe i ka nonanona, e nana i kona naoao a e hoonaauao iho." *Solomona.*

Buke 1. **HONOLULU, OAHU, IULAI 20, 1841.** **Pepa 2.**

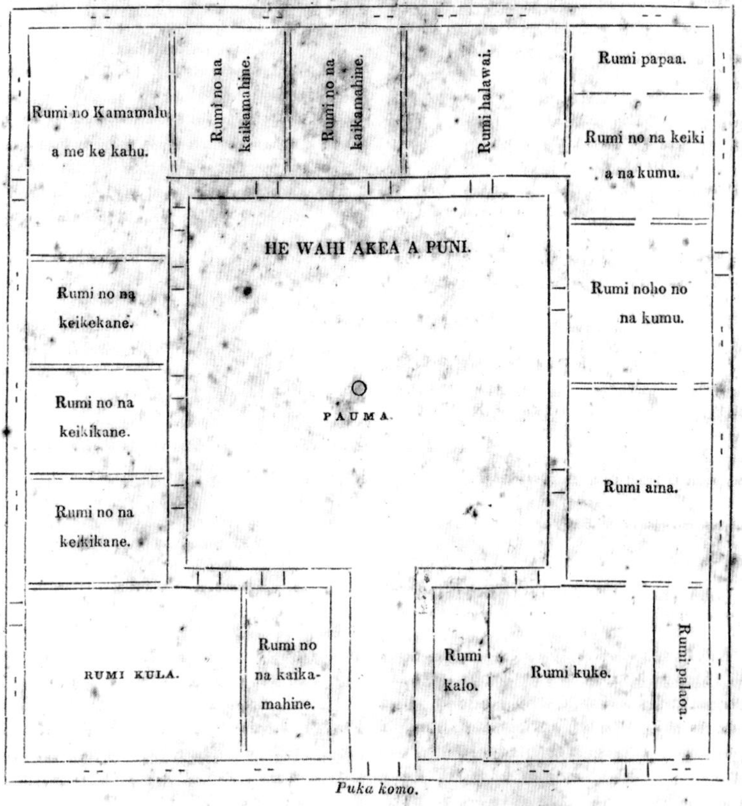

Rumi no Kamamalu a me ke kahu.
Rumi no na kaikamahine.
Rumi no na kaikamahine.
Rumi halawai.
Rumi papaa.
Rumi no na keiki a na kumu.
HE WAHI AKEA A PUNI.
Rumi no na keikekane.
Rumi no na keikikane.
Rumi no na keikikane.
PAUMA.
Rumi noho no na kumu.
Rumi aina.
RUMI KULA.
Rumi no na kaika-mahine.
Rumi kalo.
Rumi kuke.
Rumi palaoa.
Puka komo.

KA HALE KULA ALII.

O ka halekula keia no na keiki a na'lii, ma Honolulu, Oahu, mauka ae o ka hale pohaku o Kekauluohi. Ua kukuluia keia hale kula e na'lii i ka makahi o ko kakou Haku 1839. Na lakou no ka uku, aole na na misionari. Elua tausani dala paha ka uku, a ua make pono no keia uku i keia hale maikai. Na na'lii ka uku a na ke kumu no ka hoolimalima ana i na haole, a me na kanaka maoli nana i hana. Aia, maluna iho ke ano o keia hale. Ua like ka loa, me ka laula. O ka loa he 76 kapuai ia; a pela no ka laula. Ua kukuluia keia hale i na lepo kawili, a he umi kapuai paha ke kiekie o na paia, a elua kapuai ka manoanoa. O na paku he lepo no ia, a hookahi kapuai ka manoanoa. O ke pili o keia hale kula, he pili maoli no ia. E nana aku i ke kii maluna, i akaka ka puka nui e komo ai, na puka komo e ae, a me na puka ani-

The Chiefs' Children's School where, between 1839 and 1850, Pauahi and other ali'i *children were educated. This diagram of the school appeared on the front page of the Hawaiian newspaper* Ka Nonanona *on July 20, 1841.*

Courtesy of Hawaiian Historical Society

Amos Starr Cooke and daughter Mary Annis. Cooke and his wife served as the principle teachers at the Chiefs' Children's School.

Courtesy of Bishop Museum

Juliette Montague Cooke and son Amos Francis. Mrs. Cooke was Pauahi's teacher as well as her primary caregiver at the Chiefs' Children's School.

Courtesy of Bishop Museum

Pauahi at fifteen. This daguerrotype, taken in 1847, is the earliest known image of Pauahi.

Courtesy of Bishop Museum

Lot Kamehameha (the future Kamehameha V) at twenty. During Pauahi's childhood Kīna'u had planned a marriage between the two high-ranking royals that Pauahi would later reject.

Courtesy of Hawai'i State Archives

Charles Reed Bishop (1822–1915) at twenty-four.
Courtesy of Bishop Museum

Charles Reed Bishop and best friend William E. Lee, shown before their departure from Newburyport, Massachusetts, in 1846.
Courtesy of Bishop Museum

Wedding photo of Mr. and Mrs. Charles Reed Bishop taken on June 4, 1850, in the living quarters of Amos and Juliette Cooke at the Chiefs' Children's School. The young couple would have had a far grander wedding had not her parents, other ali'i, *and missionaries opposed the marriage.*

Courtesy of Bishop Museum

The He'eia fishpond on Kāne'ohe Bay where Pauahi frequently went to relax with friends. It was part of the estate given to her by her father, Pākī.

Courtesy of Bishop Museum

Hale'ākala, built by Pauahi's father, Pākī, was completed in 1855. The Bishops moved to the home and lived there with Pauahi's mother Konia, Pauahi's hānai sister Lili'u, and a large number of retainers. The home was located at the present site of Tamarind Square on the corner of King and Bishop streets. Hale'ākala was the center of many important social events while the Bishops lived there. The figure shown seated on the lower veranda is Charles Reed Bishop.

Courtesy of Bishop Museum

Pauahi and her hānai *sister, Lili'u, in 1859.*

Kamehameha Elementary School students viewing a section of the tamarind tree that once grew at Hale'ākala and provided shade for Pauahi as she counseled her people. The tree was cut down in 1901 and this portion saved. It rests now on the grounds of the Kapālama Campus of the Kamehameha Schools.

Pauahi on one of her several trips to San Francisco.
Courtesy of Bishop Museum

Princess Ruth Ke'elikōlani (right of center) with her son (seated to her left), Prince Leleiōhoku. Ruth was the mother of Pauahi's adopted son who died in infancy.
Courtesy of Bishop Museum

*Princess Ruth Keʻelikōlani, Pauahi's cousin. Ruth inherited the
Kamehameha lands which she willed to Pauahi upon her death in 1883.
These lands form the bulk of the current Kamehameha Schools' holdings.*

Courtesy of Bishop Museum

Kamehameha V (ca. 1865) ruled from 1863 to 1872. On his deathbed he offered the throne to Pauahi, which she declined.

Courtesy of Bishop Museum

Lunalilo, the first elected Hawaiian monarch, reigned just over one year before dying on February 3, 1874, only two years after the death of Kamehameha V. Charles Reed Bishop served as Lunalilo's minister of foreign affairs.

Courtesy of Bishop Museum

David Kalākaua was elected king and ascended the throne on February 12, 1874. Charles Reed Bishop served as president of the board of education during Kalākaua's reign.

Courtesy of Bishop Museum

Queen Emma, widow of Alexander Liholiho (Kamehameha IV) was considered a possible successor to the throne after Lot Kamehameha's death.

Courtesy of Bishop Museum

The Bishops in Venice, 1875.

Courtesy of Bishop Museum

Charles Reed Bishop's bank building, on the corner of Merchant and Kaʻahumanu Streets, was completed in 1878. With partner William Aldrich, Bishop formed a business named Bishop & Co. which would later become the First Hawaiian Bank.

Courtesy of Bishop Museum

The Bishop's residence at Waikīkī where Pauahi spent a few months resting in the late summer of 1884.

Courtesy of Hawai'i State Archives

Keōua Hale, Princess Ruth's mansion which she built in 1882 to rival 'Iolani Palace. Pauahi spent her last days here before her death on October 16, 1884. Charles Reed Bishop continued to live here for ten years following Pauahi's death before he moved to California. Keōua Hale was located at the current site of Central Intermediate School in Honolulu.

Courtesy of Bishop Museum

Pauahi in San Francisco in 1875.

Courtesy of Bishop Museum

ported Lot on the importance of maintaining Hawaiian sovereignty and agreed with him again in opposing the cession of any lands to the United States. As we shall see, she would have opposed the annexation of Hawai'i to the United States at nearly any cost. And by virtue of her upbringing and commitment to the values of her *ali'i*-hood, she unquestionably supported the continuation of *ali'i* rule. The extent to which Pauahi would have accepted democratic principles and procedures in a monarchical government is not clear. For example, we do not know to what degree she agreed with Lot's abrogation of the 1852 Constitution with its liberal provisions of popular government, although she appears to have been more for democratic participation than against it. Ideologically, Pauahi was as much a political "nativist" as was Lot.

Finally, Lot had no difficulty in acknowledging the depth of Pauahi's commitment to her people and to her lineage as a Kamehameha. If he had any doubts about either, he would never have dared even to entertain the possibility of naming her as his successor. While Pauahi did not entirely share all of Lot's exuberant support of the old ways, including the use of a court *kahuna* (priest), she still was fundamentally a traditionalist, as he was. In sum, Lot had good reasons for choosing Pauahi as his successor.

But why did he wait till the last hours of his life to announce his choice? One view is that Lot had a "superstitious fear," that if he appointed a successor such an act would cause his premature death. This fear is supposed to have been due to his misplaced faith in Kamaipuupaa, his female *kahuna*. Kuykendall did not believe that "superstitious fear prevented Kamehameha V from naming his successor." He argued that Lot simply did not want to appoint Lunalilo "whom he, in common with his subjects, recognized as having the best natural claim to the throne but whom he also considered to be unfit for the position."[17] Actually, Kuykendall begs the question because, if Lot's only goal was not appointing Lunalilo, his waiting to announce his choice would not have mattered.

It seems quite plausible that Lot really was afraid to appoint a successor for fear of an early death. He had strong feelings for the ritual power of the ancient priestly order. Kamaipuupaa was not the first *kahuna* he patronized; in fact, he had had other *kahuna* in his entourage, such as Paniku Hua, as far back as the 1850s.[18] Furthermore, it was a common Hawaiian practice to wait till one's dying moments to announce a successor. This practice was followed by the master craftsman or teacher passing on his secrets and keys to his successor, and the father designating his eldest son to take over the household. Though Lot's procrastination may seem like an unnecessary gamble with death, it was consistent with traditional behavior.

Lot was acting quite naturally when he waited to the last hours of his life to offer Pauahi his throne. Had Pauahi accepted, Lot would have been vindicated, along with his "superstitious fear" and *kahuna*. What he did not count on, of course, was Pauahi's refusal. Ironically, Paniku Hua had prophesied five years before in Kona that Lunalilo would succeed Lot.[19] Lot probably knew of this prophecy but either refused to believe it or insisted anyway on acting out the final scene of his kingship.

The next question deals with Pauahi's reasons for deferring to Ruth. To begin with, Ruth was a direct descendant of Kamehameha and the half-sister of Lot. Though Lot may not have regarded her as a suitable queen, he never doubted her lineage, unlike others, such as Kalākaua and Liliʻu. Pauahi was on solid ground when she spoke of Ruth's "right." Secondly, Ruth was five years older, and Pauahi was old-fashioned enough to honor her seniority in the family. Thirdly, Ruth already had considerable leadership experience, having served as the Governess of Hawaiʻi since 1855, or nearly seventeen years. She had practical managerial experience for, since the death of her husband in 1848, she had been overseeing the vast estates she had inherited from him. Fourthly, there was no question about Ruth's political stand on the preservation of the monarchy, sovereignty, or the integrity of the Hawaiian body politic. If there was any question, it concerned the comparatively extreme positions Ruth took on not speaking English, shunning the missionaries, and minimizing contact with foreigners. That Pauahi understood and accepted this part of Ruth speaks volumes for her Hawaiianness and *lōkahi*. And lastly, Pauahi respected Ruth's natural intelligence and abilities, which she had observed over the past forty years of intimate contact with her.

In Pauahi's mind, these were sufficient reasons for Lot to appoint Ruth. She was not blind to Ruth's inadequacies, and this was why she emphasized that she and Charles and the others would *kōkua* or help Ruth. But plainly, Lot had thought about Ruth in the same way as he had thought about Lunalilo, and nothing Pauahi could say would dissuade him.

Finally, it is necessary to deal with the question of Pauahi's rejection of the King's request. At an earlier time in Hawaiian history, it was unthinkable for any *aliʻi* to refuse such an offer; a request was a command, and to reject it as Pauahi did would have invited severe if not fatal sanctions. Besides, it was inconceivable for an *aliʻi* not to seize such an opportunity. But Pauahi refused Lot's offer with seeming impunity. Her action was a commentary on the transitional nature of the times as much as on her own character and priorities.

Pauahi had good reasons for refusing to be Lot's successor. She told Lot that she "did not need it." For one thing, she did not need all the stress and pain that came with the position. Pauahi grew up in Kīnaʻu's household and witnessed firsthand the anxieties and turmoil that beset Kīnaʻu as *kuhina nui*. Pauahi may have stored up childhood fears that still had a strong impact on her attitudes as an adult. Such fears would only have been reinforced by her intimate knowledge of the frustrations that filled the lives of Alexander and Emma and now Lot. Perhaps Pauahi knew all too well her threshold of tolerance for stress and decided not only that she did not need the added stress but that she would not be able to bear it.

The ultimate reward of kingship was power, status, wealth, glory, and Pauahi decided she didn't need any of those. That is, not at the price she would have to pay. After all, she owned one of the finest homes in the city as well as 16,000 acres of land with its fishpond, agricultural and marine resources. If she did not have all the money she needed, through Charles she had better access to funds than any other woman in the Kingdom. She enjoyed the respect of her people and foreigners alike. She held her own court almost daily under the tamarind tree and regularly had distinguished guests at Haleʻākala. And she was secure in her birth and lineage as a Kamehameha and as an *aliʻi*. Given the personal cost, the glory or status of becoming queen would have added little to what she already possessed.

Above all, Pauahi did not need to be forced into a way of life which would threaten the security and happiness she enjoyed with Charles. As Mrs. Bishop and *ke aliʻi* Pauahi, she enjoyed the best of both worlds, for she moved freely and comfortably between the traditional and the modern, the Hawaiian and the *haole*. She realized that as a monarch, her freedom, independence, and privacy would be both curtailed and exposed, for living in a palace was like living in a fish bowl. As Mrs. Bishop, she could settle differences with Charles in the privacy of their home. But as a monarch it would be difficult, if not impossible, to keep disagreements from either a very watchful press or an army of rumormongers. Charles represented some powerful economic and political interests, already at variance with some of her own positions on preserving Hawaiʻi's political independence and cultural integrity. If Pauahi were the monarch, these differences could easily be blown out of proportion and lead to uncomfortable consequences between husband and wife. In short, her partnership with Charles was the most precious and enduring relationship she had and she was not about to jeopardize it in exchange for the uncertainties of the crown.

In the end, there may have been a very simple reason for Pauahi's spurning the throne. She took careful inventory of her abilities and attitudes and concluded that she would not be effective at carrying out the myriad responsibilities the monarch would face in the crucial years ahead. She may have felt she was not capable of doing the job. Managing Hale'ākala and her estates was one thing, but administering the affairs of a hundred thousand people and six thousand square miles of land was quite another thing. Prudence dictated against her getting into a situation she could not handle. Pauahi was a cautious, not an ambitious woman.

There is one question: Did she suspect by now that she had another kind of mission, one whose consequences would far transcend the mortality of the monarchy? Whether she did or not, in a strangely serendipitous way, Lot would help her to realize that mission. The lands he left to be claimed by Ruth were those ultimately willed to Pauahi.

Conflict and Resolution

In the aftermath of Lot's death, ministers of his cabinet met to consider candidates for the election of a successor. Four names were considered: Lunalilo, Ke'elikōlani, Kalākaua and Pauahi. Pauahi's name was brought in because she had been so "pointedly designated" by the late king that the cabinet thought she should be presented to the legislature "as the formal nomination of the King."[20] Though this was a gesture to Lot, it meant little to Pauahi, who may have felt somewhat awkward about the matter. She told Judge Elisha Allen, one of the cabinet ministers, that she personally favored Ruth but recognized that the Hawaiian people would surely favor Lunalilo, because he was of the highest chiefly rank. Lunalilo was a close friend of both Pauahi and Charles. Judge Allen personally believed Pauahi was better suited to the position than Lunalilo and hoped that she would change her mind.[21] She did not, and Lunalilo was elected by popular ballot on January 1, 1873.

The new King quickly appointed his cabinet, and he selected Charles as his Minister of Foreign Affairs. Though finance was his natural field, Charles had served as a member of the Foreign Relations Committee in the House of Nobles since 1864, and as its chairman in 1870. Through his banking and personal ties with the United States, he added a great deal to his portfolio of experience. In addition, Lunalilo had some personal reasons for his selection. Charles was acting as Lunalilo's guardian, and his responsibilities included doling out a monthly allowance of $25 for spending money.[22] He and Pauahi had known Lunalilo since the days of the Royal School. They helped him to shape his will, drawn up in June 1871, in which he left his property for the founding of a home for indigent Hawaiians.[23] There was a close relationship between the Bishops and the King that went back many years.

One might wonder how Charles could manage his new cabinet post, his seat in the House of Nobles and the Privy Council, and his responsibilities at the bank, all at the same time. He was partly able to do this because of the help he had at the bank, which now included the young Samuel Mills Damon, who had joined the firm as a clerk the year before. He was also helped by his wife, who managed his domestic and social affairs with skill and grace. Charles and Pauahi had added another dimension to their busy lives with the arrival in their household of nine-year-old Emma Bernice Bishop from Stockton, California. Charles' niece and the daughter of his brother Henry, she would live with them at Hale'ākala for the next three years.

The new foreign minister faced one of the thorniest issues of the day: the cession of Pearl Harbor to the United States. This problem was both political and economic, since the cession was tied to reciprocity and sugar. The 1872 sugar crop was poor and prices were down, causing a serious business depression. One solution proposed was that the government should lease Pearl Harbor to the United States in return for duty free access into the large American sugar market.

In July 1873, Charles sent an official letter to Henry A. Peirce, now the resident U.S. Commissioner, stating that the Kingdom would be amenable to a treaty of reciprocity. If the United States would allow certain standard grades of sugar to be exported duty free, in exchange the Kingdom would cede Pearl Harbor as the site for an American naval base.[24] This meant that the land would become "the national property of the United States, be regulated accordingly by the United States, which would possess all sovereign rights of the concession, and also be free from interference by the local Hawaiian authorities."[25] A few days later the King and his foreign minister issued a joint public statement confirming the proposal.

In the ensuing reaction Hawaiians erupted with the unleashed fury of Pele, the volcano goddess. They protested vehemently at public rallies in the streets and churches. At Kaumakapili Church, the site of many political meetings, a crowd of fifteen hundred Hawaiians met to hear Judge Kapena assail the cession of Pearl Harbor. He received "unanimous applause" from the crowd who "left no doubt as to the determined sentiment of the native people of this town, not to consent...."[26] The Hawaiian-English newspaper, *Nūhou*, published by Walter Murray Gibson, spoke out especially against the proposed cession of Puʻuloa (Pearl Harbor) and championed the Hawaiian cause. It described the proponents of the idea as being "chiefly enterprising foreigners" and "merchants" who were only after their own personal gain. One of its main targets was Charles, whom it accused of turning the Foreign Office into a "real estate brokerage office." With unconcealed sarcasm the paper asked: "Our Minister of Foreign Affairs has been the guardian of the King's property; and is now the guardian of His Royal Honor; and is he proposing or doing nothing to bargain it away?"[27]

Hawaiians were not against a treaty as such. They read the papers and discussed the problems of the Kingdom, and many knew that gaining access to the U.S. market was vital to the local sugar industry. Even the most xenophobic elements of the populace appreciated the economic realities of the period. But the vast majority of Hawaiians drew the line at ceding even an inch of land no matter the trade advantage. As the *Nuhou* put it: "We can confidently say that the whole of the native people of these Islands ... if tested by ballot, have indicated a decided determination to oppose the cession of Pearl Harbor or the alienation of one foot of Hawaiian territory to a foreign power."[28]

In the eyes of the Hawaiians, cession was the twin brother of annexation. The two went hand-in-hand and Hawaiians wanted no part of either, especially annexation. The idea was first promoted in the early 1850s by advocates of manifest destiny in California and the U.S. Congress. Since that time *aliʻi* and *makaʻāinana* alike had galvanized themselves to oppose annexation at home and abroad. Alexander had been an uncompromising and brilliant opponent of the idea even before he ascended the throne. In the legislature in 1854, John Iʻi and Pākī had both argued against annexation. Lot had continued the fight throughout his reign. There were a handful of Hawaiians who favored it, but, as Emma put it to the British Commissioner J. H. Wodehouse at the end of 1867, "with a few exceptions, all the natives were opposed to annexation."[27]

So was Pauahi. Though we have none of her *palapala* (words), her feelings on the matter were clear. She was from the same patriotic mold as Alexander, Lot, Emma, Iʻi, Pākī, and the rest of the *aliʻi*. None of them would or could have thought any other way without forsaking their ancestral claims. Without question, Pauahi was against annexation.

Charles was not. He did oppose annexation at first. In 1852, he wrote to his friend, the former American Consul, Joel Turrill, that "There is no doubt that the present form of Govt. and perfect independence, is at present, the best for the nation, and all interested in it."[30] But by October of 1853 he had changed his mind. He wrote to Turrill again stating, "I'm decidedly in favor of immediate annexation, not only because I'm an American, proud of the 'stars and stripes' and expect to gain something by such a move, but because I'm an Hawaiian too, and believe that while such a change might bring its evils, it would on the whole be the best thing for the great majority of the population both native & foreign."[31] Over the years Charles did not materially change his position on annexation. If anything, as economic conditions in the islands increasingly favored sugar development, a course to which his bank was unalterably committed, his feelings on annexation hardened even more.

Over this twenty-year period in their married life, Pauahi and Charles had a fundamental ideological difference. It is difficult to tell how they managed to deal with it. As the stance each had taken could not really be altered, they both must have recognized the nature of the conflict and tried instead to build a relationship on the many things they agreed upon. This way of handling the conflict was fine as long as Charles and Pauahi led relatively private lives, but when Charles became foreign minister this arrangement could no longer be maintained. Charles' public commitment to securing a reciprocity treaty based on the cession of Pearl Harbor brought the problem to a head.

We learn about the situation through a letter Emma wrote to her cousin Peter. Emma stated: "Pauahi opposes cession of territory whilst he favors." And she goes on to say that "They have already now had several disagreements upon it, the first they have ever had."[32] Emma indicated that it was a difficult time for Pauahi, who loved her husband and did not want to oppose him, especially in public. This was an echo of the fears in Pauahi's mind when she rejected Lot's offer of the throne. But the couple's disagreement was soon resolved by circumstance rather than any initiative on their part.

The fiery heat of the opposition forced His Majesty's government to withdraw its offer to cede Puʻuloa. In November, Charles had to write to Peirce reneging on his previous offer, admitting that the "general feeling" was so adverse as to make it impossible for the treaty to be accepted by the legislature. At the end of November Charles wrote to his good friend, Elisha Allen, that "Every chief in the country was opposed to it, and only the fact that I was committed to it, kept my own good wife from so expressing herself."[33] In his retreat, Charles also left a trail of ill-will. Emma described the situation: "There is a feeling of bitterness against these rude people who dwell on our land and have high handed ideas of

giving away somebody else's property as if it was theirs."[34] Charles was
hurt by the whole affair, for he wrote to Allen in December saying "Mrs.
Bishop consoles me by saying that I ought to have known that the natives
would not favor cession." The mystery is why he persisted in a course of
action that his wife, with her understanding of *ali'i* mentality and her
"tamarind tree network," must have warned him was doomed from the
beginning.

A Final No to the Throne

In the midst of the Pearl Harbor controversy, an even greater crisis was
looming: Lunalilo's deteriorating health. By mid-August he was a very
sick man, in part due to his interminable bouts with liquor. Emma
expressed the concern of many when she wrote: "The King's conduct
sometimes certainly gives us great anxiety for our future of these Islands.
He does not seem to feel the weight of his responsibility, and who knows
what may happen when he is not sober."[35] Dr. Trousseau knew that
Lunalilo would die unless he stopped drinking.[36]

As the specter of death hovered over the royal quarters, an eerie scenario
was unfolding, reminiscent of a year ago: Despite the urgings of his
ministers and others, Lunalilo, like Lot, had not designated a successor.
Charles wrote: "We tried very hard to persuade him to appoint and
proclaim his successor, but thus far without success, and he seems unable
to make up his mind upon the subject."[37] What Charles wanted to avoid
was a repetition of last year's interregnum. This time, if the government
were without a leader, some feared there might be bloodshed.

Meanwhile, there was a good deal of speculation making the rounds
about whom Lunalilo's successor would be. Emma's letters provide a
fascinating look at what was happening. She wrote: "Various and many
are the rhumors and speculations about town connected with the King's
expected death. Some officers of U.S.S. *Portsmouth* say we must have a
Queen next and Mrs. Dominis must be it. I think myself Mrs. Bishop will
be the one whome the Ministers will ask the King's acceptance to appoint
as successor to Throne for the great objection to me is my American
antipathy and the dear dear church which I *never* will resign or place to
one side for public favour."[38] She went on to mention the other candidates
and the skirmishes taking place: "Kalakaua is playing a deep game for
himself to let no chanse slip for the family. Mrs. Dominis has written for
Keelikolani to come down, hoping she may persuade the King to have
herself appointed. Then naturally it will fall on Kalahoolewa [or

Leleiōhoku, Kalākaua's younger brother] and all of their family of course will rise to the first place now."[39]

Emma desperately wanted to be the frontrunner; this was her incentive for knowing who her rivals were and what each was doing. Emma seems to have been convinced that Pauahi was a serious contender; though there is no evidence that any of Lunalilo's ministers, including Charles, were backing Pauahi at this time. On September 2, Emma wrote Peter again, this time relating a report she had received from Dr. Robert McKibbin, Jr., who had just examined the ailing king. The doctor had told her, she wrote, that "The choice rests between Mrs. Bishop and me, as the King does not like David, and, says he, Mrs. Bishop does not sit idly back and do nothing—no, she is seeing that all influence be made in her favour. But he feels sure I would be named without any trouble, as the King prefers me to any other—he urges my frequent visits there. So I suppose my scruples must be pocketed — oh dear me — and be ambitious. Dreadful —"[40] Emma's informant was correct when he said Lunalilo did not like David Kalākaua and preferred her, but was he correct too in stating that Pauahi was actively campaigning?

Emma obviously thought so, as she stated in another letter: "Mrs. Bishop on Tuesday said to several ladies she only regretted not accepting the late King's offer of throne. Of course she will not let opportunity slip now to gain it. Of course the Missionarys all will go for her on account of her American sympathy and upholding Calvanistic religion."[41] More than a month later, in a letter to Peter dated October 27, Emma wrote that "Mrs. Bishop has exerted herself on her own and Ruth's interest." She reported hearing a story that Pauahi had urged Ruth to talk to the King about the succession. According to Emma, Pauahi "strongly urged her to offer either herself or Mrs. Bishop as candidates for his approbation, because said she (Mrs. B.) if we leave this matter entirely to the King's choise, there isn't the least doubt he will apoint the Queen — Everyone knows that. Therefore that is what we must guard against and prevent it. It will never do for her to reign Queen over us, and the King must not be allowed to choose her. If she should become successor, then, 'We will say to ourselves, the scepter of authority has been distroyed under her (misrule).' "[42]

Emma continued the story: "When she left the Governess (Ruth), the latter instantly sent for Simon Kaai—related word for word Mrs. Bishop's conversation, and asked his advise upon it. He told her not to follow Mrs. Bishop's advise. 'What,' said he, 'would the King think of you, advocating your own chanse before him, and urging to be made Sovereign? What that of itself would make him reject you. Besides, why doesn't Mrs. B. go herself to the King? You know well that the objection to your incapacity for the Throne was (your) ignorance. Do you suppose you have gained wisdome and knowledge sufficient in these 9 months since the late King's death to fit you for governing this nation and settling these vexed questions of cession and annexation? Why the work would kill you sooner than if you remained as you are. I advise you not to entertain such ideas, but rather remain as you are and enjoy the immense wealth which has miraculously fallen to your lot, and if Mrs. B. wishes to be Queen let her go for her own benefit, not you.'

"Upon these expressions of Simon, the foolish old woman readily gave an ear to and quite coincided with him—'But won't you go and speak for us, as Mrs. Bishop wants it done?' He concented. That very evening he came to tell me all about it. Next day Sunday he rode out to see the King and got a chanse for private conversation, (and) repeated Mrs. Bishop's mind word for word, saying that these two Women's object was to prevent him appointing me Queen. The King got very excited upon that and said to Simon, 'Nothing can be said against the Queen. She is a good woman. Never mind, Simon, all will be right.'

"He never said another word about it. Simon returned to town and related his interview with the King, but kept back the King's remarks upon me. Mr. Bishop told Mr. Stirling at this time his wife would accept the Throne if people would press her strong enough."[43]

Yet, in the same letter Emma related another story quite contradictory to that reported above. She wrote: "What I am about to tell you was given me in strict confidence. Therefore you must keep it as such. During the King's illness last month (i.e. September) Mr. H. M. Whitney and Judge Hartwell went to Dr. Trousseau to ascertain the King's exact state of health. When they found out how he was, these gentlemen a day or two after returned to the Doctor with a message for him to put before Mrs. Bishop, asking that she should accept the Throne. The Doctor called and had a confidential interview with her, telling who requested him.

"Her reply to him was to tell those gentlemen she could not accept the Throne even if offered by the King, on the grounds of affection for her husband, that she does not like to oppose her husband on the cession of Pu'uloa, which she would have to do. They have already now had several disagreements upon it, the first they have ever had. She opposes cession of territory whilst he favors. Then Mrs. Bishop advised Dr. Trousseau to use his influence on my behalf, as being the most capable person to fill the place."[44]

Curiously, of the two stories Emma thought the first about Ruth, as reported in part by Simon Kaai, was the "more natural and authentic." She dismissed the second as an attempt by Pauahi to "produce a good impression upon him [Dr. Trousseau] for her self-denial and hypocritical friendliness towards me."[45] Which of these two stories comes closer to depicting Pauahi's true intentions? Was Pauahi actively seeking the throne, at least during the period from August to the end of December? Did she have a change of heart and regret turning down Lot's offer? Was she conniving with Ruth? Was she as ambitious as Queen Emma?

Since Emma was conducting a private correspondence with her cousin, she had no reason not to be open and frank. Her reports, however, show her personal perceptions and interpretations of events, not necessarily the reality of the situation. For example, the story about Ruth may well be true, but why would Pauahi use Ruth as a messenger? If Pauahi wanted to bid for the throne, she would have spoken with Lunalilo herself about this important matter. Nothing prevented her from doing that, as she was on excellent terms with him. She had an excellent intermediary to the King in Charles, who headed up his cabinet. But there is no hint or any evidence that Charles had at any time asked the King to appoint Pauahi as his successor. In fact, by mid-November Charles had concluded that David Kalākaua "would probably succeed him." He wrote Allen in early December stating: "... It might save a good deal of expense and some anxiety if the King would now appoint him Kalākaua as successor."[46] In any case, Charles probably knew that the native Hawaiian population would not support Pauahi because she was married to an American, and that they would prefer someone such as Kalākaua.

Emma's other story, describing Pauahi's wish to refuse any offer of the throne partly because of her feelings for Charles, is much more consistent with Pauahi's past behavior and hence much closer to the truth. Why Emma would consider statements to this effect a form of duplicity by Pauahi is inexplicable. Granted that Pauahi may have weighed seriously a second offer of the throne, she would have acted only if there was no capable candidate, or if Charles had insisted, or if she had been assured of support by a substantial majority of the legislature.[47] None of these conditions obtained, however. In view of the irreconcilable positions on the cession of Pearl Harbor that Charles and Pauahi took, Charles would never have encouraged Pauahi on such a course. In fact, by December he was quite fed up with being in the cabinet, due to the failure of his major policy and the abuse of detractors such as Walter Murray Gibson. His feelings were revealed when he wrote to Allen on November 20: "Is it not humiliating, discouraging and disgusting to be in such a position? Do you wonder that I wish to be free and away? But what good to Hawaiians, or anybody else would come of my 'throwing in the sponge?' "[48] At this point, neither he nor Pauahi wanted any part of ruling the Kingdom. Charles is reported to have told Alfred Stedman Hartwell, his fellow minister serving as attorney general, that "under no circumstances would she accept the position of queen."[49]

By the end of January 1874, the dying king still had not appointed his successor. Charles analyzed the succession struggle as follows: "I think Kalakaua has been a good deal misrepresented. Should he have the responsibilities of a Sovereign put upon him, I trust that he will be reasonable, impartial and careful. I do not think him prejudiced against any nationality...There are strong fears, that Q. E. [Queen Emma] would be partial to a clique. Perhaps they do her injustice. The people would prefer a King to a Queen, and yet a queen who would be impartial, select the best advisers to be had and trust fully in *them*, would do better than a stupid and conceited King. The curse of this little community is, that there are so many imprudent *advisers*."[50] Not only Charles and his ministers, but Ruth and Pauahi had by now tried their best to have Lunalilo appoint Kalākaua, but to no avail.

Poor Emma! She who so ardently desired to succeed Lunalilo, came close but not close enough. Charles wrote on February 3, having been called to Lunalilo's quarters several times, that "The King never mentioned her *name* to me, nor to anybody else that I *know* of; and yet I think he had it in mind to appoint her."[51] That evening Lunalilo, the bachelor-king, died[52] without leaving either an heir or a successor.

King Lunalilo's death meant the end of nearly a hundred years of dynastic rule by the Kamehamehas. Had Pauahi accepted the challenge of queenship, the dynasty might have continued for a while longer. But in Pauahi's refusal would come, as the prophet Kapihe envisioned, the resurrection and even greater glory of the Kamehamehas.

6

REVELATIONS OF AN ODYSSEY

On May 29, 1875, Pauahi and Charles sailed from Honolulu to San Francisco and New York on the first leg of a European odyssey, a trip nearly abandoned before it had begun. But it became an epic journey that took them through more than thirty cities, from London to Geneva, Munich, Venice and Paris. They toured dozens of museums and galleries from Versailles to the Uffizi in Florence, cathedrals and castles from the Dom in Cologne to Windsor, monuments and ruins from the Arch of Triumph to the Coliseum. They attended numerous dinners, teas and parties with barons, dukes, princes and princesses and other less regal friends. They paid tantalizing visits to the gambling den of Monte Carlo, the wine-imbibing Rathskeller in Bremen, and the unholy markets of Trieste. They also saw the "dirty" beggars of Killarney, the centuries-old bones of Capuchin monks, the pigeons of Venice, the papal hand, and the "death" of Captain Cook. The adventure, beauty and enlightenment Pauahi experienced on this journey made it one of the peak experiences of her life. It was the only time she was ever able to travel this extensively.

The story of her odyssey is an interesting travelogue, but what it tells us about Europe is of less immediate importance than what it tells about Pauahi as a person. Travel, after all, can be as revealing of the sightseer as it can be of the sights. What the traveler selects to see or do and hear in a limited period of time reflects personal beliefs, attitudes and values. For example, that Pauahi elected to attend eight operas in as many months on the Continent or to see hundreds of masterpieces in gallery after gallery, shows the depth of her aesthetic interest in classical art and music. This interest began during her Royal School days and continued to blossom throughout her adult years. In her travels she showed the extent of her interest. This recounting of her journey examines some of the beliefs, attitudes, opinions, and even prejudices that characterized her later years.

Some interesting questions are raised, if not answered as well. Her enthusiasm for London and other European cities prompted Pauahi to make remarks about wanting to live there. Was she merely responding to the romanticism of the moment? Or would she seriously have considered living outside of her Hawai'i Nei? Had she become so cosmopolitan by now that she had lost her absolute patriotism to her ancestral homeland? In her awe of the achievements of European civilization, did she ever feel ashamed of her own native civilization? Was she largely a dilettante or a high culture snob? Was she a puritan in sheep's clothing? Was her interest in the churches of Italy really indicative of a deep-seated tolerance of all religions? Did the journey alter her values in any fundamental way? And finally, did she return home with a more positive view of herself and her people?

Two sources of information help to make this discussion possible. Pauahi wrote about most of her journey in a diary that has been preserved till this day. We also have the letters she wrote to her "cousin Cordie" who headed the household at Hale'ākala during Pauahi's travels. Together the diary and letters form the most detailed record of any period of her life, except for her school years. Though they cover only a year or so, they provide the best perspective we have of Pauahi in the golden years of her life.

To Go or Not to Go?

We do not know why Pauahi and Charles decided to go to Europe. Did they go because they wanted a change of environment? Did they want to escape from the politics at home? Did Pauahi yearn to see, feel, touch and hear what she had only read about in books? Or did they travel to Europe because it was the fashionable thing to do?

It has been suggested that Charles wanted to get away from Hawai'i because of his unhappiness with the way the new king, Kalākaua, was conducting the affairs of state. Charles did, in fact, become disillusioned with Kalākaua, but not until much later. He and Pauahi both seemed to be on good terms with the King after his election in February 1874, and until the time of their departure. Charles had sat as the presiding chairman of the initial legislative session convened by the King in that year. In one of his earliest appointments, Kalākaua elevated Charles to President of the Board of Education (Charles had been a member since 1869). Just after the Bishops left Honolulu, the King awarded Pauahi with the ribbon of the Order of Kalākaua, an honor which she appreciated highly as "proof of his esteem."[1] So Kalākaua's actions do not seem to have anything to do with the timing of their journey.

Another reason that has been given is that Pauahi and Charles had been advised by their doctors to seek a change of climate—ideally, a cooler and drier climate — every two years.[2] There does not seem to have been a medical reason that would have prompted this advice. Perhaps it was given less for reasons of physical than of mental health, especially to Charles, who was under constant pressure and could afford regular trips, anyway.

A more likely reason might be found in the fact that it was a relatively quiet period in Charles' otherwise hectic business and governmental career. The sugar industry and the islands' economy were already recovering from the depression of 1873, as exports reached unprecedented peaks in 1874 and 1875. Government revenues had increased to an all-time high in 1874-75 (but so had government debt).[3] If the Hawaiian economy was doing well, so was Bishop & Company. Charles had good, reliable men at the bank in John Paty and Samuel Damon, both of whom he could count on if he were away on a long trip. As for his government obligations, he held no position, such as he had had in Lunalilo's cabinet, that would have required his continual presence. In short, Charles was free to go.

After the turmoil of the politics of 1872-73, both Charles and Pauahi wanted to escape for a while. A trip to the fountainhead of Western civilization would help to take their minds off past problems and unpleasant memories. More important, perhaps, was the need to see and find out about Europe for themselves. To read or hear others tell about it—as, at the Royal School, Pauahi had heard Timothy Haalilio tell about his trip—was simply not enough. Pauahi had to satisfy her curiosity and her innate need for exploration and adventure. She was no Ulysses and nor was Charles, but there is a part of Homer's hero in almost all people. Without some sense of adventure, however small, we would not get beyond our doorways or the corner convenience store. Given the voyaging heritage of her ancestors, she may have possessed more than the average instinct for venturing beyond the next horizon. Pauahi's interest in travel had already been manifested in her previous two trips to the U.S. mainland and many inter-island trips.

In the latter half of the 1800s, a trip to Europe entailed some risk and physical hardship. Traveling in those days by ocean steamer or train and horse-driven carriages was strenuous and tiring and demanded stamina and a strong constitution. International travel was an adventure with many uncertainties. These conditions could lead to fears, such as those

Pauahi confided in a letter to her "cousin Cordie," dated February 16, 1875: "I am so glad you are coming back this week as our time for departure is very near. I have much to do. Oh dear! My heart misgives me, sometimes when I think of going away, perhaps never to return."[4]

The social and intellectual values of a trip to Europe clearly compensated for whatever risks or fears Pauahi may have felt. As a member of the *ali'i*, she was going to share an experience of the privileged in *haole* society. For touring Europe especially was more than the socially fashionable thing to do; it was *de rigueur*, prescribed by the unwritten rules of social acceptance among the sophisticated elite. And Pauahi was part of this elite group, as much as any other woman, white or brown, in Honolulu society. The trip was a status symbol and, perhaps, there was even some innocent competitiveness involved. Unlike the other *ali'i* who had traveled to Europe only on official missions, she was going at her leisure and at her own expense.

A far more important reason for undertaking the trip was that it was a practical and exciting way to continue her education. It was Pauahi's own grand tour of Europe, a practice that flourished in the seventeenth and eighteenth centuries when the young aristocrats of England traveled to the Continent to round off their education. As indicated by her activities in reading and discussion circles, Pauahi had never stopped educating herself. Now, of course, she was about to watch the abstractions of the printed page turn into concrete, physical reality. She was on the verge of exploring the mysteries of an unknown destination. The anticipation of discovery energizes the traveler and the student, who are often one and the same.

Whatever the Bishops' reasons may have been, historically speaking, they could not have picked a better time to travel in Europe than the 1870s. Nations still lived in relative peace and mutual respect. National boundaries could still be crossed with comparative ease. The tempo of life still allowed slow and methodical travel. The tradition of the Grand Tour was still observed. Europe, in short, was still basking in the last stages of the enlightened age of romantic travel.[5]

Advance planning was required for this trip of sixteen months, most of which was to be spent seeing the many sights of Europe's cities and countrysides. Part of the planning involved several months of correspondence with friends and contacts Pauahi and Charles had made in Honolulu, and who were now residing in various parts of Europe. Many or all had been entertained at Hale'ākala, including the officers of the Austrian ship *Donau* and Admiral Baron von Petz, the other members of the Austrian Legation it carried to Honolulu in May of 1869; and the Duke of Edinburgh. This calling for a return of the same favor was in tune with the hospitality code of the day. With the exception of only a handful of places, they had a pre-arranged contact in every city and town they visited. Such was their international circle of friends, a product of assiduous *ho'okipa* and aloha over many years.

Their planning also required reading about the geography and history of Europe. Of course, Pauahi had already done a good deal of this from her earliest years, as she indicated in a letter written from London in August 1875: "...We are in London, and I can hardly realize the fact. It seems like a dream, and, what seems more strange, the names of streets and places here are so familiar to me—having heard and read of them from my childhood. It seems as if I had been away for years, and had come back to renew my acquaintance with them."[6] Those places she was less familiar with, she read about in works such as Karl Baedeker's detailed guidebooks for those touring Europe.[7] By the time she arrived there, she was armed with many more facts and figures, a little more confidence and higher expectations.

Before departing from Honolulu, Pauahi installed "cousin Cordie" to serve as hostess of Hale'ākala during her absence. "Cousin Cordie" was actually Charles' niece, married to William Fessenden Allen of California. Mrs. Allen had visited "Cousin Bernice" in 1864, and the two had become fast and close friends. She had also traveled with Pauahi and Charles to New York three years before. So it is not so strange that Pauahi would have brought the Allens to Honolulu to take care of her home rather than leaving it in the hands of her local friends. Since the Allens arrived in February, they had ample time to get oriented to the house and its large staff of retainers. Whether the Allens were also given some responsibility for looking after her lands and *konohiki* is not clear, but Pauahi undoubtedly made provisions for that too. She was as efficient and caring of her people when she was away as when she was at home.

One of the last things Pauahi did before leaving was to make sure that her Sunday School class at Kawaiaha'o Church would be properly cared for. She had been teaching the class for some time and enjoyed it. Apparently, she had entrusted the responsibility to some senior members of the class.

Having seen to the care of her people and her God, Pauahi, with Charles and young Bernice, left aboard the *City of Melbourne* heading for San Francisco and Europe.

The Itinerary

Though Pauahi was used to the ocean, it was unkind to her during the eight-day crossing, for she was "sick nearly all the way over." So San Francisco was a welcome sight. There Charles visited with officials of the Bank of California with whom he had close business ties. He did not realize it then, but he would be rushing back four months later to deal with a crisis that threatened the existence of his own bank.

Pauahi and Charles enjoyed the company of young Bernice too much to leave her behind with her parents in San Francisco, so the three continued on to New York City by train. They arrived at Grand Central Station on the morning of June 21, and at least Pauahi was "tired and used up." As she wrote later that day to "cousin Cordie" in Honolulu, "I am writing this under difficulties—am so tired and used up, and my head is in such a whirl. I can scarcely think. The journey across was pleasant—and the eating-places all along were clean and neat, and the food excellent. But, under the circumstances it is a very fatiguing journey."[8] She was not so fatigued, however, as to be unable to see her French dressmaker or to make what she called "Herculanean" shopping expeditions or to attend concerts during their time in the big city. Her better-than-average recuperative powers would stand her in good stead in view of the ambitious itinerary they were about to undertake. They left New York on July 7, for the port of Queenstown (or Cobh) near the city of Cork, in Ireland.

Why they chose to start with Ireland is not clear, for it was one of the few places where they did not have friends to greet them. It may have been because of the natural beauty of the country. Pauahi described as "fairyland" the scenery on each side of the River Lee, that wended its way through and beyond the city of Cork with rolling hills and castle ruins covered with ivy. She wrote in her diary: "I thought I never saw anything so lovely and picturesque in all my life."[9] Or it may have been because of her desire to see Blarney Castle with its famed "Stone of Eloquence" which she kissed not once but "*three* times." (Italics hers) She noted, with slight tongue in cheek, that she of course "believed" in the power of the stone. Her skepticism did not stop her from climbing 108 steps to see the Stone, while Charles waited at the bottom. Perhaps she only betrayed a traditional Hawaiian belief in the *mana* of certain stones. At any rate, she was very impressed with almost everything about the Irish landscape except for the O'Sullivan Cascade, which she said was "very pretty, but nothing to compare to some of our waterfalls at home."[10] Every traveler is a hometown chauvinist at heart.

It was in Ireland that Pauahi had the harshest things to say about her fellow humans. Because it is so uncharacteristic, the incident is worth mentioning. She observed: "Truly the poor Irish are a pitiable class such poverty I never saw before and everywhere you go the beggers are after you — heaping blessings upon you — all for a penny."[11] In Killarney, "[We] were besieged by two beggar women to buy some milk and whiskey. They were so persistent that they even ran after us for some distance when we had assured them, over and over again that we did not want any."[12] After several more encounters, she lost her patience and stated: "What a disgrace to the nation! At every corner these creatures run after you and insisting upon your buying whiskey, milk, woolen stockings—however, at last we passed these nisances [sic] ..."[13] Yet, when it came time to leave Killarney, she did not want to leave. She wrote to Mrs. Allen at Hale'ākala, "We were in Killarney two days and such a delightful time as we had!"[14]

In Dublin, Pauahi and Charles saw the first of the many art galleries they would visit throughout Europe. She complained about the lack of time and wrote: "...We regretted so much that our time was so limited and were obliged to hurry thro' from room to room which was very unsatisfactory...I really enjoy looking at picture(s) and sculpture(s) and must have plenty of time, and to study the beauties of each one...."[15] This statement underscores her appreciation for art. She intended to take as much time as she could to study and view the masterpieces of Europe. Charles apparently agreed with this aim because he was to remain at her side in every single gallery.

Liverpool was the first place where the Bishops met and dined with friends formerly of Honolulu. They included Theosophilus Davies, the founder of Theo H. Davies & Company, Mr. Janion, a partner in the firm Starkey & Janion, who was now the Hawaiian Consul in Liverpool, and Charles G. Hopkins, who once served on the Privy Council under Kamehameha III. It was also one of the few places where Pauahi did not go out much at all because she was "too miserable from fatigue."[16] She was also resting in preparation for the myriad attractions of London and its environs.

Westminster Abbey, Hyde Park, Regent Park, Coventry, the Tower of London, Parliament, Windsor Castle—Pauahi was absolutely enthralled with the city. Of her visit to Windsor Castle, she wrote: "I wish you could have seen us start from the White Horse Cellar, Piccadilly, on the top of the coach with four horses, the driver in livery, the man behind blowing the horns as we drove down Piccadilly in grand style... We went through all the suburban villages of London along the Thames ... For twenty-eight miles we were in this blissful state, and I only regret it that it was not longer."[17] She would later write of London: "... I long to be in London once more. It is a charming place to be in, and live in. I don't think one would ever tire of the life there...."[18] This first visit was to be only a few days, but she would return for a longer and even more thrilling stay.

From London, Pauahi and Charles made a detour to Greenwich with its celebrated Observatory. They also visited a nearby naval training school's picture gallery, composed entirely of portraits of naval heroes and scenes of their victories. One picture caught Pauahi's eye. She recorded it in her diary: "There was one picture which interested me much; but it was however not a victorious scene. It was a picture of the encounter of Capt. Cook with the ancient Hawaiians and of his death. It was a spirited scene, but doubtful, as being a true representation of the actual encounter with the natives."[19] She did not explain why she thought the picture an inaccurate representation.

They then headed for Scotland via the small town of Dalmellington to meet and visit with the Stirlings. As Minister of Finance, Mr. Stirling had served in Lunalilo's cabinet along with Charles. Pauahi and Charles arrived just in time for the grouse season and she had her first taste. "Delicious eating they were," she said. After playing euchre, one of her favorite card games, she wrote: "We almost believe ourselves back again in dear old Honolulu it was like old times to hear '16 trumps!' "[20] Not once in her diary or letters did she mention being homesick, and one of the reasons may have been that, with so many friends like the Stirlings around, she felt right at home.

After a couple of days, they continued on the way to the Highlands as far as Inverness, which Pauahi called "this most wonderful city."[21] Back down at Edinburgh they reunited with Bernice, who had been staying with friends while Charles and Pauahi went north. Pauahi noted at this point, "We are well and are enjoying every moment... But it is very fatiguing for all that."[22] They returned to London, where she intended to have a dress made, since, as she put it, "I am quite *pilikia* for a nice *warm* dress." They planned to go for a sail on the Rhine, with young Bernice in tow. But this was not to be.

When they arrived in London, Charles learned from the newspapers that San Francisco's Bank of California had closed its doors on August 26. Because of that bank's close connections with Bishop & Company, Charles worried that his own bank might be forced to close too. Besides, all of Charles' letters of credit abroad were through the Bank of California, which meant that they would soon be out of travel money. As Pauahi put it, "it gave him a great shock, and he instantly decided for our return, as far as San Francisco at least."[23] The situation was a "great disappointment" to them, but Pauahi was quite resigned to it. She wrote: "... so it is, — 'man proposes but God disposes,' "[24] revealing the sense of fatalism that seemed to characterize the last years of her life.

They returned to New York in September, but by the time they arrived, the condition of the Bank of California had improved somewhat. Charles decided to go on to San Francisco anyway, while Pauahi and young Bernice remained in New York. Despite the good news that the situation had improved, both Charles and Pauahi were furious with the bank's people for not having been completely open about its affairs when Charles was there in June. Before Charles left, however, they decided that they would start again and complete their European travel upon his return to New York. Pauahi wrote Mrs. Allen that they were not about to come home. "I don't care to go back yet. I am enjoying myself too well to wish that."[25] And so, in late October they sailed direct to Bremerhaven, Germany, but this time without Bernice. A sad Pauahi wrote, "I am sorry to leave her behind me ... for I shall miss her while travelling, she was so companionable. I shall feel lonely without her." She left her young companion at a "very nice" boarding school in Stamford, Connecticut.[26] Curiously enough, this was probably the only school that Pauahi visited throughout her journey.

They met old friends in Bremen: the Hackfelds, who founded one of the major mercantile companies in Hawai'i (that years later would become American Factors); and the Pfluegers who would also establish a business name in the islands. No sooner had they arrived, it seemed, than they were taken to see the first of many operas they would attend while in Europe. This one was "La Dame Blanche" and Pauahi judged the singing to be "very fine."[27] When it came to operas or concerts she exercised a critical ear, for she never failed to comment upon them in her diary. For example, a few evenings later she was taken to a concert and wrote: "The music was good and the orchestra very fine—but altogether the concert was nothing extra."[28]

Travel abroad tends to lower one's inhibitions, and Pauahi did something she probably would have thought twice about doing at home. She went with her friends to the "Rathskeller," a "favorite place of resort for ladies and gentlemen," as she put it, where they drank, ate and smoked in very cozy and very private booths with doors. She commented on the age of the wines in the cellar, some 250 years old, and then stated: "We drank of several of the choices(t) wines and also of that called the 'Rose.' "[29] The next day she went to church, but she was not much edified because the service was conducted in German. During the coming days in Germany, she would become increasingly sensitive to "the disadvantage of not knowing the German language." As a matter of fact, she probably felt a linguistic handicap in Italy and France as well, because she did not speak any of the Romance languages.

Pauahi and Charles went on to Cologne, where they visited the Church of St. Ursula with the bones of 11,000 virgins preserved in cases placed round the church. As she explained it, "the skulls are encased in crimson velvet, most beautifully embroidered in gold and silver and different colored silk threads...."[30] They also visited the twinspired cathedral or the Dom, at the time still under construction but today the largest Gothic edifice in the world. On the day Pauahi saw it, about 500 workmen were working on it. She noted the famed doors which are "each a perfect work of art" and the "flying buttresses beautifully carved." She seemed to be fascinated with the architecture and art of the churches, and almost everywhere she went in Europe took time to examine them with care and thoughtfulness.

The two travelers went down the Rhine on a boat, but "it was fearfully cold and windy and part of the time rainy, so that we could not be much on deck, yet we saw a good deal from the windows of the steamer and when ever it was practicable we rushed up on deck and thereby manage to see the towns and villages(,) castles & vineyards everywhere...."[31] They stayed overnight in Coblenz, and continued on to Frankfurt for another night, and then to the castle town of Heidelberg. There they spent a "very pleasant evening" with Dr. William Hillebrand "talking of old times and answering many questions." Dr. Hillebrand had returned to Germany from Hawai'i in 1871 after distinguishing himself as head of the Queen's Hospital and as an authority on Hawaiian botany. After viewing Heidelberg Castle, Pauahi concluded: "Truly the ancients understood the art of building castles for their works are remarkable not only for their beauty in architecture, but also for their solidity and durability."[32]

On November 15 they arrived in Bern, Switzerland, and were greeted by old friends, Mr. and Mrs. Williams, who acted as their guides and hosts. They visited the Castle of Chillon, made famous by Lord Byron's poem "The Prisoner of Chillon." Pauahi must have known the story quite well, because in her diary she described in detail the place of the execution, the spot where the bodies were thrown into the lake, the room where the celebrated prisoner was confined, the pillar to which he was tied, and so on. The poem may well have been one of those read aloud in her reading circle, with favorite lines having been committed to memory.

Appropriately enough, it was in wintry Switzerland that she experienced her very first snowfall. She described the novel event: "On getting up this morning it was snowing (the first time I had seen anything of the kind) and I enjoyed seeing the tops of houses, trees, and the ground gradually covered with snow—and in a little while everything was white—it looked for the world like frosted sugar—It was a beautiful sight."[33] Though it was beautiful, she also had to adjust to the accompanying cold.

Pauahi's appreciation of great art was clearly shown by her experiences in Munich, their next stop. She and Charles went to the renowned Old Pinakothek art museum which contained a superb collection. The works were primarily those of fourteenth and fifteenth century masters, including Rubens, Correggio, Titian, Rembrandt and Murillo. She wrote: "Some of them were very fine—but the greater portion to my poor judgement were ordinary. We spent a greater part of the morning [from ten to two] at this gallery and as there are 1400 or more pictures in it—I can't say that our inspection of them were [*sic*] satisfactory—time was too short—we had to hurry thro' to see them all...."[34] Fourteen hundred paintings in four hours! As if that wasn't enough, they then went to Baron Schack's Collection of modern paintings for more viewing during the rest of the afternoon.

There was also the New Pinakothek which, of course, she insisted on seeing too, all eleven rooms "covered to the ceilings with pictures." It contained contemporary nineteenth-century paintings. She was enthusiastic about them and said: "I think they are by far the finest paintings... They are excellent." She still complained, however, about the lack of time "to do justice to these wonders of art and skill."[35]

She was also interested in sculpture and visited the Glypthothek which exhibited thirteen rooms of ancient works. She was discriminating enough to notice two statues in black and white marble which she had never seen before. But she was a lover of paintings, and on their last day in Munich they went back to the Old Pinakothek to savor her favorites once more.

At night they went to the opera, this time to see Wagner's "Lohengrin." Her verdict: "It was well-performed—the orchestra good—but I must say I don't appreciate Wagner's music—it is too monotonous for my taste."[36] It was a courageous thing to say in the composer's own backyard.

Moving on to Vienna, they went on their first night to another opera, "Le Prophete" by Giacomo Meyerbeer. Pauahi clearly preferred Meyerbeer to Wagner, as she commented: "We have had a splendid time—the

installed in a fine room
of the "Hotel Grant" — This
city is situated at the
confluence of the Rhine
and the Mosel — which
latter river we crossed
over a fine bridge just
before entering the city —
It was dark when we
arrived, so we saw nothing of
the place — and went
to bed —

  Frankfort Thurs. Aug 11 —
This morning we left
Coblenz in a steamer, so
as to have a fine view of
the prettiest part of the
Rhine — and we were just
disappointed — altho'
it was fearfully cold
and windy and part
of the time raining, so
that we could not be
much on deck. yet
we saw a good deal

Pauahi's journal entry on November 11th, 1875, describes a trip down the Rhine River from Coblenz, Germany as: "fearfully cold and windy..."

Courtesy of Bishop Museum

music excellent as well as the acting."[37] This was the second Meyerbeer opera she had seen in two months, since she had attended "Les Huguenots" while waiting for Charles in New York City.

Vienna being Vienna, their week in the Austrian capital was a musical feast. Besides the opera they spent one evening listening to the "far famed Strauss band," another taking in an operetta, and another at a ballet which she termed "a most delightful evening—the dancing was wonderful, the dresses ... all very beautiful ... [and] the scenery ... the most beautiful and grand I ever saw."[38]

Pauahi took her first sleigh ride thanks to her host, Mr. Schonberger, the Hawaiian Consul, who made the arrangements. "I have had today my first and probably my last sleigh ride and enjoyed it exceedingly." The ride entailed a twenty-mile round-trip to the Emperor's summer palace outside Vienna and "it was bitterly cold." Of the ride back she wrote: "We retraced our steps back to the sleigh and away we went back to the city—the horses feeling very fine the bells jingling merrily as we rattle on...."[39]

She was having difficulty adjusting to the temperatures. Her fingers were constantly stiff and she felt that her back was freezing. She wrote to Mrs. Allen: "The streets and the tops of the houses are covered with snow and my fingers are stiff, although there is a fire in the room. But stoves in this country are so wretched that they do not warm the rooms at all, only when you are close to them do you feel the heat in front, while your back, at the same time, is freezing."[40] Pauahi was not one to complain, but no Austrian could blame a Hawaiian for remarking upon this one discomfort.

On December 5 they arrived in Trieste "tired and weary to death." She noted that "We did not get up until 10 o'clock" the next morning. That morning she took a walk and saw the "ends of the world." As she described it: "... walked to the Molo ... to hear the band play and to see the motley population of this strange city — all sorts of nations were represented — Greeks, Armenians, Egyptians, Turks, Europeans ... and finally one Hawaiian appeared on the scene — truly the ends of the world come together."[41] She showed her bias for keeping the Sabbath holy when she wrote: "Afterwards we took a walk thro' some of the streets and saw the people with their little booths, buying and selling toys, worsted things, fruits, gingerbread and other small ware...along the sides of the street and this on a Sunday!"

The stopover in Trieste seemed to be for renewing acquaintanceships with the officers of the Austrian frigate *Donau* and meeting members of the local nobility. They met Baron Benko and Admiral Von Petz, whom they shook hands with "over and over again," and dined with the Admiral and his wife. That evening they also met Baroness Sutteroth and His Royal Highness the Archduke William of Wurtemburg. Pauahi wrote to Mrs. Allen about leaving Trieste, "we left ... with many regrets, for we were received so warmly, not only by our friends, but also by friends of our friends. As C_____ remarked to me afterwards: 'Trieste was a cold place, but it contained warm hearts.' "[42]

A delay on the train as they left Trieste led Pauahi to vent her frustration at the Italians. She described the incident: "We left Trieste at 6 this morning. At Nebresina, we waited 1 hr and more — at this horrid place only about 15 miles I should think from the latter, we are to remain two hours more for the Lord knows what reasons — these Italians have a queer way of arranging things...." Though it was very cold, she still observed that "the sky however is clear and blue as that of my dear native land."[43] At moments like this it was easy for Pauahi to become a little nostalgic.

Pauahi's spirit soared when they got to Venice which was "like a dream" come true. She could not get over the sensation of stepping off the train and right into the waiting gondola that carried them to the Hotel Royal Danieli, one of the leading hotels of the time. "Everything I had read of Venice," she wrote, "of her glory, her magnificence & her pride in days gone by, came up before me — and I could hardly believe that I was really looking at the homes of these people, who made Venice famous & envied."[44] She seemed barely able to contain her excitement as she and Charles hired a gondola and rowed up the Grand Canal on their own "Voyage of Discovery," as she put it, to see all: the churches of Santa Maria della Salute and the Frari with their masterpieces by Titian and Tintoretto, the renowned Rialto and Shylock's bridge, the historic *palazzi* that line the Canal, the art galleries and museums, and the Piazza of St. Mark. Like any other tourist, she stared happily at the "far famed pigeons" fed by the promenaders in the arcades and on the great square where people "sat around little tables, drinking coffee and eating ice cream altho' the thermometer was down to freezing point." She added: "The scene was new & novel & we greatly enjoyed it."[45]

From Venice they traveled by train en route to Naples, stopping in Rome overnight. The stop was long enough for Pauahi to write an overdue letter to Mrs. Allen in which she confessed to being "all mixed up" and to not really liking the "Old Masters." "If you could only know our daily life —it is trot, trot, trot, from morning till night, through picture gallery after picture gallery, churches, museums, etc., etc., until the whole thing is all mixed up in my mind — Titian, Rembrandt, Veronese, Rubens are one composite mass; I must confess I do not appreciate the old Masters. I much prefer modern art... Of course there are some few paintings of the old Masters, particularly Murillo, and two or three of Titian's, which are very fine—perhaps the finest in the world, but as a general thing I failed to appreciate their merits. No doubt it is owing to my want of culture."[46] No such confession appears in any part of her diary. Perhaps her words were just an impulsive outburst, coming at a moment of fatigue.

They spent the next week in Naples, which they enjoyed very much because "The climate is mild, like our own, but it is not so hot."[47] They again trotted to see churches, palaces, museums and an "Aquasium" where Pauahi saw the "finest collection" of sea anemones she had ever seen. And what else should she be doing on December 19, her forty-fourth birthday, than spending "the morning in the Museum admiring and wondering anew the vast treasures kept there"?[48]

She was fascinated with Pompeii, "a place full of interest—sad interest," perhaps because she could easily imagine at Vesuvius the presence of a fire goddess Pele. She wrote about an unearthed city "so replete with interest of a past race of a people who had their own joys and sorrows, but in a moment were buried out of sight by the erupting of Vesuvius... The paved streets with high stepping stones at the corners and the ruts made by carriages, are just the same now as on the day of the calamity... Now no sounds are heard in the silent streets but the steps of the tourists...."[49] These are words that could only have been written by a person with the poetic soul of a *haku mele*.

Pauahi and Charles spent the next four weeks in Rome, the capital of world Catholicism. This was the longest period of time they had yet spent in any city. While in Rome, Pauahi did not show any feelings against the Mother Church or the Holy See, such as those harbored by her mother Kīna'u and Mrs. Cooke. Perhaps she suppressed her feelings in the interest of rest and recuperation, or perhaps she had gotten rid of many of them in the course of her grand tour. In any case, by the end of their stay, she could only leave Rome "with regret for I was beginning to know the place pretty well and to become attached to it."[50]

Their stay began rather inauspiciously because on Christmas day Pauahi was ill in bed with "a most dreadful headache." It was serious enough for Charles to summon a doctor who came and diagnosed her trouble as "rhumatic affection [*sic*]."[51] While she lay in bed, Charles went to St. Peter's to witness the high mass being performed by a cardinal. Three days later, Pauahi was up and about and ventured out to see her first church, the St. Giovanni in Laterano. She eventually saw others such as

St. Maria Maggiore, St. Paul's and, of course, St. Peter's, but a handful of the city's 500 churches. Pauahi showed more than a cursory interest as she attended several services, mainly to hear the music. In one church, she was taken down to the basement filled with the bones of monks of the Capuchin Order who had died as long as four hundred years ago, all of which she regarded as "disgusting."[52] She had far more enlightened feelings for the paintings, frescoes, sculptured altars and naves, and so on, that make the churches structures of enduring art. Amidst Rome's maze of churches, she found her way to a non-Catholic American church to attend several Sunday services.

Pauahi was able to meet Pope Pius IX. She described the scene as follows: "... After waiting nearly an hour — several people had in the meantime come in, altogether 70 — his holiness finally entered the room tottering along on a cane, preceded by a priest who inquired after the names of each one as they passed in front of the line, every one kneeling, most of those present kissed his hand others merely held it — while I touched my forehead with his hand."[53]

She toured the monuments and ruins of ancient Rome such as the Coliseum, Arch of Constantine, the various Forums, and the Appian Way. Needless to say, she also saw the galleries and museums, from the Palazzo Borghese and Spada Palace to the Vatican Museum. She proved that her deep interest in art had not waned, as she attended one evening a lecture on the Vatican Museum and then the next day toured "all the rooms" with the lecturer acting as guide.

Pauahi was too interesting and attractive a person for Roman society to ignore. Through the Countess Suchtelan of Naples, whose company she enjoyed while there, Pauahi and Charles became acquainted with the Marquis de Campenari. On one evening at the countess' home, Pauahi stated, "We met some of the first people of Rome," including Princess Faconieri and the Contessa Carpegna, among others. On the other hand, they also became acquainted with the Roman "middle class," through a banker named Camellas who had won a grand lottery and gave a dinner party for sixty or seventy friends to celebrate his good fortune. She wrote of this experience: "We were fortunate enough to be invited and I was very glad of the opportunity to mix in purely Italian society. I like them exceedingly. They are so simple-hearted and good-natured. They remind me of our own people, and that is why, no doubt, they have won my heart."[54] Though she took an interest in many peoples and cultures, in the end Pauahi favored those most like her own. She seemed to value the good and simple heart above all the sophistication and erudition of the cold and the arrogant.

While Pauahi had a critical eye for art, she also had a critical eye for the appearance of the people she met. For example, she commented on her impression of one of the sons of the Marquis de Campenari: "I never saw such a superb young man in my life. He was a perfect Apollo..."[55] She was only slightly less complimentary about the Princess Margarite, whom she described as "very pretty, handsome eyes and complexion—nose perhaps a little too long."[56] Her diary and letters are sprinkled with similar observations, generally both aesthetic and emotional in content.

On January 24, Pauahi and Charles left Rome for Florence, Genoa and then Nice, France. They visited the Uffizi Palace and the Gallery which, Pauahi noted, had a collection of "500 paintings." Since it was considered "one of the finest in the world," she tried to see all of the paintings.[57] The peripatetic pair also went to Pisa to see *and* to ascend the Leaning Tower. She thought the Cathedral was the "most unique church" she had ever seen.[58] In Florence, they saw another opera and a ballet, and a royal funeral which Pauahi described in detail, particularly the procession. The scene piqued her interest because of the many funeral processions she had witnessed, and would yet have to witness, at home.[59] Before departing the city, they attended a party with the nephew of James Jackson Jarves. Pauahi described Jarves as one "who wrote the best history of our islands."[60]

Their stay in Genoa was notable for the number of people they met, including old friends and "some charming Russian ladies," and for the two operas they saw, one being Verdi's "Aida." From Genoa they went for an overnight visit to the seaside resort of San Remo. Pauahi reported how the town had become a popular spot for invalids, and how its growth was evidenced by the construction of many new buildings and homes, and that it would soon compete with Nice as a winter destination for invalids.[61]

On the morning of February 22, they left San Remo by carriage for Nice. Pauahi described the trip as "very charming—passing thro' villages—orange and lemon gardens, plantations of olives and palms [*sic*]—the road ascending to a considerable height above the sea—from whence is seen magnificent prospect of the coast — near and far — and then again descending, in and out of valleys—and around promontories—an ever varying [*sic*] view to the beholder...." They stopped at Mentone on the French border for customs and at the local "Hotel de Russie" for lunch, after which they resumed their ride passing villages and the "most beautifully terraced" fields. Years later, Charles would say that this was "the most delightful drive" he had ever taken and that the day "was almost, if not quite, the happiest day" of his life.[62]

Nice was at the end of its season, but they were in time to enjoy its famous and riotous Carnival and ball. Both Charles and Pauahi had enjoyed the balls at home and they were looking forward to this one. They went to the Carnival's masquerade ball with some friends they met at their hotel and did not get home until two in the morning, "pretty well tired out." Pauahi wrote in her diary the next day, which was Ash Wednesday, that with "the commencement of Lent no doubt every body went to church to repent of their sins."[63] She did not say whether she went with them.

In Nice they saw two more operas, "Le Reigne Indigo" (actually an opera bouffe) and "Lucia di Lammermoor." Pauahi showed she could be a devastating critic, as she said of the former production: "We could not make out the story being in French—even from the acting—all the actors but one were third rate—and this one distinguished himself principally by her shameful costume—the singing was very poor."[64] As for the latter, she thought the singer who took the part of Lucia sang and acted beautifully, but that the rest were all "mediocre singers."[65]

Charles and Pauahi made two excursions to Monte Carlo, their only excuse being "curiosity." Pauahi, who had learned enough from Charles to recognize a promising money-making venture, saw the gambling casino as "profitable business." She described some of the players and the general scene inside the casino: "old women and old men, bald-headed and toothless, some of them, and the young of both sexes, all intent upon the game as if their very life depended upon it." As for her own role, she said, "I was generally more interested in watching the countenances of the players than in the play, the earnest, rapt expression of some, the stoical independence of others, as they lost or won."[66] To keep people near the gambling tables, the casino offered dining as well as "the most delicious music possible" all of which, she concluded, were designed to "allure poor, weak human nature. No wonder many are caught in the snare!" She related how several people had committed suicide because of their losses. "Is it not shocking? I will not relate any more dreadful stories, dear Cordie, for, no doubt, you are sufficiently shocked with me for being there, let alone relating other people's misdeeds — our only excuse being, curiosity."[67]

They went to Milan and Turin but stayed only a short time, as they were anxious to get to Paris. They arrived in the French capital on or about March 18th and reveled in its magnificence and beauty for six delightful weeks. As in almost every other city in Europe, they were the recipients of the hospitality and kindness of many old and some new-found friends. Among them were Mr. and Mrs. Charles de Varigny. He had served as minister of finance and foreign affairs in the cabinet of Kamehameha V. In Honolulu Mrs. de Varigny had been a member with Pauahi of both the Sewing Society and the Amateur Music Society. These friends took the Bishops on a grand tour: On one day to Versailles, on another to Fontainbleu, then on another to the Louvre, Notre Dame, the Champs Elysees, the palaces, museums, *et cetera, et cetera.*[68] Pauahi summed up her six weeks: "I never worked so hard in my life as I did ..., not only in trying to have some clothes made but in shopping, and, at the same time, sightseeing."[69] This probably explains why she failed to keep a daily journal in Paris: She could not share her last precious moments on the Continent with lifeless pen and paper. Pauahi found it painful to leave Paris and the Continent for London, where they would then head home to Honolulu. She wrote to Mrs. Allen: "I hope you and my other friends will forgive me if I say that I am not yet ready to go home. Of course I wish to see you all again, but this European life is so charming that I wish it could be prolonged indefinitely."[70]

By May 5 they were back in London for one final act of ritual: to be presented to the Queen of England. Charles had contacted the Duke of Edinburgh. The Duke apparently remembered him, because promptly the next day Charles was informed that the Duke would be happy to present him at court on whatever day he pleased. Pauahi stated that they "were much surprised at the great condescension of his Royal Highness and very grateful for the honor he has done us."[71] The great day was set for the 12th. Pauahi wore a silk dress in two shades of rose, a light and a dark. The dress was made in Paris, but in London she had added a three and three-quarters yards-long train and low bodice for the occasion. She would write afterwards: "I had plumes the color of my dress, flowers and lappets in my hair and I flatter myself that I looked almost as well as some of them."[72] On this special occasion there was no reason for any false modesty.

Pauahi saw nothing flattering about the costume Charles chose to wear. She described him as "dressed in an ex-Minister's uniform — sword, cocked hat with a red ribbon, and as I never before saw him in a uniform, he looked funny enough." And she added, "But he had to wear it, or else go in silk breeches."[73]

Pauahi related the actual event in a letter to Mrs. Allen: "I was nervous at first, but soon got over it. The Duke of Edinburgh presented C _____ and me to the Marchioness of Salisbury. As my name was announced by the Lord Chamberlain, the Queen, much to my surprise, came forward and bowed with a kind smile of recognition, which of course, pleased me, very much. I bowed next to the Princess of Wales and to others of the Royal family, and when I was opposite the Duke of Edinburgh he extended his hand to shake hands with me, and he did the same with C_____, who was behind me. We then, with the rest, went to the outer rooms and did not see the Royal family again."[74] So it was one *ali'i* paying respects to another, perhaps wondering what sacred claims, if any, each had on the other.

A week later they had left London and arrived back in New York on May 30. They made several trips: One to Washington, D.C., another to Boston, and a pilgrimage to Charles' birthplace, Glens Falls, and to Sandy Hill, which he had left for Hawai'i thirty years before. Perhaps their principal, if not most interesting, trip was to the Philadelphia Exhibition, held to celebrate the centennial of America's independence. They spent about a week there looking at the displays, mainly of machinery as Charles was no doubt interested in their application to Hawai'i's agriculture, especially sugar development.[75] Many other people from Hawai'i were there, too, with the same kind of interest.[76] Moving from the ancient and classical culture of Europe to the futuristic and industrial culture of capitalist America must have been quite a leap for Pauahi. By the end of September they were back in the security and warmth of Hale'ākala.

7

THE SEEDS AND THE CORPUS

Years of quiet are often lived within the eye of a storm. So it was for Pauahi during the next several years after her return from Europe. While the principals in her life, such as Charles and Ruth, battled against the elements, mostly political and financial, Pauahi seemed secure in the sanctuary of Hale'ākala or Kawaiaha'o Church. Not that she was oblivious to what was happening around her, for that was impossible. But for the burdens she would soon have to bear, peace and quiet were what she now needed most.

Part of the focus of this period is on Charles as President of the Board of Education. It was through him that Pauahi gained much of her understanding of the needs and problems of Hawaiian education. Some of the seeds of the concepts that led to the founding of the Kamehameha Schools may have been sown in their discussions of Charles' reports to the Government.

Most of the focus is on Ruth and the tempest of her last years that would forever change Pauahi's life. The major events include Ruth's attempt to be designated heir apparent following the death of her son Leleiōhoku; her successful appeasement of Pele as the lava flow encroached on the city of Hilo; her financing and construction of Keōua Hale as a challenge to the Kalākauas and as a symbol of unrequited pride; her celebration of its completion as a reaffirmation of her *ali'i*-hood; her death and funeral. Finally, in her will Ruth deeded all her properties to Pauahi. These lands would form the essential corpus of Pauahi's final estate and the foundation of the Kamehameha Schools.

Decompression

Pauahi came back from Europe psychologically reinvigorated but physically exhausted. As she mentioned in her diary and letters, she was too often tired, not to have returned bone weary. All that she needed to recover was a slower pace and some time, at most a few weeks. At forty-four years of age she was still a vigorous person and, so far as is known, free of any afflictions. Still, she needed time to readjust, just as any returning traveler requires time to get back to the routine of being at home again. And if the trip was a long and exhilarating one, as it was for Pauahi, the adjustment is even more difficult. She needed a period of decompression.

Although Charles returned in more or less the same condition, he did not have either the time or the leisure that Pauahi had. In fact, he had hardly arrived home when construction started on a new two-story bank building, located on the corner of Merchant and Ka'ahumanu Streets. The business had outgrown the old space and needed a larger area. An important factor in the bank's potential for growth was the fact that the reciprocity treaty had been renegotiated and signed with the United States. Charles had fought hard for the treaty three years before. Now Charles and the bank would accumulate wealth on a scale neither had known before. Twenty months later the building was completed and Honolulu had one of its "handsomest edifices."[1]

Besides his business, Charles had to resume his legislative duties in the Privy Council and House of Nobles, his presidency of the Board of Education, membership on the Board of Immigration, plus his positions on other private boards such as that of Punahou School. Charles had to take the time to become current with the issues and business that had transpired during his trip abroad.

In the meantime, Pauahi resumed her responsibilities at Hale'ākala, as Mrs. Allen left with her husband and went back to California. Pauahi checked on the management of her estates and apparently went to He'eia before the year was out. She also resumed her literary, musical and civic activities, with even more energy and confidence now, and the teaching of her Sunday School class, with more stories to tell. By December 19th, on her forty-fifth birthday she was probably well settled into the routine of her old life-style.

But even after a year and a half of being home, Pauahi still had occasional thoughts of being elsewhere. In January 1878, she wrote to her "cousin Cordie" who was back in New York visiting her brother, who was then the Hawaiian consul there. After telling her of events here and that her passion vine was *make* (dead), and that she was planting some more (still showing her interest in gardening), she said, "I wish to goodness I were in New York, now. I long to hear the 'divine Patti' again. I envy you your enjoyment of music, etc."[2] What she missed was the fine music, the opera, the symphonic concerts, and the like she had heard there and in Europe. In this sense, being in Honolulu would never be enough for Pauahi, who longed for the quality of music and art that only a metropolis could really offer. Honolulu had little to offer except the band music of Henry Berger, who had arrived in Hawai'i in 1872, and the occasional visiting concert pianist or singer. After 1881, the city's musical offerings would improve, however, with the construction of the Music Hall (later known as the Opera House). This was a rather impressive edifice for a city of Honolulu's size, and it symbolized the efforts that Pauahi and others made to enrich their cultural life.[3]

In 1877, two significant events took place. The first was another encounter with succession to the throne, although this time the situation centered on her beloved cousin Ruth. On April 10, the heir apparent Prince William Pitt Leleiōhoku, Ruth's adopted son and the blood brother of Kalākaua and Lili'u, died after contracting pneumonia while attending school in San Mateo, California. Ruth was enormously fond and proud of her son, whom she had renamed after her first husband, and had great ambitions for him.[4] Notwithstanding her public posture of maintaining anti-*haole* ways, she spared no expense in seeing that he received the best education possible. Unlike Pauahi or Lili'u, who were educated in Hawai'i, Leleiōhoku was sent abroad for a purely *haole* education. When it came to her most vital self-interests, Ruth acknowledged that the *mana* of the future resided in learning the principles and techniques of the *haole* world. Though she herself did not exemplify this principle in her own personal life, she had, in effect, been following it vicariously through her son. It was to be through his power and achievements as king that she would gain a measure of the self-respect she craved not only for herself but for her people.

At the news of Leleiōhoku's death, Ruth immediately petitioned the King to proclaim her heir apparent. This impulsive and unrealistic act was made in the throes of grief and most likely without counsel. She probably did not discuss the matter with Pauahi, who would surely have advised against it. Ruth may not have sought her cousin out because of the sadness that surrounded her adoption of Leleiōhoku. As described earlier, in 1862 Ruth gave Pauahi her infant son Keolaokalani. Lot was furious and in his anger forced Ruth to renounce all ties with the infant as her heir. Then he insisted that she adopt Leleiōhoku and make him her heir. Having lost her first husband, then Keolaokalani and now her last and only child, Ruth was understandably in no mood to argue the pros and cons of her action with a rational Pauahi. Perhaps Ruth's impulsive petitioning of the King symbolized a desperate final tribute to her hopes for the continuation of the Kamehameha dynasty.

At a cabinet meeting her petition was placed before the King and his ministers. According to Lili'u, they objected on the grounds that if her request was granted, Pauahi "would be the next heir to the throne, as they were first cousins."[5] It was a legitimate objection based, perhaps, on the fear that Pauahi could not leave any heirs as she was barren. But the main objection to Pauahi and Ruth was a matter of dynastic politics: The Kalākauas were in command and they were not about to relinquish control to the Kamehamehas, certainly not to Ruth. Kalākaua himself, through his "skillful" genealogists, had repeatedly cast doubt on the legitimacy of Ruth's claims to being a descendant of Kamehameha, and in the process, he cast doubt on Pauahi's claims as well. So it was a foregone conclusion that the decision of a successor would be made in favor of a Kalākaua, namely, Lili'u. It did not take the cabinet long to decide. By the afternoon of the 10th, the booming of the cannon announced that Lili'u was heir apparent to the throne of Hawai'i.

But the significance of this episode does not lie in the fact that neither Ruth nor Pauahi became the successor to the throne. It lies in the death of Leleiōhoku, which left Pauahi the only real heir to Ruth's lands, the lands of the Kamehamehas.

The second important event in 1877, was the death of Pauahi's aunt 'Akahi. From 'Akahi, Pauahi received a legacy of 9,557 acres, almost double the amount she had been left by Pākī. The bulk of the land was 7,300 acres in Kealia, South Kona. There were other separate parcels: 656 acres in Makalawena, North Kona; 1,106 acres in Ke'eiiki, North Kona; 466 acres in Pu'uwepa, Kohala; and 19.49 acres in Ulupa'alua, Kohala. An additional 10.25 acres were located at Kaipu, Mānoa on O'ahu. The total area of land Pauahi now owned was 25,600.58 acres.[6] While the land increased the size of her estate, she also incurred the additional responsibilities for *konohiki*, tenants, and the natural resources that these acreages contained.

In bequeathing her land to Pauahi, 'Akahi at the same time reaffirmed her genealogical ties to Kamehameha. 'Akahi was the daughter of Kalua'i and Pauelua. Pauelua was in turn the issue of Kai'ilipaakalua and Kaleiwohi, and Kaleiwohi was the child of 'Akahi I and Keōua. Keōua was 'Akahi's great-grandfather. As we recall from the recounting of Pauahi's genealogy, he was also the father of Kamehameha I. Pauahi, of course, was the great-granddaughter of Kamehameha I. Since 'Akahi and her husband Kepa'a had no children, they had designated Pauahi as their closest kin and legitimate heir.[7] This was a large inheritance, but Pauahi's largest inheritance was still five years away.

The Seeds of Conception

Strangely enough, though her contributions to education would ensure Pauahi's place in the memory of her people, Pauahi and those who knew her did not write specifically about her ideas about education. It can be inferred, of course, from her avid interest in reading, discussions, teaching (whether sewing, piano or Sunday School), and travel that she was interested in education in general. But was she really aware of the educational situation, the schools, problems, and needs of the Hawaiian populace? If so, how did she become aware? What were her probable views on the subject? And how were her views shaped? These questions may be approached indirectly by looking at Charles' work as a member and then President of the Board of Education.

Pauahi's partnership with Charles meant that she shared in what he was doing, especially in an area as important to him as education. Charles was a self-educated man, a very knowledgeable individual although he had had no formal education beyond the eighth grade. He had been (and would always be) a firm and unstinting supporter of education, both private and public. His interest was evidenced in the fact that he had served on the Board now for nine years.

In 1878 Charles submitted to the Legislative Assembly his second biennial report on the conditions of the schools in the Kingdom. It seems reasonable to assume that Pauahi knew of the general conditions described in the report, and that she would have read it in any case. More than likely, she and Charles discussed its contents at one time or another. She would have known, then that 6,991 pupils were in attendance at the schools. The majority or 61 percent were in "Government common schools" open to all children. Another 13 percent were in "Government select schools" such as the Lahainaluna Seminary. Twenty-six percent were in independent or private schools such as Punahou and Iolani.[8] Since Hawaiians still counted for most of the total population, the majority of the students were Hawaiian, and most of them boys.

Charles indicated in his report some of "the causes of retrogression" or problems such as "the difficulty of procuring competent teachers; the indifference of parents to the interest of the Common Schools; the withdrawal of children from the Schools before the expiration of their lawful School age; in some districts, the inconvenient location of the Schoolhouses; also the lack of supervision." He stressed the latter point by stating that "Intelligent supervision is the life-giving principle of every educational system."[9]

The report then noted that "the popular demand is for English." But though English was the common medium of instruction in all the select and higher schools, he stated the case for the continued use of Hawaiian in the public schools: "... the English language, which, under the most favorable circumstances, is difficult to master, is so little used that there is no practice in it outside the School-house, and until many more natives are available as teachers in English, the expense of such teaching will be too great to be generally afforded. In the Schools away from the centres of business the knowledge which may be acquired in a few years, through the medium of the language of the people, is of more practical value than any mere smattering of a foreign tongue, which may cost more than double as much in time and money."[10]

To say that English was in "popular demand" was an understatement. Like a slowly building tidal wave, the English language movement in the schools was sweeping the land. It had started as far back as 1851 when the government set up its first English language school. By 1866 there were 28, and by 1874 there were 46. In 1878 there were 53 English schools with 2,678 students or 38 percent of the student population. Even the venerable Lahainaluna, where classes had been taught only in Hawaiian since 1831, decided to drop all its instruction in the language that year.[11]

By 1878 Hawai'i had become virtually an English enclave: English was the language for business, diplomacy, and much of government itself. When Charles urged the continuation of Hawaiian language instruction in the common schools, he was really vying for time and for more public funding for education. Charles' view may be contrasted with that of Pākī, who in 1854 had served on a committee with similar functions. Pākī also opposed the spread of English but for different reasons: He believed the Hawaiian language was essential for the maintenance of Hawaiian culture. Now, the issue was whether Hawaiians could survive economically without fluency in English, and the general feeling in the Hawaiian community was that they could not. This view was shared by Pauahi and the other ali'i who had attended the Chiefs' Children's School, where the precedent of English language instruction had been established.

A major section of the report dealt with the "manual labor" program which Charles fervently believed would "promote health and industrious habits." Essentially, the idea was to give three or four hours a day to intellectual studies and from two to three hours to manual labor outdoors. It was hardly a new idea; Lahainaluna and the Hilo Boarding School, both of which were familiar to Pauahi, had developed similar programs many years earlier. In 1874, at the Board's urging, the legislature had legalized the inclusion of training in agriculture and other industrial subjects. The girls were taught sewing and other domestic arts, while the boys did farm work in school gardens. In exchange for their labor, the students received four-fifths of the profits and their teacher the other fifth, providing that he "worked just as hard."[12]

Charles' motives in backing the program were moral and economic. He stated: "It is frequently remarked that the rising generation are not as industrious as their ancestors were; that they — and especially those educated in the higher schools and in the English language—have wrong ideas about labor — in short, are lazy and idle, and have much more of pride and conceit than is good for them."[13] Charles chose these words carefully for they are insightful and sensitive. Though many of his *haole* contemporaries indiscriminately labeled Hawaiians as lazy, he did not follow suit here. He said that some of the present younger generation were "not as industrious as their ancestors." He made an important distinction, clearly recognizing that the Hawaiians of old were not lazy but industrious.

Pauahi surely agreed, given her knowledge of the ways of her ancestors and of the standards she herself tried to exemplify. She would have also concurred with Charles' implied condemnation of those students who, after getting a little bit of knowledge, felt they were somehow above doing any manual labor. Through her willingness to do her own yard work, house cleaning and gardening, Pauahi tried to demonstrate that working with one's hands and with the soil was never demeaning. She would probably have had a difficult time containing herself, had she met *maka'āinana* students who, in their conceit, looked down upon those who did work of this nature.

A key word in Charles' statement was "industrious" — a word that would resound among Pauahi's beneficiaries for years to come. Courses in manual labor were designed to produce industrious habits: working hard and long, being well-motivated, planning ahead, completing every task, doing flawless work, setting up objectives, and following through, among other things. Industriousness was equated with a whole ethos of ideas about how a student should carry out his responsibilities as an individual and as a citizen contributing to the common good. The opposite ethos was associated with the habits of idleness or laziness. Pauahi knew, and Charles probably did too, that idleness was as much condemned and despised in traditional Hawaiian society as it was in even the most rigid Calvinist doctrine. Both Charles and Pauahi disliked and feared what would happen if the schools and changes in the larger society continued to cause more and more young Hawaiians to become lazy. Such a trend would surely threaten their very survival in an increasingly competitive and Westernized society.

Charles had cause to be concerned because the manual labor program was not going as he had hoped. In fact, it was failing and some in government were ready to get rid of it. So in this 1878 report he argued the case anew, this time taking a slightly different tack. He declared: "A well alleged objection to our Common School system has been, that it too often gives pupils a distaste for agricultural and industrial pursuits. But it is evident that a large portion of our community must depend upon such occupations for means of subsistence. And hence the instruction of our youth should have for its object, not only mental culture; but also the development of those faculties which most facilitate industrial effort. So far from industrial culture interfering with intellectual culture, the Board believe it really lends to it a powerful support, by strengthening the character and developing the energies of the pupil; and that 'work of hands and mind combined is quite essential to render education an efficient means of mental development'; and hence they are of opinion that judiciously managed manual labor should still remain a part of our Common School system."[14]

Here Charles was making the case for manual labor (1) as industrial training and (2) as an indispensable ingredient for the total development of the mind and body. In 1874, he had stressed the moral or character-building basis for manual labor, but now he emphasized the more practical and vocational benefits. As a businessman he saw more clearly than most the value in such training, which would help students become better fitted for jobs in the rapidly developing sugar and ancillary industries. As a financier who necessarily worked on the basis of projections for investments and loans, part of his vision was always focused on future developments and needs. His visit to the Philadelphia Exhibition on machinery opened his eyes even more to the future possibilities. Pauahi had accompanied him to the Exhibition and so must have had some appreciation of the impact of industrial or mechanical advances on Hawai'i's educational and economic future.

Charles also showed that he was aware of the newest theories and practices in American education, because manual or industrial training was just becoming popular in the 1870s. The first real manual training school would be set up in St. Louis, Missouri, in 1879. Exponents of the new training schools argued that they represented the broadest kind of education because "We put the whole boy to school," that is, by training the student in the use of his mind, hands, eyes and senses, the entire person was being developed.[15] The statement in Charles' report that "work of hands and mind combined is quite essential to render education an efficient means of mental development" reflected exactly the thinking of those like Dr. C. M. Woodward, who founded the St. Louis School.

The manual labor scheme in the government common schools did not prove successful and was eventually abandoned. But in Charles' rationale for the scheme may lie the seeds of some of the educational concepts in the last will and testament of his princess.

The Lull Before the Knell

1879 did not seem to be a very eventful year for *ke aliʻi* Pauahi or for Charles. She continued to oversee the development of her estates, particularly at Heʻeia where she had leased her lands for other crops besides taro. As early as 1871 *kuleana* lands were being leased to Chinese for rice cultivation,[16] and most of the taro *loʻi* (irrigated terraces) were being turned into rice paddies. Rice was thriving not only in Heʻeia but in Kāneʻohe and Kailua. It is also possible that rice was being cultivated on Pauahi's lands at Lumahaʻi on Kauaʻi. The *Advertiser* reported on August 5, 1879, that while "sugar is King...rice may be styled its Prime Minister." Over five million tons were being produced throughout the islands.[17] Some of her lands may also have been converted to sugar cane as well. In either case, Pauahi, the landlord, was engrossed in the economics and management of her estate.

Pauahi still led an active religious life, especially at Kawaiahaʻo. Besides tending to her Sunday School class, she was attending services regularly, including the occasional organ and other musical concerts. Pauahi loved to listen to the organ at Kawaiahaʻo. She had helped to raise the funds for its purchase back in 1867. Liliʻu played the organ for the church, alternating with Henry Berger. Pauahi may have attended the concert held in 1879 when Berger performed at the organ, accompanied by four brass instruments.[18] The Kawaiahaʻo choir often met for rehearsal at Haleʻākala. Members of the choir looked forward to meeting there, but, as one of the members remarked, "they had to behave when they went there. Something restrained them from doing anything out of the way in the presence of Mrs. Bishop."[19]

Pauahi's presence was commanding, as she demonstrated once in an incident at the church. The church's Hawaiian-speaking pastor, Rev. Henry H. Parker, or Paleka as his Hawaiian parishioners called him, described it: "On a certain Sunday morning a drunken chief entered the Kawaiahaʻo Church during public service and started to make things unpleasant. An attempt to lead him out only made matters worse. Governor Kekūanaōʻa called loudly on the church officers to force the disturber out of the house but none dared approach him. Mrs. Bishop took in the situation at once, and stepping out from her pew crossed the aisle, went behind the man, touched him on the shoulder to attract his attention, and as he turned about motioned him to follow her, and he went out as quiet as a lamb."[20] Her faith went beyond the walls of the chapel into the houses of great and small alike on errands of mercy. Paleka was fond of telling how "about nine o'clock one Sunday evening he went down to a little side street to see an old Hawaiian lady who was very ill. On his arrival he found Mrs. Bishop making an egg-nog. After a few minutes he went away, leaving her attending the old lady. He remarked that when he saw this he said to himself, 'in as much as ye have done it unto one of the least of these ye have done it unto Me.' "[21]

The hostess of Haleʻākala still took part in the social hubbub of the capital, mingling with high society from home and abroad. With Liliʻu, now heir apparent, Pauahi was in the center of the ceremonies and entertainment given in honor of Prince Henry, younger brother of Emperor William of Germany, when the prince's ship dropped anchor in Honolulu harbor on April 19, 1879.[22] Pauahi could be an even better hostess than before, because her trip to Germany gave her more to say to the Prince and members of her entourage. Among the Hawaiian nobility at this time, she was the only one who had made a grand tour of the Continent.

Pauahi was still on good terms with the King, but feelings began to sour the next year. Charles, for example, did not care for the results of the 1880 election. He thought the King had chosen some "nincompoops" for friends. On February 14, 1880, after the voting results were announced, Charles wrote to E. H. Allen: "... The worst of it is that H. M. (His Majesty) took quite an active interest in electing some nincompoops who are mere tools of his, and has expressed some plans which are so weak and useless that he has lost a good deal of the confidence and respect of foreigners and the most intelligent natives. I think he sees his mistake and I wish he would profit by it. He has a great fancy for military and carries it so far as to make himself almost ridiculous."[23] Pauahi probably agreed with Charles. She strongly opposed the actions Kalākaua took in September, when he dismissed his cabinet and appointed the adventurer Celso Caesar Moreno as Premier and Minister of Foreign Affairs. The appointment was also opposed by Charles, Ruth and a whole coalition of Hawaiians and *haole*.[24] Gradually, Pauahi and Charles became alienated from the Monarch.

Pauahi was still in good health in the fall of 1880, but her cousin Ruth did not seem to be. The unexpected loss of her son Leleiōhoku had taken its psychic toll on Ruth, and her enormous body weight continued to tax her heart. Because of their close relationship, Pauahi was no doubt concerned about Ruth's health and, perhaps, so were the ancestral guardians of the destiny of the Kamehamehas.

Ruth's Years of Glory

On November 5, 1880, Mauna Loa, a volcano on the island of Hawai'i, began one of its most massive and long-lasting eruptions. The fury of Pele could be measured by the tremendous flow of lava that plunged down the slopes of the Long Mountain, over the high basaltic wastelands and then the lower cultivated and inhabited areas. The lava flow approached the edge of the city of Hilo, some thirty-six miles from its source. The fire and the heat caused a glow visible in the night from as far away as Honolulu. For ten months the volcano kept spewing hot magma from its northeast flank and some geologists estimated the material amounted to two billion cubic meters. By August 1881, the unending flow of lava threatened Hilo and its nearly 8,000 inhabitants. While nervously and helplessly pondering the city's seeming destruction, sightseers gawked in wonder at the dancing flames. Among those viewing the spectacle were the heir apparent Lili'uokalani and her party of friends.[25] While ministers prayed to Jehovah and the *kāhuna* turned to Pele for deliverance, the river of fire edged closer to the city. On August 4th, a meeting was held with the visiting Lili'u to see whether anything could be done to save Hilo, and attempts were made to construct earthen barricades to divert the flow.[26]

In the meantime, Hawaiians were appealing to Ruth to intercede with Pele, believing that as a descendant of Kamehameha she would have the *mana* to do so. Though Ruth was safely ensconced in Honolulu, she in her own mysterious faith decided to make the trip. She endured the rough passage in sailing to Kailua. From there she endured what was probably an even rougher trip to Hilo by wooden carriage. The story of what happened next is best told by Ruth's longtime bookkeeper, Oliver Kawailahaole Stillman:

"Things looked desperate for Hilo. As the lava came through the forest, trees would burn. Everything went before the hot lava.

"We went down to see it one morning when it was three quarters of a mile from Hilo near the stone wall of a sugar mill. I went back and told Ruth about it.

"She didn't do anything for a little while, as she sat quietly musing. Then she said: 'I wonder if there are any red silk handkerchiefs in Hilo. Go and get as many as you can,' she told me.

"I bought out the town and got some 30 of them mostly from Turner's Dry Good Store. I took them to Ruth.

"'Now bring me a bottle of brandy,' she said and gave me the money for it. I brought a quart of brandy to her.

"'Now,' she announced, 'I am going to the flow.'

"It was very dramatic. I remember it clearly because I was quite concerned for the Princess who wasn't in any too good health.

"There was but one hack in Hilo and I went to get it. It was some job getting her into it but we succeeded. Accompanying her of course was her retinue of servants, some 25 to 30. Ruth always liked to travel with a group. They surrounded her carriage.

"Ruth remembered to take two roast pigs, for our own consumption, not for Pele. We also took along a couple of tents, as it rains in Hilo ...

"When we got to the flow it was advancing slowly but unmistakeably. The Princess walked to the flow, and I heard her give a long prayer. I was about 20 ft away from her. Then she took off her own red silk handkerchief and threw it into the red hot lava. Pele likes red silk.

"Then Ruth took other handkerchiefs and did the same thing.

"After the handkerchiefs were all gone, she took the brandy bottle and broke it by smashing it on the hot lava. It blazed into fire right away. Then she prayed again to Pele.

"We left the fire then and went to the tents where we spent the night.

"Early the next morning all of us went to the lava flow and we couldn't believe our eyes. The flow had stopped right there. Suddenly our feelings towards the Princess changed. We were one and all awed. The whole thing was awe-inspiring. Some may laugh and say that it happened by lucky coincidence, that there's nothing to it.

"But one must remember that Ruth knew nothing of the rapidity of the flow. She had not been there for several days ... I was the one to report to her that it was getting close to Hilo.

"When the Princess returned to Honolulu, a tremendous crowd greeted her at the dock. The streets were lined. It didn't take long for the story to flash around the Islands."[27]

Was Pauahi one of those to welcome Ruth back? Unquestionably. She probably wondered why Ruth undertook the strenuous trip in the first place, and may have been quite skeptical about Ruth's faith in Pele. Lili'u was dubious enough to have dismissed any appeals to Pele, as she indicated in writing of her own visit to Hilo at the time Ruth was there.[28] The difference between the attitudes of Lili'u and Pauahi, of course, was that Pauahi had a deeper understanding and empathy for her cousin Ruth. Pauahi was consistently and sympathetically tolerant of Ruth's beliefs and practices, however different they were from her own. Her tolerance was based on love, as well as respect for Ruth's natural intelligence and abilities. Perhaps, as she greeted Ruth on her triumphant return, Pauahi regarded her with new respect. Pauahi may have been in awe, not of Ruth's mystical powers, but of her courage in risking not only her health but her self-respect. What if Ruth had failed? She would have been an even greater object of whispered and sometimes open scorn and ridicule. Pauahi may have marveled at Ruth's faith and confidence in herself. Pauahi, along with others, wondered also at the coincidence between Ruth's incantations and offerings and the halting of the lava flow on August 9th. *Lōkahi* was still available to her, particularly at moments like this that transcended her rational and theological powers to explain.

While all of this was happening, Ruth was building her elaborate Victorian mansion, Keōua Hale, on her Emma Street property. Only a couple of blocks away, construction of the King's palace was also proceeding. It was no accident that these two extraordinary projects were taking place simultaneously. Keōua Hale symbolized Ruth's final challenge to the Kalākauas, inspired by her competitive instinct, her resentment, perhaps, of their attacks on her genealogy, and mostly her pride and ego. But Ruth was to pay dearly for all this. In order to finance the building, she initially sold 10,500 acres of her lands at Kīpū and Kīpūkai on Kaua'i for a price of $27,500. Halfway through the construction, the estimate of its cost was leaping skyward and Ruth was forced to sell several large pieces at Hāmākua, Hawai'i and on Lāna'i, all for a total of $80,000.[29] Her honor, it seems, justified selling the *'āina*.

To a frugal businessman such as Charles, who would have been quite satisfied with a modest cottage, the project was too extravagant, if not intolerable. On September 28, 1882, he wrote to Albert F. Judd of Ruth: "... although I would willingly do anything in reason to aid and protect Keelikolani, she is so peculiar that I do not feel like offering my services or advice unasked. Almost anybody else can do so better than I can, for my motive would be likely misrepresented by parties who wish to keep or gain an influence with her for their own advantage. She has been greatly misused and deceived, and she greatly needs honest and wise advice."[30] But Charles may not have understood Ruth's motives.

It was indeed an extravagant enterprise, for Ruth spared no expense in its construction or furnishings. When completed in early 1883, two years after it was begun, Ruth's mansion exceeded in grandeur anything that had ever been built in Honolulu. In some people's view, her home was the equal of the King's still unfinished palace. As one wag put it, the dimensions of the structure were as stupendous as Ruth's own physique. For example, the two drawing rooms on the first floor occupied a combined area of more than 1,650 square feet, the entry hall was 66 feet long, the vestibule to the rear verandah stretched 65 feet in length and 13 feet in width, and the dining room was 30 feet by 24 feet or 720 square feet. The interior, with its plaster finishings and fresco ceilings painted by an Italian artist, was judged "admirable."[31] The newspapers had a field-day describing this grandiose display.

Ruth celebrated completion of the mansion along with her fifty-sixth birthday on February 9. The celebration lasted three days. The first day began with a grand *lū'au* for a thousand guests including Kalākaua, Pauahi, other *ali'i*, missionaries, diplomats, and anyone of importance. Ruth took pains to make this a Hawaiian statement of tradition and hospitality. The *lānai* was decorated with coconut fronds, fern lei, and *ti* leaves. Everyone sat on the floor, with the *ali'i* sitting on fine mats from the island of Ni'ihau. The most precious of her *kāhili* were positioned behind His Majesty. The tables were covered with *kapa* (bark cloth) of great value, some pieces being more than a century old. At the table, the *ali'i* ate from calabashes made either of coconut or *kou* (a beautiful native wood). Around her neck Ruth wore a priceless *palaoa* necklace.[32]

The *Honolulu Advertiser* described the chiefly abundance as follows: "Great preparations had been made to supply this multitude sumptuously and also to make this a thoroughly typical native feast. There had been a perfect holocaust of bullocks, hogs, chickens, turkeys etc. The sea had given its toll in the shape of quantities of fish and limu. The soil was mulched in taro, poi, sweet potatoes, coconuts and fruits...(and) bowls of poi, of excellent quality stretched in long lines down each table...."[33]

On the third day, Ruth was true to the ideal that the great chiefs tried to emulate: *'E ōpū ke ali'i* or "Be as kind and as generous as a chief should be." She lavished her generosity on "natives only." Tables were spread underneath a great tent "and bountifully filled with all the good things of native Hawaiian fare, which seemed to be produced from an absolutely inexhaustible store. A very large number took advantage of the Princess' hospitality...."[34] And after they had eaten their fill, Ruth ordered entertainment for the even larger crowds that had assembled on the premises throughout the night. The program consisted primarily of the traditional *mele* with an occasional modern song.

What Charles did not understand, perhaps, was that the building of Keōua Hale was a symbolic assertion of Ruth's power and status. The ensuing celebration was but a reaffirmation of her chiefly values: *ho'okipa* (hospitality) and *lokomaika'i* (generosity). Like the *ali'i* of the past, Ruth was claiming renewed honor and aloha from her people through her giving. To an *ali'i* this respect was worth more than anything else. The building was merely a monument to her pride and glory. Yet, Ruth did not care to stay here, preferring to sleep on the *lānai* (porch) of her old home nearby, or on the floor among her favorite pillows in her grass house in Kailua, Hawai'i. In fact, the only time she would ever rest in her mansion was during the weeks her body lay in state in the high-ceilinged drawing room.

Symbolism aside, Ruth could well afford to build herself such a mansion. She was the richest woman in all Hawai'i. It was not that she had no understanding of money or its value—she had gained too much business experience managing her estates to be accused of that. From her viewpoint, Keōua Hale was well worth its expense. Except for Pauahi, Ruth had lost everyone she loved dearly. She had all the money she would ever need, and so little time left to enjoy it. She was ill and, like many Hawaiians, may have felt that death was approaching. Stillman stated: "I think she had a premonition of what was coming. Hawaiians often feel death before it comes."[35] The mansion was Ruth's last extravagance.

Her timing was uncanny: the day after the end of the celebrations, she fell ill and was ordered by her doctor to go to Kailua to "improve her health." There she retired to her thatched cottage near the spot where her great-grandfather, Kamehameha I, had died. She was prepared. On January 24, she had made out her final will. It was the most important document she was ever to sign.

During the weeks that she "lay propped up by her familiar stacks of yellow cushions," Ruth was visited by many of her people. All had shared in her bounties and perhaps a few had experienced her tantrums and rebukes. They had come to show their concern and to share in her last days.

Unbeknownst to Ruth, someone sent a note to Pauahi and Emma, urging them to come at once. Ruth had an intermittent fever and her condition was worsening. Ruth herself became alarmed and finally asked

Judge Hoapili to summon her friends. But they, including the King himself, were already on their way.

Meanwhile, Ruth had finished her last remaining task: the composing of her own *kanikau*, the chant to mourn her passing. In it, Ruth bid a poetic farewell to her favorite island, the great mountains, the waves, the ocean, the beach, the familiar places, the houses, the friends. So reported the *Hawaiian Gazette* of May 30, 1883, but no copy of her lament has yet been found.[36] In this exquisite moment Ke'elikōlani was the incarnation of the Hawaiian of the classical past.

Ruth was quite conscious when the King, Pauahi and Emma arrived. Believing that she was in no danger, the King proceeded to Hilo. Pauahi and Emma watched at Ruth's bedside throughout the night. The next morning, May 24th, at nine o'clock, she died.

Ruth's body was taken back to Honolulu, where Samuel Damon was already making arrangements for the funeral. For the next three weeks or so she was to lie in state in her mansion, amidst the *kāhili*, the wailing, the mourners, the memories. Pauahi was there as one of the chief mourners, along with Emma, throughout this long vigil. As Pauahi sat during those many hours, a parade of other loved ones may have passed through her mind: Kīna'u, Moses, Pākī, Konia, Kekūanaō'a, Alexander, Kamāmalu, Lot, Keolaokalani. And now Ruth. Who would be next?

During her adult life, Ruth had successfully avoided the inside of almost every Christian church. Finally, on the afternoon of June 17th, she was the subject of a Christian service. The Kawaiaha'o choir sang and the Rev. Henry Parker preached and prayed for her soul. And then, accompanied by three alternating bands (of firemen, policemen, and U.S. Marines), the undertaker led the funeral procession to Mauna 'Ala, site of the Royal Mausoleum. The procession included the King's guards and household troops, Pauahi and Emma, His Majesty and the Queen, Lili'u, other *ali'i*, legislators, officials, diplomats, the cavalry, and a hundred *po'olā* (stevedores) drawing the hearse. In the Royal Mausoleum, to the dismay of her detractors, Ruth was laid to rest alongside other *ali'i* of the Kamehameha line.

The Corpus

While the rituals of death were taking place, Charles was taking care of the legal rituals attendant to Ruth's will. Ruth had appointed him as one of two executors, the other being Rudolph Meyer, who managed her properties on Moloka'i. The role was not an unfamiliar one to Charles, for he had served as the executor for Pākī, Lot, and Lunalilo, among others. Upon hearing of Ruth's death, he moved swiftly for the law required that notice of her death be published in the *Hawaiian Gazette* and *Kū'oko'a* newspapers for three consecutive weeks, before a will could be admitted for probate. The last notice had to appear at least seven days prior to the probate hearing. Ruth had died on May 24th, and the Court approved Charles' probate petition on June 22nd.[37]

While Charles hoped that probate proceedings would go smoothly, he had reason to fear that they might not. Ten years ago when the will of King Kamehameha V (Lot) was in probate, a man named Kahoukua went to court claiming that Ruth was not the rightful heir to Lot's lands. He argued that she was not Lot's sister since her true father was Kahalai'a (at one time the *kahu* or guardian of Kamehameha II or Liholiho) rather than Kekūanō'a. Besides Kahoukua, Charles Kana'ina, Lunalilo's father, had also issued essentially the same challenge. The court had turned away the challenges and declared Ruth to be the legitimate heir. Charles must have been greatly relieved to find that as probate progressed, no one came forward to take issue with Ruth's will.

Ruth had declared Pauahi sole heir to her entire estate: "I give and bequeath forever to my beloved younger sister (cousin), Bernice Pauahi Bishop, all of my property, the real property and personal property from Hawaii to Kauai, all of said property to be hers."[38] The amount was mind-boggling: about 353,000 acres, Keōua Hale and other homes in Kailua, Kona and Waikīkī; her precious heirlooms; and some cash. The total value of her assets is difficult to estimate, but it was around half a million dollars.

The lands, of course, were the real prize. The corpus of Ruth's estate comprised lands from the estates of her first husband Leleiōhoku, Victoria Kamāmalu, Mataio Kekūanaō'a, Namau'u (her father's brother), Moses Kekū'aiwa, and Kamehameha V (Lot). The bulk of the estate came from Kamāmalu's lands, which had reverted to her father Kekūanaō'a at her premature death in 1866, when she left neither will nor heir. Kamāmalu's lands in turn had come from Kamehameha III, who in 1848 had redistributed the lands in accordance with the *Māhele*. These were the Kamehameha lands, handed down from the greatest *ali'i* of all, Kamehameha the Great.[39]

The inventory is too long to list all of its individual parcels, but a few sample areas will indicate the magnitude of the lands. On the island of Hawai'i there were 38,298 acres in Keauhou in Ka'ū, 153,618 acres in North Kona, and 17,457 acres in Puna. On O'ahu there were 14,207 acres in 'Ewa and 25,486 acres in Waialua. There were 2,546 acres at Lahaina, Maui; 4,715 acres on Moloka'i; and 7,585 acres on Kaua'i.[40] There would have been more acres had Ruth not sold lands on Kaua'i, Maui and Hawai'i in order to finance the construction of her own "palace."

Ruth's will contained no instructions or hint as to how she might want the lands to be used. Had Ruth ever discussed the topic with Pauahi? Or did Ruth consider it inappropriate to impose any conditions? Or did she prefer to leave the ultimate disposition of her lands entirely to Pauahi's good judgment? Given the vast lands involved, their dynastic origins and great symbolic importance to the Kamehamehas, Ruth might have well raised the matter with Pauahi. What they might have discussed, we will probably never know. Even if such conversations never occurred, Pauahi must surely have known that she would most likely be inheriting this vast estate even before Ruth wrote her will in January. Pauahi was Ruth's closest relative (Emma was a distant cousin). Charles may have suspected, if not assumed, this when he was asked to be executor of Ruth's will. Whatever the case may be, Ruth granted her estate to Pauahi, not only because she was her logical heir, but also because Ruth had faith in Pauahi's abilities, loyalty, and commitment. Pauahi could be counted on to consider the feelings and values of Ruth and her forebearers in whatever she decided to do with her inheritance.

In an instant, Ruth had turned Pauahi into the largest landowner and the richest woman in the Kingdom. At the same time, she presented Pauahi with the greatest challenge and responsibility of her life. Pauahi now owned a giant estate, and she would soon have to decide to what ends it would be used.

8

HELE LĀ O KAIONA

In moments of doubt, Pauahi may well have wondered about Ruth's generosity. Her legacy only complicated a very secure and comfortable existence. After all, Pauahi didn't need to be the richest woman in the Kingdom; she was already married to one of its richest men. She certainly didn't need a bigger house, especially one the size of Keōua Hale, or the army of retainers that came with it. And what would she do with another 353,000 acres of land? It was fourteen times as much as she had and meant that many more problems. At fifty-one years of age, she suddenly found herself having to take on an enormous responsibility, one that would have severely challenged a person many years younger. Pauahi, who had turned aside the status and glory of the throne, certainly did not want the lesser status that might accrue from being a big landlord. In purely selfish terms, she really didn't need Ruth's legacy and surely neither did Charles.

Here was a woman who had the least need for more material goods, being showered, if not burdened, with more than she had ever asked for or wanted. Why? The answer is found in her sacred birth; the genetic linkage to Kamehameha, Keōua, and Keawe; her chiefly status; experience; leadership; intelligence and education; integrity, loyalty, aloha and other qualities; and her commitment to her people, their past, present and future. But while these combined factors make a rational and persuasive case, in the end, the why is bound up with circumstance, the confluence of events, fate. There are just so many twists and turns in Pauahi's odyssey that the historian's logic or scholarship cannot fully explain.

Pauahi no doubt wondered about the course and purpose of her own existence. At last she may have concluded that, for all the reasons above, she had been brought to the eventide of her life to perform one crowning act, to be accomplished through the lands of the Kamehamehas. This final chapter tells how she barely completed that task.

The Preliminaries

Events moved quickly and seemingly all at once. As the executors of Ruth's estate worked to satisfy claimants and to ready the estate for transfer to its new owner, Pauahi had to ponder not only how best to manage it but, paradoxically, how best to dispose of it. According to Charles, when years later he recounted what happened in this period, he and Pauahi began to talk about her own will after the probate of Ruth's will was admitted.[1] Apparently, Pauahi had not given the matter of a will much thought before. For one thing, she had always enjoyed good health and had never thought her time was at hand. For another, her previously small estate had seemed of no great import. Now, however, the value of her estate was so high and its potential for good so promising that it seemed prudent to make a will. Though prudence was one motive, her intuition may have been another, because in a few months she was to fall victim to serious illness.

We have no record of the conversations between Pauahi and Charles, but if she was formulating a will, there were two questions that had to be answered: To whom should she leave her estate? And for what purpose? Pauahi had no close relatives left, excepting, of course, her Charles. There was Emma, who was a distant cousin, and Lili'u, who was an adopted sister, though in almost every sense she and Pauahi were as close as sisters. But these two were well along in years and had their own estates. The ideal heir would have been a child of her own. Strange as it may seem, either just before or during the planning of her will, this ever-present wish almost came true.

Some details of the story are unclear, but the essential outline is as follows: Sometime between 1882 and the summer of 1883, Pauahi and Charles tried to adopt the infant William Kaiheekai Taylor, who was born on April 28, 1882. His parents were Keomailani Crowninburg and Wray Taylor. Pauahi had known Keomailani ever since she was a young girl. Keomailani was sent to school in England under Emma's auspices and returned to Hawai'i in 1880. Pauahi had expressed an interest in the baby and had in fact taken it home for a short while soon after its birth. Pauahi and Charles attended the boy's christening at St. Andrew's Cathedral and became his god-parents. Sometime in 1883, they asked for permission to legally adopt the boy, but were turned down and instead offered one of Keomailani's just-born twin daughters.[2]

While the young Keomailani declined to give her son for adoption, Pauahi made up her mind about her legacy. She would adopt the children of her people and make them her heirs.

Charles recalled that, when it came to the question of purpose, it came down to two choices: health care and education.[3] Health care was considered because, for social, religious and personal reasons, Pauahi had a deep interest in it. She showed a compassion for the sick, caring for the ill whether they were family, friends or strangers. Her Christian as well as her own native values were a powerful motivating force. An even greater force was her concern over the dreadful fact that the race was dying at a rate that put its whole future in doubt. Pauahi still had vivid memories of the devastating effects of the measles, influenza and whooping cough epidemics that swept through Hawai'i during her last year at the Chiefs' Children's School. The epidemics had killed more than 10,000, and they had continued to break out as recently as 1879 and 1881. Despite private and public efforts in establishing hospitals, health prevention and other facilities, the needs were not being met, especially for Hawaiians. So the whole field of health, from hospital construction and patient care to research and training, offered many possibilities for Pauahi's largess. But, in the end, Pauahi decided against health care. Perhaps it was because Emma's activities with the Queen's Hospital had, in a sense, pre-empted the field, or because Charles himself had already been actively involved, as a member of the hospital board and as a generous contributor.

This left education: a natural if not inevitable choice for Pauahi. If education fundamentally involves the development of the person by improving the desirable qualities of the mind, body and character through the acquisition of knowledge, wisdom, and skills, her life reflected its value. We have showed how Pauahi genuinely enjoyed being an active part of the educational process. She spent ten years being a bright and serious student at the Royal School — being, in Mrs. Cooke's opinion, the best and brightest of the lot—seeking to be educated in the truest sense of the word by developing her entire self intellectually, physically, morally, and artistically. Though she did not continue in higher education, an option not readily available to her, she sought to educate herself throughout her life. She demonstrated this aim in her lifelong habit of reading extensively; her continual involvement in discussion groups; her participation in the work of various organizations, invariably in leadership roles; her travels, which were educational as well as pleasurable; and her own teaching activities, whether in music, sewing, or Sunday School. For Pauahi, education did not take place only within the walls of a classroom; learning was an endless pursuit in the School of Real Life Experiences. While such thinking would have been considered progressive by educational theorists of the time, in a very real sense Pauahi was only emulating a philosophy of education followed for centuries in traditional Hawai'i.

Pauahi's interest in education reflected her own personal values. Since she was a product of at least two cultures, her individual philosophy was made up of both Hawaiian and Western, particularly American values. Her zeal for learning came in part from the enthusiasm that her missionary teachers brought to the classroom and the premium that Americans such as Richard Armstrong and Mrs. Cooke placed on learning. The American belief in education rested on utilitarian assumptions that it would lead to progress, freedom, opportunity, success and achievement. These were heady notions that must have impressed Pauahi and other *ali'i* who strongly supported the educational system of the islands. Other values came from her traditional culture. These included excellence, respect for the intellect, industry and diligence, and belief in the *mana* in knowledge and expertise. Such values were partially based on the belief that the process of learning was sacred; hence, all the essential elements of that process, from the teacher to the place of learning and the students, were consecrated to the gods. While Pauahi had not been educated following traditional forms, she was still imbued with the substance of that process that elevated the pursuit of knowledge above all else. These were complementary, if not universal values, which she came to personify in her life.

Pauahi understood the value of education to her own life, but why did she think it was good for Hawaiians in general? The answer to this question is at the heart of her will. In her idealism, she must have believed that education would help to lift her people out of their plight and restore their pride and hope for the future.

In the summer of 1883, the Hawaiian people were in a terrible condition. The numbers stood out in bold relief: In the year Pauahi was born there were 124,500 Hawaiians, and now there were approximately only 40,014 left, along with 40,500 foreigners.[5] Pauahi probably never really believed that she would live to see the time when foreigners would outnumber her own native people. Many of the remaining Hawaiians suffered from diseases such as leprosy, tuberculosis, diabetes, gonorrhea, syphilis, and cancer. Following the earlier epidemics, still more would fall victim to new sicknesses such as the mumps, beriberi, and diphtheria. Hawaiian adults did not live as long as those of other races, and rates of infant mortality were also higher.

As if sheer physical survival of the race were not enough of a challenge, there was the complex problem of psychological, cultural and economic, not to mention political, survival. Psychologically, many Hawaiians were being crippled, having lost much of their sense of identity and self-esteem. They had been stereotyped as lazy, promiscuous, and dumb, the descendants of an uncivilized, savage and pagan civilization. As individuals and as a group, Pauahi's people were being traumatized by a compelling sense of inferiority. Pauahi was not an armchair observer of these devastating problems. Through regular contact with her people, whether under her tamarind tree or on her estates or in the streets of Honolulu, she knew what was happening and how they felt.

Culturally, much of the traditional fabric of customs, symbols and values was rapidly being tattered. Kalākaua made valiant efforts to revive the old myths, the *hula* and the *mele,* and adapt the new to old, in music and other areas. But the cultural lifeline of the Hawaiian people had been reduced to a few threads. One of these threads was the language. But Walter M. Gibson, who had just replaced Charles as President of the Board of Education, had completely substituted English for Hawaiian in public schools.[6] With the loss of their language as a functional medium in formal education, Hawaiians would slowly but surely lose the single most important tie to an understanding of their past.

The psychological and cultural devastation was mirrored in the social and economic conditions of the Hawaiian community. The litany of broken homes, absent fathers, drunkenness, crime and delinquency, truancy, and other social dislocations, was already being heard throughout the Kingdom — and is still being heard more than a hundred years later. The breakdown of the family system was one of the direct causes of the educational predicament of the Hawaiians. Traditionally, it was the family, especially the *kūpuna* or grandparents, who carried on the teaching of the children. But by now grandparents were missing or being relegated to places like an old folks home, leaving children without mentors and models. Family disintegration increasingly left Hawaiians without their customary refuges of security and love and respect. Their alienation gave them feelings of rebellion and resentment against all others, including the *ali'i.*

There was an economic antecedent to most if not all of these problems. Hawaiians had long lost control of their economy, partly through the loss or sale of their lands and through being driven out of certain traditional occupational fields like farming (even taro and the making of *poi*), small-scale shipbuilding and retailing. On the sugar plantations they were being replaced by immigrant laborers. Increasingly, Hawaiians were forced to compete with Japanese and Chinese whose drive to succeed and to become educated would make them all but invincible in the race for the spoils left by the *haole* oligarchy. More and more were less and less equipped with the skills to find jobs in the open market. All of this, of course, did not happen in a year, but incrementally over several decades. What Pauahi now saw was the cumulative impact of death, despair, waning prestige, feelings of inferiority and fear.

Pauahi and many others had concluded that the survival and salvation of the Hawaiian people would have to come through education. There was God, too, and hard work and sacrifice and government assistance, but the key was in all the advantages a good education would bring to those who wanted it and applied themselves. The largess of Pauahi and Charles would always be predicated on those conditions. Specifically, Pauahi saw the power of education to awaken the mind and spirit of the people to the world of possibilities and to their own potential. Education could strengthen their self-image and restore their dignity, and above all teach them the skills to become gainfully employed, so they would be able to raise their families and their living standards, educate their children and help them to stake out their rightful place in society. Only this process could ensure the survival of the Hawaiian people.

Pauahi may not have referred to these ideas in exactly these terms, but they probably come close to describing her frame of mind as she sat down to write out the conditions of her *kauoha* or will.

The Formulation of Her Will

Once she had decided on education, the next step was to determine exactly how the will would be formulated, specifically for whom and under what terms and conditions, plus a host of other factors. To make these decisions, she no doubt sought out the best advice she could get from friends and experts,[7] both Hawaiian and non-Hawaiian, including some of the men she later selected as trustees for her estate. Then she made her own final decision. It would have been totally out of character for her to let anyone else, including Charles, decide things for her. As her life shows, she was entirely able and willing to make large and important decisions in the best or worst of circumstances. Now in her last days, making the most critical decisions of her life, perhaps without realizing then just how critical they would be, she and she alone would decide.

Pauahi's decision is set out in the thirteenth section or paragraph of her will. It reads in part:

"I give, devise and bequeath all of the rest, residue and remainder of my estate real and personal, wherever situated unto the trustees below named, their heirs and assigns forever, to hold upon the following trusts, namely: to erect and maintain in the Hawaiian Islands two schools, each for boarding and day scholars, one for boys and one for girls, to be known as, and called the Kamehameha Schools. I direct my trustees to expend such amount as they may deem best, not to exceed however one-half of the fund which may come into their hands, in the purchase of suitable premises, the erection of school buildings, and in furnishing the same with the necessary and appropriate fixtures furniture and apparatus. I direct my trustees to invest the remainder of my estate in such manner as they may think best, and to expend the annual income in the maintenance of said schools; meaning thereby the salaries of teachers, the repairing of buildings and other incidental expenses; and to devote a portion of each years income to the support and education of orphans, and others in indigent circumstances, giving the preference to Hawaiians of pure or part aboriginal blood; the proportion in which said annual income is to be divided among the various objects above mentioned to be determined solely by my said trustees they to have full discretion. I desire my trustees to provide first and chiefly a good education in the common English branches, and also instruction in morals and in such useful knowledge as may tend to make good and industrious men and women; and I desire instruction in the higher branches to be subsidiary to the foregoing objects. For the purposes aforesaid I grant unto my said trustees full power to lease or sell any portion of my real estate, and to reinvest the proceeds and the balance of my estate in real estate, or in such other manner as to my said trustees may seem best. I also give unto my said trustees full power to make all such rules and regulations as they may deem necessary for the government of said schools and to regulate the admission of pupils, and the same to alter, amend and publish upon a vote of a majority of said trustees. I also direct that my said trustees shall annually make a full and complete report of all receipts and expenditures, and of the condition of said schools to the Chief Justice of the Supreme Court, or other highest judicial officer in this country; and shall also file before him annually an inventory of the property in their hands and how invested, and to publish the same in some Newspaper published in said Honolulu;... I also direct that the teachers of said schools shall forever be persons of the Protestant religion, but I do not intend that the choice should be restricted to persons of any particular sect of Protestants."[8]

In the fourteenth paragraph she named her five trustees — Charles, Samuel M. Damon, Charles M. Hyde, Charles M. Cooke and William O. Smith — and designates that the vacancies on the board of trustees be "filled by the choice of a majority of the Justices of the Supreme Court, the selection to be made from persons of the Protestant religion."9

There are other provisions in Pauahi's will providing bequests of money, land and life stipends to various persons, including Lili'u, Emma, Keomailani Taylor, Bernice Bishop Dunham, some of her faithful retainers and servants, and Charles. She also stipulated that $5,000 be given to Kawaiaha'o Church and an equal sum to the Kawaiaha'o Family School for Girls. Charles and Samuel Damon were named her executors.

Pauahi completed her will, with the help of Francis M. Hatch, a highly respected local attorney, on October 31, 1883.10 She signed two copies written out in eleven pages of English (instead of Hawaiian), giving one of them to Samuel Damon. Actually, she was not finished yet, because within a year she would revise and add other terms in two more codicils. But the essence of her will is contained in this document, which has been praised by some legal specialists for the quality of its formulation.

Elucidations

In the intervening years, many questions have been asked about certain ideas, words, and phrases contained in Pauahi's will. Since conditions in society change constantly, it is not surprising that the will has been subject to reinterpretation, in ways sometimes drastic enough to invite a great deal of public and private reaction. In Hawai'i today no other will has undergone as much scrutiny as Pauahi's. It is useful, then, to pause and consider a few of the more important aspects of the will as Pauahi might have viewed them.

To begin with, some have wondered why she chose to establish two schools, one for boys and one for girls, physically and administratively separated. The founding of separate schools seems both inefficient and costly. Besides, educating boys and girls apart seems artificial, not true-to-life and therefore socially and psychologically unhealthy. Most schools in Hawai'i at the time, whether common, select or independent, were coeducational, and Pauahi's own alma mater, the Chiefs' Children's School, had also been coeducational.

Pauahi and her advisers were quite aware of these arguments but still rejected them. A coeducational boarding school would pose the same kind of problem that hounded the Cookes' of boys and girls getting in each other's beds. In a school for students of one sex there would be fewer distractions, students would concentrate more on their studies, and discipline would be more easily imposed. Pauahi, perhaps familiar with some of the best private schools in America and England, such as Phillips-

Exeter and Eton which were not coeducational, may have used them as a model. But, in the final analysis, she may just have felt that a separate arrangement would be more conducive to good scholarship.

As for the choice of a boarding over a day school, a good case could be made for boarding. If the populace from which students were to be selected had lived in one central area, a day school would have made sense. But because Hawaiians were scattered all over the islands, bringing students together in a residential arrangement was a logical move. In addition, Pauahi may have been reminded of John Iʻiʻs recommendation that the Royal School assemble the children of the chiefs from different areas in order to foster a common understanding and greater unity. Most important, however, would have been the need to create an environment where students would be protected from harmful and distracting outside influences, whether from the city or their own homes and be given a better chance to learn good habits and proper morals. Finally, the school would need to exercise maximum control over the students' time, and the residential arrangement would be the best means to do so.

Over the years a good deal of controversy has been stirred by the omission in the will of a restrictive clause specifically providing only for the admission of students of Hawaiian ancestry. The reference to Hawaiian ancestry is somewhat oblique and more directly related to the admission and education of orphans and indigents. Then, the will only makes it a matter of giving "preference" to "Hawaiians of pure or part aboriginal blood." Some have interpreted this wording to indicate that Pauahi actually meant the schools of the Kamehamehas to be open to all nationalities. Of course, this interpretation is untenable in the light of Pauahi's beliefs and deeds in a life so inextricably bound with the destiny of Hawaiians.

Pauahi's actual intention is best summed up in the phrase "exclusive but conditional." She founded the institution for the exclusive use of Hawaiians. This was and is her first premise or the general policy. She attached a condition, however, to serve more as a challenge than a threat. In effect, the condition sets out Pauahi's view that, while the educational opportunities of the schools would be offered to Hawaiians, Hawaiians would have to take advantage of them. The problem in interpreting this point in the will arises only when the subordinate condition is not viewed in the context of the first premise. The condition is only a "but," although an important one. It does not alter the general, fundamental principle that the schools were established to serve the interests of Hawaiians, first and foremost. That this was Pauahi's meaning and intention is very clear from a review of her history.

Above all, Pauahi was a champion of her people, and the principle of exclusive use derives from this fact. She was a Hawaiian, an *aliʻi* and a Kamehameha before she was anything else. Her identity as a person and purpose in life were always defined by ethnic and national bonds with her *ʻāina*, her people and her ancestors. Though she epitomized the blending of *haole* and Hawaiian ways, she did not surrender or alter her fundamental commitment to her essential being as a Hawaiian. Given the context of the times when Pauahi wrote her will, she had to be most concerned with the plight of the Hawaiians, not anyone else. After all, in the summer and fall of 1883, her people were on the verge of racial extinction and cultural disintegration. Who needed help more than her own people? At such a juncture she could not have been thinking of helping all nationalities, for that would imply that she was incapable of discriminating those in desperate need from those whose need was far less.

Though in a legal sense she was the sole founder of the schools, Pauahi was heir to the lands of the Kamehamehas — Keʻelikōlani, Lot, Kamāmalu and Konia — and Kekūanaōʻa and Pākī. In a real sense they had entrusted the lands into her keeping and disposition. Pauahi accepted this responsibility and trust, because she insisted that the schools bear not her name, but the name of the Kamehamehas. If Pauahi had given the matter any less thought, she would have omitted any reference to naming the schools, in which event the schools would most likely have been named after her. But when she established the schools, she was acting not only on her own behalf but for her royal predecessors as well. Each of them, but most of all Ruth, was, in effect, a co-founder of the schools. None of them would have assigned major assets to a cause whose beneficiaries were not Hawaiians. Pauahi, of all people, certainly knew this. And just as she memorialized them in the name of the schools, so she would have respected their wish to provide for the needs of their people first and foremost.

All the *aliʻi* who left charitable trusts appear to have thought about their beneficiaries in the same way. In 1874, Lunalilo willed his estate to the care of the "poor, destitute and infirm" old people of Hawaiian blood. It should be recalled that Charles and Pauahi helped him to formulate his last testament. When Queen Emma set up her trust, funds were specifically provided for Hawaiian patients.[11] When Queen Kapiʻolani established the Maternity Home in 1890, the facility was intended for Hawaiian mothers.[12] And when Queen Liliʻuokalani provided for the trust that created the Liliʻuokalani Children's Center, Hawaiians were clearly given preference.[13] Since Pauahi was from the same ideological mold as the other *aliʻi*, it would stand to reason that she intended her assets to be used for the benefit of Hawaiians.

If Pauahi intended the schools to be for the exclusive use of Hawaiians, why didn't she state this intention in the will? The answer lies in the condition. By not stating her intention explicitly, Pauahi set an implicit challenge before her people. Her challenge was like the *kaona* or hidden meaning found between the lines of Hawaiian poetry. To have stated the condition in so formal a document would have been indelicate. But to leave it implicit would have been the Hawaiian way. Attaching the condition was perfectly consistent with Pauahi's outlook and understanding of the psychology of her people. They would respond to the challenge because it recognized their dignity and their potential.

One might ask why a similar condition was not found in, say, Lunalilo's will. It stated simply and clearly that only Hawaiians would be served by the old folks home. The reason is to be found in the difference between the nature of a school and an old folks home, a hospital or a maternity home. The latter institutions are humanitarian with admission based on need, not competence, intelligence, motivation or ability to learn. A school by its very nature is a challenge and so must lay down conditions.

Charles stated the "exclusive but conditional" idea as a policy many times while he served as a trustee. He wrote in a letter dated February 11, 1897: "There is nothing in the will of Mrs. Bishop excluding white boys or girls from the Schools, but it is understood by the Trustees that only those having native blood are to be admitted at present, that they are to have the preference so long as they avail themselves of the privileges open to them to a reasonable extent."[14] Here, of course, the meaning of the condition is carried to its logical conclusion: if Hawaiians do not take advantage of the schools, their places will be given to others. But Pauahi clearly preferred not to make an explicit statement to this effect in her will. In her darkest moments she might have acknowledged the possibility the time might come when the race disappeared physically and spiritually, but she was too hopeful to believe that such a time ever would come.

At the heart of the will is her injunction that the trustees, above all else, provide her beneficiaries a "good education" that will make out of them "good and industrious men and women." A "good education" consists of "the common English branches" and "instruction in morals." That is all she says about the matter in her will. What she does not say seems again to be of as much importance as what she does say.

What did Pauahi mean by "the common English branches?" For one thing, it is clear that English would be the medium of instruction. It was plainly a decision based on acceptance of the fact that only those with a mastery of the English language would have access to the kinds of knowledge and skills necessary to compete and succeed in Hawai'i. The choice of English was based purely on practical socio-economic considerations. Pauahi wanted Hawaiians not merely to survive but to achieve. As she demonstrated in her own life, mastery of English was a vital tool for achieving success in the *haole* world. She may well have bemoaned the loss of fluency in the Hawaiian language and the negative implications of this loss for the vitality of the culture. But here she was dealing with the overriding problem of preparing young Hawaiians for making a living, something they could not do if fluent only in Hawaiian.

By the phrase "the common English branches," she undoubtedly meant those subjects normally taught as parts or branches of the study of English, namely, reading, speaking, composition, spelling, grammar and penmanship. In addition, she may also have had in mind those subjects offered in the then government-supported English schools. If so, the subjects would have included some or all of the following, contained in the high school curriculum of 1881, and shown by grade:

Grade Nine

Algebra commenced	Physical Geography
Bookkeeping	Ancient History
Botany and Physiology	French, German or Latin

Grade Ten

Algebra finished	Rhetoric and English Language
Geometry commenced	Medieval History
Zoology	French, German or Latin

Grade Eleven

Geometry finished	Modern History
Chemistry	English Literature
Natural Philosophy	Latin and Greek

Grade Twelve

Trigonometry	English Literature
Geology	Mental Philosophy
Astronomy	Latin and Greek

There were also "collateral studies" which included elocution, declamation, drawing, music, and orthography.[15]

Besides the above, Pauahi specifically mentioned "morals" as a subject of instruction. In so doing, she was taking a page from the statutes of the Hawaiian Kingdom which mandated schools "to instruct the children in good morals." The Education Board understood good morals to include "honesty, truthfulness, charity, temperance, obedience to parents and teachers, kindness, chastity, gratitude, control of temper and passions, benevolence, generosity, cleanliness, helpfulness to the weak and the poor, avoidance of profanity and obscenity, humanity toward animals as well as man, patriotism, respect for one's superiors in age and position, and much more."[16] Pauahi herself might have added others such as aloha, *lōkahi*, hospitality, frugality, prudence, promptitude, diligence, respect of ancestors, reverence, courage, persistence, and tolerance.

"Instruction in morals" did not mean religious instruction. Morals had everything to do with character-building, in terms of developing positive attitudes and clarifying values, but it had nothing to do with theology, ritual, or priestly practices. Good morals might generally be the same as religious or Christian teachings. At the time the Board of Education took the view that morals were to be taught by example and precept, but not by presentation of any particular set of religious doctrines. Pauahi no doubt accepted this philosophy as well, for there is no provision in her will for religious instruction. However, neither is anything said against it.

In fact, Pauahi studiously avoided detailing school subjects in the will, realizing all too well that the world of knowledge constantly changes, with accompanying implications for changes in school curricula. Wisely, she left the responsibility of determining subject-matter to others, but she also left them a standard by which to judge what would be appropriate for the schools' curriculum. That standard was, in effect, the same as the schools' objective: the making of "good and industrious men and women." In other words, if a subject would help to turn students into "good and industrious men and women," that subject would be acceptable. It was a simple but brilliant solution to the problem she faced when formulating her will and trying to define what a good education should be. Only let the ends justify the means. But what did she mean by those ends, "good and industrious men and women"?

Making "good and industrious men and women" has come to be accepted as almost scriptural in its authority by those who have to explain the schools' *raison d'etre* today. This statement is the only one of its kind in her entire will. It is elegant and enduring in its simplicity and brevity. That, perhaps, is the nature of great ideas: they tend to be uncomplicated, memorable and almost universal. But, more often than not, they are the distillation of many complex and intricate concepts and hypotheses, failed experiments, good and bad experiences, profound insights, and unresolved questions. After all, Pauahi was dealing with the central issue of educational philosophy, a topic with a long and voluminous history. If not Pauahi herself, certainly her advisers were aware of the varied and conflicting opinions and theories then prevalent about education and its role in society. She may even have been familiar with the notions of one of the most famous educators of the time, Horace Mann, whose son she entertained many times at Hale'ākala. It is entirely plausible that she had discussed the subject with Charles and others many times over the years. In writing Section Thirteen she was forced to reduce all of her beliefs, impressions and feelings about education to its bare essentials and her conclusion was: it ultimately serves to make "good and industrious men and women."

She might have stopped with "good." Thus, "a good education" would produce "good men and women." The logic is irrefutable, its meaning universal, and its relevance timeless. The term "good" is all-encompassing — it includes everything and excludes nothing of any worth. It is also an excellent word to express a mandate that she hoped would last in perpetuity, because it offers those who are entrusted with the schools the widest latitude to exercise their creativity, judgment and responsibility.

But the term "good" was not enough, because she added "industrious" — it had to be "good *and* industrious men and women." Why did she feel compelled to add the word? Why was it so important to single out this specific attribute? And what did it mean? At first glance, it appears to be a word that Charles might have suggested. As noted in the previous chapter, the term is included in his 1874 report to the Legislative Assembly, in which he complained about students in "the higher schools and in the English language" having "wrong ideas about labor — in short [being] lazy and idle." The general feeling was that the "rising generation" was "not as *industrious* as their ancestors" (italics added). If Charles raised the issue in a public document, it was certainly a matter of public concern and knowledge. The widespread perception of the Hawaiian as being "lazy and idle" must have troubled Pauahi deeply, enough so that it came to occupy a dominant place in her mind. She knew from his traditional habits and values that the Hawaiian should be as industrious as any other person. She was keenly conscious, though, of the psycho-cultural crisis of the Hawaiian and the effects it was having on his self-confidence and performance. If the Hawaiian was to be saved, he had to break out of this predicament by being industrious, but to do so he would need help. Pauahi would offer that help in the form of a good education that would make him not only an industrious but a good person.

The word "industrious" comes from the Latin "industriosus" which means "diligent." Specifically, it means being zealous, energetic, dependable or steady in applying one's skills or abilities, especially in a job. Thus, to be industrious presupposes that a person has a skill or a job. A person without any skills or employment, without anything to do, cannot be diligent or zealous. An unskilled or unemployed person cannot help but be idle and lazy. Pauahi understood that, in order to help a person to be industrious, it was first necessary to provide the person with an opportunity to develop a skill leading to gainful employment. It is fine to be good, but better to be good and industrious. That was the whole point of a good education, as far as Pauahi was concerned.

In the will the term "industrious" is not used in the modern sense of "industry," as in the "sugar industry" or the "tourist industry." Its antecedent is not business or commerce. A person can be industrious in any line of work or field of endeavor, from playing music, to gardening, to studying, to making money. Confusion can result if the term "industriousness" is given a different interpretation. For example, there is no necessary connection, causal or otherwise, between "industrial training" and being "industrious."[17] Pauahi's will does not endorse any special type of training except that in the English branches and morals.

One more issue requires elucidation. Some have been troubled because Pauahi's declaration seems to imply a bias against higher education. The will states that "instruction in the higher branches" should be "subsidiary to the foregoing subjects." Pauahi did not say precisely what she meant by the "higher branches" of knowledge. Did she have in mind such subjects as logic, physics, intellectual philosophy, political economy and anthropology? These were considered "higher branches" then, but they were university subjects which would not have been in a high school curriculum in any case. Or did she view certain subjects in the English school curriculum as falling into that category of "higher branches"? Would she, for example, have thought of rhetoric, trigonometry, or Greek and Latin as "higher" subjects? Would it have been out of place in her scheme of things for a Hawaiian student to learn Cicero's first Catilinarian oration or Plato's *Republic?* It is difficult to tell, and probably just as well that she did not say, because what one generation may consider a "higher branch" of knowledge may not be considered so by the next generation.

Pauahi did not state or even hint that she was against "higher branches" of knowledge *per se,* but only that they should be "subsidiary." That is, they were to be supportive of but in a subordinate position to the "foregoing objects," that is, the "common English branches" and "instruction in morals," and above all, the making of "good and industrious men and women." Clearly, she did not intend the Kamehameha Schools to be a college.[18] In 1883, the urgent need was not for a college. No part of Pauahi's will should be interpreted to mean that she was, in principle, against higher learning. Her own learning activities after leaving the Royal School, and her own values regarding personal development and achievement, suggest that she would have wanted her schools to encourage students to go on to the "higher branches" of knowledge.

No special religious qualifications were required for admission as a student, but Pauahi felt it was necessary to impose a condition on teachers and trustees. Her will clearly stipulates that teachers "shall be forever of the Protestant religion," although not of any particular Protestant sect. This restriction is said to have found its way into her will because of the strong influence of one of her advisers, a Protestant clergyman. The implication is that this provision in the will is uncharacteristic of Pauahi, at heart a tolerant person married to a man who had "little respect for sectarianism," as he said himself.[19] This explanation finds some support in that the Cookes did not judge her a "pious" person, at least as a student. From all indications, she did not become much more pious as an adult. She enjoyed dancing, the theater, merry parties, card-playing and, perhaps, other social pastimes which the missionaries of an earlier period might have frowned upon. But however tolerant she may have been, the fact remains that her will bars all but Protestants from serving as teachers or trustees.

There is a reasonable explanation for this fact. Pauahi was a Congregationalist, though not pious, still devout. Her regular attendance at Kawaiahaʻo Church, her Sunday School class, singing in the choir, her interest in the girls' school, and her posthumous bequests to both the church and the school, attest to her faith. She was born into and raised in the Protestant religion. Kīnaʻu, whom she tried to emulate in some ways, Pākī, Konia, Kekūanaōʻa, John Papa Iʻi, who were so influential in her younger years, and her close *haole* friends such as the Cookes, Damons, and many others, were all strong Protestants — and many equally strong opponents of Catholicism.

Pauahi was not raised in an atmosphere of tolerance for Catholicism. As an impressionable child, she saw her regent mother Kīnaʻu locked in bitter battle with the French who were supporting the proselytizing efforts of the first Catholic priests. Kīnaʻu viewed these moves as part of a conspiracy which threatened the sovereignty and unity of the Kingdom. Her feelings against the priests were not only doctrinal but political. In this highly charged atmosphere, fueled by the vehement opposition of the Protestant missionaries, it was easy for deep-seated suspicions to turn into feelings of intolerance. Pauahi was only one of many who got caught up in the religious and political conflicts of the time.

Although she was never able to resolve her inner feelings completely, Pauahi had apparently achieved partial resolution in her later years. This is suggested in part by her enthusiasm for the great architectural and artistic accomplishments of Catholicism in Europe and the contentment she discovered in Rome. She also developed warm friendships among Catholics at home and abroad. She did not hold their faith against them when she wrote that she loved the Italians because they reminded her so much of her own people.

In a sense, the insistence on teachers and trustees, but not students, being Protestant is a compromise that reflected an evolution in her view of religion in the world as it was in 1883. To her everlasting credit, Pauahi did not impose any sectarian limitations on students, thus forever encouraging their rights to speak, to read, to listen, to think and to believe according to the dictates of their conscience. She understood the need to let the spirit of inquiry soar high and free.

She was not yet done with her will, but time was running out.

Hele Lā O Kaiona

As her fifty-second birthday approached, Pauahi had cause to celebrate. She had completed the formulation of her will, and she had a far better understanding of the workings of her giant estate, under good management thanks to the *konohiki*, business agents and managers. Rudolph Meyer had just been given power-of-attorney to take charge of the lands on Molokaʻi belonging to Pauahi and Charles, including Molokaʻi Ranch with its cattle and sheep.[20] Samuel Damon apparently assumed overall management responsibilities for Pauahi's holdings, although he was still taking care of matters for Ruth's estate.[21] Pauahi took an active part in the management to the extent that she was in regular contact with Damon and was regularly called on to approve leases, financial reports, and the like. For example, on December 28, 1883, Damon wrote to Meyer: "I have closed the Estate account and given my report to Mrs. Bishop of the receipts and disbursements during the last twelve months."[22] Again, Damon asked and secured Pauahi's consent for the sale of a parcel of land in Līhuʻe as revealed in the following letter to W. H. Rice: (Mrs. Bishop) "considers that an offer to sell the whole for $100 a fair settlement."[23]

But by the end of 1883, it is quite possible that she was feeling the first pain of her still undiagnosed illness. It must have been a shock, for having always been in good health she had "never experienced pain" before.[24] Sometime before or right after the new year, she was examined by Dr. George Trousseau, who had attended most of the *ali'i*. His preliminary diagnosis is not known, but whatever it was, it did not deter her from working. In a letter to Meyer, Charles wrote on February 9, 1884: "Mrs. Bishop is hard at work gardening."[25] Not even pain could keep her away from a lifetime passion. Anyway, she would not have shown it if she could help herself, because she was not one to complain or to indulge in self-pity.

By March her condition had worsened, and Dr. Trousseau advised her to go to San Francisco for a change of scenery and further consultations. Charles wrote to Meyer on March 10: "Mrs. Bishop will go to SF in the "Almeda" April 1st to be absent about seven weeks."[26] Evidently, neither he nor Pauahi knew at the time how seriously ill she was. After arriving in San Francisco, she did not go to see her doctor immediately. Instead, she wrote to her cousin Cordie: "We have now been in Frisco nearly a week, and, as usual, I have been out to see the dressmaker, milliners, etc., etc., to say nothing of shopping, although I have not indulged much in that respect for myself... The weather has been perfectly atrocious since we came. It has rained every day — cold and damp, and we have been obliged to have fire in our room a great deal... I feel very much better for being here, and, for a wonder, have not had a cold ..."[27] Young Bernice Bishop from Stockton, who had gone along partway to Europe with Pauahi and Charles, was with her in San Francisco. Princess Likelike, Lili'uokalani's sister, was also there seeking her own medical relief.[28]

Pauahi eventually got around to seeing a Dr. Lane, who diagnosed her problem as a malignant cancer, on her left side below the arm, that had already reached an advanced stage. He advised immediate surgery, which was done in the annex of the Palace Hotel "where a comfortable room had been made ready."[29] The operation probably took place in May. Samuel Damon wrote to Meyer on May 10th: "Mrs. Bishop's health is not good and an operation performing in S.F. gives Mr. Bishop some anxiety. At last accounts, Mrs. B was improving and not in danger. Very few know of her illness here and I would ask you to keep this quiet."[30] Coincidentally, Mrs. Damon was in San Francisco at the time and spent a "pleasant" half-hour visit with Pauahi after the operation. Mrs. Damon wrote: "I haven't the least faith in the knife for a cancer."[31]

Charles, too, wrote to Meyer on the same day informing him that: "I am going to S F in the "Mariposa" next week. Mrs. Bishop was not quite well at last report and cannot come home this month, consequently I shall go over, and may or may not return in one month. I hope to find her so well that I may return immediately in the Mariposa whether she comes with me or not. She will not be expecting me because she knows how inconvenient it is for me to leave home now; and she also knows that I know that she has every attention and comfort possible where she is. While I expect to find her better I feel that I must go...."[32]

When he arrived, he found an improved Pauahi who expressed "a strong desire that she might live, and go back to Honolulu 'to do more for her people.' "[33] After a few weeks of rest, she returned with Charles on June 9. On board the *Mariposa* with them was Likelike. Shortly after their return, Damon wrote to George Campbell, Pauahi's agent in Ka'ū, Hawai'i: "Mr. & Mrs. Bishop have returned from San Francisco and I am pleased to report that Mrs. Bishop is in much better health and gaining rapidly."[34] She spent the next few weeks at Hale'ākala.

In the meantime, it is worthwhile to see how her managers conducted the affairs of her estate and how much she was involved in their activities. While she was in San Francisco, in late April, Charles had sent out a letter, signed by Pauahi, informing the appropriate parties that Keau had been appointed the agent for their lands in Ke'ei, Kona.[35] A few days later, Charles wrote a letter for Pauahi to R. F. Bickersten, of the Commission for Boundaries for the Island of Oahu, asking for a hearing to settle the boundaries of her lands at Maunalua, Kona, O'ahu.[36] On May 5th, Damon wrote a similar letter on Pauahi's behalf for a hearing to settle the boundaries of the *'ili* (section of land) of Pāhoa in Wai'anae. And in June, Damon wrote to F. S. Lyman asking him to survey the *ahupua'a* of Umauma "which belongs to Mrs. Bishop" in order to have the boundaries settled.[37]

In addition to boundary matters, a variety of other business matters required attention. For example, cattle brands. Damon discussed this in another letter to F. S. Lyman: "With reference to brands, if the plain brand 'R.K.' is not already recorded, you will please have it done in the name of Mrs. Bernice Pauahi Bishop and in future, that will be her only brand used in Hawaii."[38] Pauahi's estate was also involved in the selling of rock. On May 8th it was announced that an agreement had been entered into between "Mrs. Bernice Pauahi Bishop and the Minister of Interior, Charles Gulick, to pay Mrs. Bishop 10 cents per ton for 8,500 tons of rock of road work and limestone from the Kapalama quarry at 12½ cents per ton."[39] And, since land matters involve property rights with disputes needing to be resolved by lawyers or the courts, Pauahi's estate was involved in legal battles. For example, Damon, acting in his capacity as

Pauahi's attorney, protested to the Minister of Interior for trespassing upon Pauahi's rights by leasing a portion of her property to the "Honolulu Yacht Club."[40]

Pauahi kept informed about what was going on with her lands, as indicated by the communication Damon sent to George Campbell in Ka'ū, Hawai'i. After inquiring about Campbell's general expenses, the condition of the ranch's stock, feed, and so on, Damon stated: "These items of interest assist me in forming opinions as to the condition of affairs and in that way, I am always posted and can answer questions when asked by Mr. or Mrs. Bishop."[41] In sum, Pauahi was not a passive spectator when it came to the management of her estate; after all, she had been in the business since 1855, nearly twenty-eight years.

Meanwhile, her convalescence at Hale'ākala was up and down, at best. On July 7th, Charles wrote to Meyer: "Last week Mrs. B was quite unwell for several days with diarrhea and threatened with dysentery, but she is now much better again."[42] And on August 12th, he communicated with Meyer again: "I am sorry to say that Mrs. Bishop is not quite well as well as she has been."[43]

Sometime in the late summer she moved to her villa in Waikīkī (near the present site of the Royal Hawaiian Hotel) to take advantage of the sea breezes and air. When Lili'u called one day, as she wrote in *Hawaii's Story*, Pauahi "besought me to come and stay with her, which I did...."[44] In the first week of October Mrs. Cooke visited Pauahi. Pauahi had had sporadic contact with her during the years since her days at the Royal School. Mrs. Cooke draws a graphic picture of Pauahi's physical condition. "...She is failing. The tumor is again growing with rapid strides. It commenced in the old wound about 2 weeks ago. Now there are several lumps that are very painful. Some lumps under the arm & on the back of the neck! The head, limbs, neck & heart are all painful. She takes opium a half grain once in four hours & still suffers *great* pain. Says that the medicine does not help her much...I asked how she was and she replied, 'I do not know how to think of myself!'... Mrs. Allen feels very bad about B.'s condition. She says the Dr. shakes his head."[45]

Despite her terminal condition, Pauahi found the presence of mind to add the first of two codicils to her will, which she had written nearly a year ago. In the codicil filed on October 4,[46] she continued to add bequests of both land and money to a long list of persons and institutions, some not named in her original will. For example, she bequeathed to "my friend Samuel M. Damon, of said Honolulu, all of that tract of land known as the Ahupua'a of Moanalua...and also the fishery of Kaliawa; to hold with the appurtenances to him, his heirs and assigns forever."[47] This was an exceptional legacy, larger by far than any she had given except to Charles. Moanalua covered more than 7,000 acres from the Koʻolau Range to the marshes, ponds and the sea (the area known today as Keʻehi Lagoon). It was, perhaps, her way of honoring the services of a *konohiki* who remained loyal to her during her lifetime and thereafter; who had served as an equally loyal friend and employee of Charles; and who had befriended Ruth and taken good care of her estate. Damon's father had offered Charles the first hand of friendship when he arrived with his friend William Lee in 1846. Damon, who privately referred to Pauahi as his "Chiefess,"[48] had high regard and affection for her, as revealed in his letters. Though the market value of the undeveloped *ahupuaʻa* was relatively small at the time, it was eventually worth a fortune.

Pauahi revised several bequests made in her original will. Instead of the premises situated on Emma to Fort Street known as the *ʻili* of Kaʻakopua, she now left to Emma the parcels of land in Nuʻuanu Valley known as Laimi. The *ʻili* of Kaʻakopua she gave to Charles, along with Waiʻalaenui and Waiʻalaeiki. This was in addition to her earlier bequests of Molokaʻi Ranch, all the lands she had inherited from Pākī, Konia and ʻAkahi, plus any lands in Waikīkī. Charles was no doubt thankful for her generosity, but a few years later he returned to her estate almost every acre he had been given. Her bequest to Charles did not include Lumahaʻi on Kauaʻi or Kealia in Kona (which were also part of Konia's legacy), since these had previously been promised to Liliʻu.[49] But to Liliʻu's bitter disappointment, Pauahi did not grant her what she desired most— "the wish of her heart" — Haleʻākala.[50]

Pauahi said nothing about the schools in the first codicil, although she added an important qualification regarding the purchase or sale of real estate. She emphasized that no real estate or property of any kind was to be sold unless it was "necessary for the establishment or maintenance" of the schools or in "the best interest" of her estate.[51] Clearly, Pauahi's insertion of this injunction in the codicil was to remind her future trustees to preserve the corpus of the estate. Perhaps she was prompted by what she saw happening to Lunalilo's estate. His trustees were selling off lands in order to raise funds to build an old folks home. They were acting in full conformity with the terms of his will, selling and investing the income. But after ten years a good deal of the real estate had been sold, and in a few years almost all of it would be. Unfortunately, expenses kept rising, finding good investments became more and more difficult, and interest rates sometimes fell.[52] In the meantime, as more lands were sold, the corpus of

Lunalilo's estate was getting smaller and smaller. The estate's growing predicament was well known to Charles, if not to Pauahi as well, by October 1884. She was well enough to realize what would happen to her own estate if a similar course were pursued.

On October 8th, Mrs. Cooke telephoned Pauahi's Waikīkī villa to find out about her condition. The ever-faithful cousin Cordie answered and advised her to come the next morning. Mrs. Cooke recalled: "... I went. She is failing!...She seems willing to go or to stay as God sees best. Talked of that part of it very freely. She said that a lady said to her once that she must be very happy as she had so much property. She said happiness is not money, for having so much she felt responsible and accountable. I was so much comforted with what she said! She asked me to pray...and to bid all her friends to pray, for she needed help from on high."[53]

Incredibly, though wracked by intense pain and falling in and out of consciousness, Pauahi wrote her second and last codicil on October 9th.[54] She wrote it from her sickbed, because the two signed witnesses are Drs. Trousseau and J. Brodie. What was important enough to be recorded in her hours of agony? Apart from a couple of bequests and an additional gift to Lili'u of land at Kahala, she added three important terms regarding the school: (1) the boys' school should be established first and the girls' school next, but only after the former was "in efficient operation"; (2) the trustees should have the power to determine "to what extent said school shall be industrial, mechanical, or agricultural"; and (3) the trustees should also be empowered "to determine if tuition shall be charged."[55] The reason for giving priority to the boys' school may be that she saw a more urgent need to get the future breadwinners schooled, trained and into jobs. Also, she may have felt that there were, at the time, more and better schools existing for girls than for boys. The provision for having the trustees determine the extent of the schools' industrial, mechanical or agricultural program, seemed to round out the curriculum of the "English branches" and "morals" Pauahi emphasized in the original will. But it also reflected the interest Pauahi and Charles had in these technological and land-based fields. The rationale for incorporating these subjects in the schools' curriculum was suggested in Charles' 1874 report to the government. As mentioned earlier, the report stressed the importance of putting "the whole boy to school" by training the student in the use of his mind, hands, eyes and senses, in other words, his entire person. This was a rather advanced and unconventional approach to education in the 1880s. Finally, although Pauahi properly left the decision of whether tuition should be charged to the trustees, she would probably have opted for charging tuition. Requiring payment would have been in keeping with her attitude of reciprocity—of giving but getting something in return—a value as deeply ingrained in her Hawaiian character as that of industriousness. Charging tuition would be viewed as part of the condition.

With the completion of the second codicil, she had finished with the construction of her will. Or had she? If she had lived longer, would she have added other conditions or other bequests? Did she leave anything unfinished?

On the same day, October 9th, Pauahi was moved from Waikīkī to Keōua Hale, never to return to Hale'ākala. She and Charles had planned to move to Keōua Hale after her return from San Francisco. Mrs. Cooke reported that, during her conversation with Pauahi, on the 6th "B. told me that when they returned they expected to live in Ruth's home. They have been altering it so that it would be convenient." In one of her last acts, Pauahi paid deference to her beloved cousin Ruth, by living in the mansion she had never lived in herself.

On October 11th, Damon wrote to George Campbell: "Mrs. Bishop's health is very precarious and this has been a very anxious week for all of us. Her disease is cancer and of a malignant type."[56] All these weeks, Damon seems to have kept even the nature of her illness a secret, perhaps out of respect for Pauahi's dislike of having her health discussed. The next day he penned a note to Meyer stating: "Mrs. Bishop has slept well and takes nourishment and has gained slightly. She is kept constantly under the influence of morphine taken hyperdermically — under the skin."[57] Morphine was a common treatment, but it only dulled the pain and did not arrest the cancer.

On October 14th, Damon wrote to Meyer again: "It is with heavy heart that I write you of Mrs. Bishop's state of health. Since Monday her decline has been very rapid and during the night after her removal to Ka'akopua which occurred on Thursday and every hour since, her death has been expected at any moment and the Doctors (four) have predicted certain death. Her courage and endurance is wonderful as in a moment after a convulsion or acute attack of cancer pains she will speak cheerfully to those about her. Mr. Bishop is near her constantly and bears [up?] well. Next June they will have been married thirty-five years — and separated only for a month at the longest. They have the concern and sympathy of many friends."[58]

It was Thursday, October 16, 1884. The rains had been falling since early morning. Pauahi was unconscious and Charles was at her side. In a heavy downpour the rains reached a crescendo just about the time Pauahi died. It was twelve minutes after noon.[59]

"Kulu ka waimaka, uwē 'ōpua." "The tears fall; the clouds weep." So was it said in ancient days when rain fell at the time of a person's death or funeral, for the gods mingle their tears of affection with those who weep in sympathy and aloha.[60]

While the gods wept, so did the mortals in Honolulu. Not since the passing of the little Prince of Hawai'i, more than ten years ago, had Hawaiians displayed as much genuine grief.[61] Since Pauahi's death was not unexpected, word spread quickly. Within half an hour, most of the offices and shops in town closed and the flags were lowered to half-mast. Hawaiians thronged to Keōua Hale all that Thursday noon and night and for days after. Her retainers and *konohiki* from her outlying estates came and encamped on the premises. The spontaneous outpouring of sorrow and aloha was matched only by the rains that continued to fall.

For the next two weeks, her bier lay in the same room where Ruth's had been. Every hour and every minute during that period the black *kāhili*, historical heirlooms with names of their own, like Malulani (shade of the heavens), waved over her coffin. Many *kama'āina* (native born or longtime residents) observed that never on any similar occasion had they seen so large and so beautiful a display of *kāhili*. There were more than a hundred.[62] The *uwē helu*, the wailing, rising and falling in rhythmic cadence, also continued without stopping. Among the mourners were those who chanted her *mele inoa* or name songs. One of them, *Ka wahine hele lā o Kaiona* or "The Sunbeam-Chasing Lady of Kaiona," was her favorite.

> "Answer to thy name, Sunbeam-Chasing Lady of Kaiona, Chasing the mirage of the ohai flowery desert, My companion of the cold double night-rain of the Ko'olau, And of the ki and kukui shaded groves of Kahoiwai..."[63]

Without pause, for fifteen days and nights, her *mele inoa* were sung along with the *kanikau* or chants of lament. And, as the gods would have it, throughout this period the rains continued to fall unceasingly. It was all grimly beautiful.

On November 2nd, after a short service, Pauahi's coffin was placed in the hearse which then proceeded to the Royal Mausoleum. The procession was spectacular, long enough to take twenty-three minutes to pass by. There were over 900 people in the cortege, exclusive of school children, and seventy-five carriages. The procession included her servants, *konohiki*, Sunday School class, attending physicians, members of the Bar, the *ali'i*, nobles, *kāhili* and pall bearers, the King, Lili'u, Emma, Mrs. Allen and Charles. Among the accompanying clergy were not only the Protestants but the Anglicans and the Monseigneur Right Reverend Bishop of Olba and other Catholics of the cloth. In the procession, the police led the undertaker, while the cavalry followed in the rear.[64] As the cortege wound its way up Nuʻuanu Valley, the rains halted and the sun broke through. Samuel Damon, who had coordinated the entire funeral, could not have orchestrated heaven and earth any better.

Pauahi was laid to rest next to Ruth and Lot and the other Kamehamehas.

From the press and pulpits, impressive eulogies paid homage to her memory. Had Pauahi been forced to hear them in life, she might have winced in embarrassment. But their words were sincerely and honestly given. For example, *The Friend* editorialized with rare insight:

> Through the combined influence of birth, wealth, culture and character, she occupied a position not only peculiar but unique. The representative of the most powerful line of chiefs of the olden time, she was also an exponent of the best type of foreign habits and mode of life. Retaining a natural and proper pride of ancestry and an interest in the welfare of her own people, she so perfectly assimilated the essential spirit of Anglo-American culture as to take easily and naturally that high position in the best foreign society to which her birth and fortune entitled her. She was thus a link between the old and the new, between the native and the foreign, in a sense which was not true of any other person whatever. It should be a source of pride and satisfaction alike to the native Hawaiians and to those foreigners who have labored for their elevation and improvement, that this peculiar and in some respects trying position should have been so gracefully and so worthily filled. The Hawaiian race may yet develop many noble characters, manly, brave, intelligent, patriotic men and loving, devoted and virtuous women, but the peculiar niche occupied by the lady who just passed away, is vacant and must ever remain so.[65]

The Reverend J. A. Cruzan, Pastor of the Fort Street Church, spoke of the "last and best of the Kamehamehas" movingly and prophetically at a Sunday Service:

> ...The great loss which Hawaii sustained last Thursday was not that the last of this great line of High Chiefs died, nor that the possessor of great wealth died, but that a true woman died. "Who can find a virtuous (i.e., a strong, noble, true) woman; her price is far above rubies." True in all times and among all races—pre-eminently true in these days among our native Hawaiians. And all the more valuable is such a rare jewel of womanhood when there is joined to it rank and potential influence and wealth.

That Bernice Pauahi Bishop was such a true woman her life bears witness. Refusing a crown, she so lived that she was crowned. Refusing to rule her people, she did what was better, she served them, and in no way so grandly as by her example... "The world can do without its masters better than it can without its servants."

... For fifty-three years her royal life here has borne unswerving witness in favor of virtue and purity ... She hated that which was impure with an intense hatred. She had only loathing and contempt for that which was coarse and low. Place, power, wealth, nor influence could win her favor or regard if it was joined with degraded character. And her womanly example was all the more potent for good because it was so quiet ... The things that are most noisy are not the most powerful. Nay, things that make no noise, and make no pretension, may be really the most powerful. This quiet, modest, true womanly life has been for years, and still is, and will be for years to come, a mighty power for good here in Hawaii. Only the God who loveth purity and righteousness can measure this one true woman's influence for good upon her people....[66]

The Fort Street pastor did not know how prophetic his words were, but who could have known then how great an influence for good she would be? Could Pauahi ever have dreamed of her lands — the lands of the Kamehamehas—still largely intact and worth billions of dollars a century later? Could she have conceived of not hundreds but thousands of boys and girls—gathered from all islands, of all social and economic strata and all creeds — seeking and receiving a good education at her schools? What would she think of those graduates who have gone on to become good and industrious mechanics, farmers, mothers, and teachers; and also writers, judges, generals, professors, corporate executives, opera singers, professional athletes, hula masters, engineers, physicians, scientists, artists, and legislators? Could she have foreseen the enormous expectations to advance the achievement of her people, that Hawaiians and others have for her estate and schools today? And could she and her advisers have imagined the vast social, economic and political impact that her largess has had, and will continue to have, on the life of these islands?

Maybe and maybe not. What truly matters, of course, is that Pauahi had the vision and courage to make a noble and fateful beginning. The rest was left up to the faith and hope, the diligence and integrity, the dedication and achievement of others over the last century. The story of their collective efforts, in transforming a princess' will into the most successful institution of its kind anywhere, is an exciting and fascinating sequel to the story of her life.

Yet there is another story, the unhappy and frustrating litany of the many Hawaiians whose educational needs and aspirations have not entirely been met by Pauahi's legacy. She would be pleased with what has been accomplished, but she would surely be moved by the magnitude of the unmet needs of so many others. Of course, she could not have foreseen in the bleak 1880s the fivefold increase in the Hawaiian population that has taken place since. Nor could she have anticipated the diversity and complexity of the needs and goals in the lives of modern Hawaiians. Were she to return, Pauahi would see that not even two, three or more estates equal in size to hers could meet all the pressing needs of all of her potential beneficiaries. Yet it is her trust that remains today as the major catalyst for spurring the efforts of all agencies, public and private, in satisfying the educational aspirations of Hawaiian youth.

Her greatest legacy of all cannot be overshadowed, either by the growth of the Hawaiian population or by its unmet needs. This is the legacy of her example and the ideals she personified. Her lands would be worth much less were it not for the example of her life as a Kamehameha. Ultimately, the most enduring and enriching form of wealth is that of the spirit. Pauahi's legacy is the *mana* of her goodness — *mana* forever limitless, renewable, and accessible to all.

NOTES

Prologue

1 William Ellis, *Journal of William Ellis* (Rutland, Vermont: Charles E. Tuttle Co., 1979), p. 93.

1/Hawaiian Roots

1 James Hunnewell and Henry A. Peirce were both young traders who arrived in Hawai'i in the 1820s and formed a business partnership that was the start of today's C. Brewer & Company. See Josephine Sullivan, *The History of C. Brewer & Company, Limited, One Hundred Years in the Hawaiian Islands 1826 to 1926* (Boston: Walton Advertising & Printing Co., 1926).

2 Samuel M. Kamakau, *Ruling Chiefs of Hawai'i* (Honolulu: Kamehameha Schools Press, 1961), p. 235.

3 Kathleen D. Mellen, *The Magnificent Matriarch, Ka'ahumanu Queen of Hawai'i* (New York: Hastings House, Publishers, Inc., 1952), pp. 253-54.

4 *Ibid.*, p. 352.

5 *The Hawaiian Kingdom, Volume 1, 1778-1854, Foundation and Transformation* (Honolulu: University of Hawaii, 1938), p. 133.

6 *He Inoa no Pauahi—Birth Chant.* Unpublished chant, *Helen Roberts Collection of Meles, No. 24, 1923-24,* in the Bishop Museum Library. Roberts obtained the chant from Mrs. Emma Ahuena Taylor, a noted authority on Hawai'i at the time. The complete text in Hawaiian along with its English translation is in Appendix A. The translation was done by Mrs. Taylor and appeared in the *Paradise of the Pacific Magazine,* April 1934, p. 5. Some Hawaiian scholars may disagree on Ahuena Taylor's translation of the Hawaiian, especially the initial lines of the chant. Note that although this is the only birth chant of Bernice Pauahi we know of today, it is highly likely that others were composed, too. The possibility that these existed at one time is suggested by the Kamehameha Schools newspaper, the *Handicraft,* Volume XIV, January 1908, No. 1.

7 Uli is also the name of a goddess of sorcery, invoked by Hi'iaka in her prayers of resuscitation for Lohi'au. Pukui-Elbert, *Hawaiian Dictionary,* p. 397. *Uli* may also mean "darkness" as in the darkness of the eternal abyss.

8 *Kaihi* means a very sacred chief, but it may also refer to "flowing sea."

9 Paihikalani is another word meaning the same as a very sacred chief, but is used here as a poetic device or "linked assonance."

10 Regarding the moment of Kamehameha's birth, Joseph Poepoe writes it was "on a certain night of heavy down pouring rain— the lightning struck its wrathful flashes into the sky—the thunder pounded with all its might —the stormy wind veered every which way— the red water churned in the streams...." Edith Kawelohea McKinzie, ed., *An Original Narrative of Kamehameha the Great Written in Ka Na'i Aupuni (1905-1906) by Joseph M. Poepoe: Hawaiian Text with English Translation and Brief Comparative Reviews of Earlier Historical Biographers of Kamehameha I,* a paper submitted in partial fulfillment of the requirements for Master of Education degree, University of Hawaii, Honolulu, 1982, p. 20.

11 *An Account of the Polynesian Race; Its Origin and Migrations and the Ancient History of the Hawaiian People to the Times of Kamehameha I,* 3 vols. (London: Trubner & Co., 1878), pp. 129-30.

12 *Ibid.,* pp. 129-32.

13 Kamakau, *Ruling Chiefs,* p. 208.

14 *Ibid.,* p. 79.

15 *Ibid.,* p. 109.

16 Edith Kawelohea McKinzie, *Hawaiian Genealogies Extracted from Hawaiian Language Newspapers*, vol. 1, ed. by Ishmael W. Stagner, II (Laie, Hawai'i: The Institute for Polynesian Studies, Brigham Young University-Hawaii Campus, 1983), p. 40.

17 E. S. Craighill Handy and Mary Kawena Pūku'i, *The Polynesian Family System in Ka'u, Hawai'i* (Rutland, Vermont & Tokyo, Japan: Charles E. Tuttle Co., 1958), p. 17. I'i's view differs markedly from Handy's and Pūku'i's. He suggests that Kamehameha was "taken" or seduced by Kanekapolei because, like other chiefesses, she could not resist his "perfect" physique and "admirable" features. Indeed, not only did she take Kamehameha but his younger brother, Kalaimamahu as well. When Kalaniopu'u found out, I'i writes that he "was peeved and would not allow his nephews to see his face. Keawemauhili, who stepped in as mediator, told his half brother Kalaniopu'u to stop resenting his nephews because everyone knew that a woman was like an easily opened calabash, or a container with a removable lid. Upon these words, Kalaniopu'u's anger ceased, and he sent for his nephews to come and see him." John Papa I'i, *Fragments of Hawaiian History* (Honolulu: Bishop Museum Press, 1959), p. 147.

18 *An Account of the Polynesian Race*, p. 334.

19 *Ibid.*, p. 335. For those who claim that Kamehameha did not father Ka'ōleiokū, the case is advanced by John F. B. Stokes in "Kaoleioku, Paternity and Biographical Sketch," *Forty-third Annual Report of the Hawaiian Historical Society*, Honolulu (1935), pp. 15-44.

20 I'i, p. 66.

21 Stokes, "Kaoleioku," pp. 27-30.

22 Samuel M. Kamakau, in *Ka Nupepa Ku'oko'a*, October 5, 1867.

23 Clarice B. Taylor, in *Honolulu Star-Bulletin*, February 13, 1961.

24 Kuykendall, *The Hawaiian Kingdom*, Vol. I, pp. 3ა-34.

25 Abraham Fornander, *Collection of Hawaiian Antiquities and Folklore*, Vol. 4, Memoirs of the Bernice Pauahi Bishop Museum (Honolulu: Bishop Museum Press, 1917, 1918), p. 12. See also, Mary Kawena Pūku'i, E. W. Haertig, and Catherine A. Lee, *Nānā I Ke Kumu* (Look to the Source), Vol. II (Honolulu: Hui Hānai, Queen Lili'uokalani Children's Center, 1972), pp. 290-91.

26 Clarice B. Taylor, in *Honolulu Star-Bulletin*, February 15, 1961.

27 *Ibid.*, February 16, 1961. Note that Pākī, nonetheless, is reported to have had a special attachment to Liliha that went beyond their political relationship.

28 *Nānā I Ke Kumu*, p. 290.

29 Mary H. Krout, *The Memoirs of Honorable Bernice Pauahi Bishop* (New York: The Knickerbocker Press, 1908), pp. 19-20.

30 E. S. Craighill Handy and Mary Kawena Pūku'i, *The Polynesian Family System in Ka'u, Hawai'i* (Rutland, Vermont & Tokyo, Japan: Charles E. Tuttle Co., 1972), p. 78.

31 Cited in Krout, p. 19.

32 *Nānā I Ke Kumu*, p. 36.

33 At the time, this area was located behind the present site of the Hawai'i State Library (main branch). See Mary Kawena Pūku'i, Samuel H. Elbert, and Esther T. Mo'okini, *Place Names of Hawai'i* (Honolulu: University Press of Hawaii, 1974), p. 187.

34 *Ruling Chiefs*, pp. 271-72.

35 Kinau Wilder, *The Wilders of Waikiki* (Honolulu: Topgallant Publishing Co., 1978), p. 22.

36 *Ruling Chiefs*, p. 330.

37 *The Wilders of Waikiki*, p. 24.

38 I'i, *Fragments*, p. 147.

39 Laura Fish Judd, *Honolulu, Sketches of the Life; Social, Political and Religious, In the Hawaiian Islands, From 1828 to 1861* (Honolulu: *Honolulu Star-Bulletin*, 1928), p. 39.

40 *Ruling Chiefs*, p. 304.

41 I'i, p. 177.

42 Marion Morse, *The Father of Kings: The Story of Keku-ana-oa* (Unpublished manuscript), n.d. This is disputed by others who believe that Chief Kahalai'a was the true father of Ruth.

43 *Ruling Chiefs*, p. 329.

44 *Ibid.*

45 *The Polynesian Family System*, p. 201.

46 Mary Kawena Pūku'i, *Ōlelo No'eau, Hawaiian Proverbs & Poetical Sayings*, Bernice P. Bishop Museum Special Publication No. 71 (Honolulu: Bishop Museum Press, 1983), p. 201.

47 *The Polynesian Family System*, p. 201.

48 *Nānā I Ke Kumu*, p. 54.

49 I'i, p. 164.

50 *Ibid.*, p. 163.

51 Krout, p. 21.

52 I'i, p. 163.

2/At the Chiefs' Children's School

1 Kathleen D. Mellen, *The Lonely Warrior, The Life and Times of Kamehameha the Great of Hawaii*

(New York: Hastings House, Publishers, Inc., 1949), pp. 30-35.

2 Kuykendall, *The Hawaiian Kingdom, 1778-1854,* I, p. 110. See also George A. Odgers, *Education in Hawaii, 1820-1893,* Ed.D. thesis, Stanford University, 1933.

3 I'i, p. 164.

4 Mary Atherton Richards, *The Chiefs' Children's School* (Honolulu: *Honolulu Star-Bulletin,* 1937), p. 27.

5 Linda Kristeen Menton, *"Everything Lovely and of Good Report" The Chiefs' Children's School 1839-1850,* Ph.D. thesis, University of Hawaii, 1983, pp. 52-56.

6 *Ibid.,* p. 68.

7 Richards, p. 70.

8 "Report of the Chiefs' Children's School, 1841."

9 Richards, p. 77.

10 Juliette Montague Cooke to Martha Montague, 2 November 1847, ML, HMCS.

11 Menton, p. 104.

12 "Report of the Chiefs' Children's School, 1846"; Menton, p. 148.

13 Menton, pp. 165-66.

14 *The Diary of Bernice Pauahi Bishop.*

15 Menton, p. 164.

16 *The Diary of Bernice Pauahi Bishop.*

17 Samuel M. Kamakau, *The Works of the People of Old, Na Hana a ka Po'e Kahiko,* Bernice P. Bishop Museum Special Publication 61 (Honolulu: Bishop Museum Press, 1976), p. 132.

18 Laura Fish Judd, p. 121.

19 Gerrit P. Judd, IV, *Dr. Judd, Hawaii's Friend* (Honolulu: University of Hawaii Press, 1960), p. 80.

20 Letters of Amos S. and Juliette M. Cooke, 1836-1850, Aug. 25, 1844.

21 *Ibid.,* Mar. 12, 1845.

22 *Ibid.,* Dec. 11, 1845.

23 *Ibid.,* Nov. 6, 1847.

24 *Ibid.,* Jan. 28, 1848.

25 Amos Starr Cooke to Rufus Anderson, Feb. 22, 1850, ABCFM-Hawaii Papers, HMCS.

26 *Nānā I Ke Kumu,* p. 295.

27 Richards, p. 173.

28 *A Report of Voyages to and Travels on Hawaii, Maui, and Molokai Undertaken by the Students of the Chiefs' Children's School in the Summer of 1846* (Honolulu: Bishop Museum Press, 1981).

29 Amos Starr Cooke to Fanny Montague, ML, HMCS.

30 Juliette Montague Cooke to Fanny Montague, Nov. 2, 1847.

31 ASC, Nov. 12, 1847.

32 Amos Starr Cooke to Rufus Anderson, April 8, 1843.

33 Mrs. Cooke said of Pauahi that she "likes history and is well versed in it for a girl of her age." Juliette Montague Cooke to Fanny Montague, Nov. 2, 1847.

34 Amos Starr Cooke to Rufus Anderson, April 8, 1843.

35 Juliette Montague Cooke to Fanny Montague, Nov. 2, 1847.

36 George S. Kanahele, ed., *Hawaiian Music and Musicians, An Illustrated History* (Honolulu: University Press of Hawaii, 1979), p. 136.

37 ASC, Aug. 27, 1841 and May 2, 1846.

38 *The Diary of Bernice Pauahi Bishop,* June 30, 1843.

39 *Ibid.,* Jan. 24, 1844.

40 *Ibid.,* Oct. 16, 1843.

41 ASC, May 25, 1846.

42 *The Diary of Bernice Pauahi Bishop,* Oct. 16, 1843.

43 *Ibid.,* Mar. 6, 1844.

44 Lili'uokalani, *Hawaii's Story by Hawaii's Queen* (Rutland, Vermont: Charles E. Tuttle Co., 1964), pp. 30-31.

45 *The Diary of Bernice Pauahi Bishop.*

46 *Ibid.,* Nov. 7, 1844.

47 *Ibid.,* No. 1, Mar. 1, 1844.

48 "Report of the Chiefs' Children's School, 1841."

49 Juliette M. Cooke to Fanny Montague, Dec. 5, 1840.

50 *The Diary of Bernice Pauahi Bishop,* Jan. 16, 1844.

51 *Ibid.,* Jan. 26, 1843.

52 *Ibid.,* Feb. 2, 1843.

53 *Ibid.,* Jan. 31, 1843.

54 Richards, p. 313.

55 *Honolulu, Sketches,* p. 138.

56 "Report of the Chiefs' Children's School, 1849."

57 "Report of the Chiefs' Children's School, 1841."

3 / From Courtship to Marriage

1 Handy & Pūku'i, *The Polynesian Family...,* pp. 105-106.

2 I'i, p. 163.

3 ASC, Sept. 7, 1849.

4 Amos Starr Cooke to Miss Fanny Montague, Sept. 18, 1847, Missionary Letters Collection.

5 *Ibid.*

6 Richards, *Chiefs' Children's School,* p. 230. She was 14 years of age.

7 *Ibid.,* p. 270. She weighed about 115 pounds at this time and was 5 feet 2 inches in height.

8 ASC, June 8, 1843, v. 7, pp. 102-103.

9 Some married at a later age such as Lili'u who married John Dominis when she was 24 and Emma who married Alexander when she was 20 years old.

10 Lot drank a lot as a young man, but had apparently tapered off considerably when he ascended the throne in 1863. It is also said that he had a female *kahuna* in his retinue and that he was indulgent of the *hula*. Menton, *"Everything Lovely...,"* pp. 302-306.

11 Harold Winfield Kent, *Charles Reed Bishop Man of Hawaii* (Palo Alto, California: Pacific Books, 1965), pp. 1-14.

12 Ethel M. Damon, *Samuel Chenery Damon* (Honolulu: The Hawaiian Mission Children's Society, 1966), p. 24.

13 Donald Warren Griffin, *The Life of William L. Lee, First Chief Justice of the Supreme Court of the Hawaiian Kingdom*, M.A. thesis, Vanderbilt University, 1956, p. 13.

14 *Ibid.*, p. 17.

15 Henry M. Lyman, *Hawaiian Yesterdays* (Chicago: A. C. McCurg & Company, 1906), pp. 123-24.

16 Kuykendall, *The Hawaiian Kingdom, 1778-1854,* I, p. 244.

17 Kent, *Charles Reed Bishop*, p. 16.

18 ASC, Feb. 25, 1847.

19 ASC, Mar. 18, Apr. 23, June 28, 1847.

20 Griffin, p. 13.

21 ASC, Sept. 4, 1847. Charles was about 5 feet 11 inches tall.

22 ASC, Nov. 29, 1847, Mar. 14, Apr. 24, July 5 and 22, Aug. 5, 1848.

23 ASC, Sept. 2, 1848.

24 ASC, Oct. 4 and 9, Nov. 4, Dec. 27, 1848.

25 *Polynesian,* Jan. 6, 1849.

26 Kent, *Charles Reed Bishop*, p. 17.

27 Sullivan, *A History of C. Brewer,* p. 97.

28 Kent, p. 17.

29 *Ibid.*

30 *Ibid.*, p. 20.

31 ASC, Mar. 14, 1849.

32 ASC, Jan. 12, 1849.

33 ASC, Jan. 17, 1849.

34 ASC, Aug. 16, 1849.

35 ASC, Aug. 30, 1849.

36 ASC, Sept. 4, 1849.

37 *Ibid.*

38 ASC, Sept. 6, 1849.

39 Pūku'i *et al., Nānā I Ke Kumu,* p. 119.

40 ASC, Sept. 7, 1849.

41 *Ibid.*

42 A traditional Hawaiian proverb.

43 ASC, Sept. 7, 1849.

44 *Ibid.*

45 *Ibid.*

46 ASC, Sept. 11, 1849.

47 ASC, Nov. 16, 1849.

48 *Ibid.*

49 ASC, Nov. 1, 1849.

50 ASC, Nov. 14, 1849.

51 ASC, Mar. 12, 1844.

52 ASC, Dec. 10, 1849.

53 Amos Starr Cooke to Miss Fanny Cooke, Jan. 28, 1850.

54 *Ibid.*

55 *Ibid.*

56 ASC, Mar. 28, 1850.

57 *Ibid.*

58 ASC, Mar. 14, 1850.

59 ASC, May 11, 1850.

60 ASC, May 25, 1850.

61 ASC, May 30, 1850.

62 ASC, June 6, 1850.

63 Krout, p. 99.

64 Krout, p. 100.

65 ASC, June 6, 1850.

66 ASC, June 15, 1850.

67 Edward Joesting, *Tides of Commerce* (Honolulu: First Hawaiian, Inc., 1983), p. 72.

68 ASC, July 2, 1850.

69 Kent, p. 27.

70 *Ibid.*, p. 32.

71 *Ibid.*, p. 40.

72 ASC, July 17, 1850.

73 Kent, p. 40.

74 Ray Jerome Baker, *Honolulu in 1853* (Honolulu: R. J. Baker, 1950), pp. 63-69.

75 *Ibid.*, p. 30.

76 Kent, p. 32. Note that John Ladd was the brother of William Ladd, one of the partners of Ladd & Company.

77 The house was completed sometime in 1851. Clarice B. Taylor, *Honolulu Star-Bulletin*, Mar. 1, 1961. Note that this would have been well after the two or three months that Pākī indicated to Pauahi in March 1850 it would take to complete it.

78 Richard J. Lyman, Jr., and others explain that the "Pink House" is the better translation. The stone came from the ballast rock that ships discarded in Honolulu Harbor, material that was easily shaped by masons into building blocks, curb-stones, and so on.

79 Clarice B. Taylor, *Honolulu Star-Bulletin*, Feb. 28, 1961.

80 Krout, p. 103.

81 *Honolulu Star-Bulletin*, Feb. 28, 1961.

82 Krout, p. 103.

83 Kent, p. 27.

84 *Ibid.*

85 ASC, Aug. 2, 1851.

86 Joesting, p. 20.

87 *Ibid.*, p. 22.

88 Frank E. Midkiff, *The Origin, Objectives, and Development of the Bernice Pauahi Bishop Estate.* Unpublished report, July 7, 1961, p. 2.

4/Life at Hale'ākala

1 Handy & Pūku'i, *The Polynesian Family...*, p. 175.

2 Although Pauahi attended services at Kawaiaha'o, she did not become a member of the church until 1867. Krout, p. 120.

3 Charles may never have developed fluency in Hawaiian. This is suggested by a reference of his inability to write in Hawaiian contained in a letter he wrote to J. H. Hoapili, on May 11, 1886: "I have recd your letter of the 6th inst. Mr. Damon is not at the office today and I *cannot write you in the native language.*" (Italics ours) Mr. Damon was fluent in both spoken and written Hawaiian.

4 Lili'uokalani, p. 10.

5 *Ibid.,* p. 11.

6 *Ibid.*

7 Midkiff, *Origin, Objectives...Bishop Estate*, p. 2. There is a discrepancy with Pākī's probate (No. 1061, Oct. 22, 1855) which gives the acreage total as 3,737 acres.

8 *Ibid.*

9 Bishop Estate memo.

10 Office of the Commissioner of Public Lands of the Territory of Hawaii, *Indices of Awards Made by the Board of Commissioners to Quiet Land Titles in the Hawaiian Islands* (Honolulu: Star-Bulletin Press, 1929), pp. 80-81. Acreage totals are from Midkiff, *Origin, Objectives...Bishop Estate*, p. 2.

11 Victoria Kamāmalu was by far the largest landowner, having just inherited the Kamehameha lands from Kamehameha III, who had died the year before. Ruth had also received from her first husband, Leleiōhoku, upon his death in 1848, vast tracts in Kona, Hawai'i; Maui and 'Ewa, O'ahu. Pauahi would probably rank in the next tier of landowners.

12 Robert C. Schmitt, "The Missionary Censuses of Hawaii," *Pacific Anthropological Records*, No. 29, May 19, 1973. Bernice Pauahi Bishop Museum, p. 19.

13 *Ku'oko'a,* June 18, 1920.

14 Schmitt, p. 26.

15 Marion Kelly, *Loko I'a O He'eia: Heeia Fishpond* (for the Bernice Pauahi Bishop Estate), Department of Anthropology, Bernice Pauahi Bishop Museum, Honolulu, Sept. 1975, p. 8.

16 *Ibid.*

17 *Ku'oko'a,* June 18, 1920.

18 Bishop Estate.

19 Krout, p. 204.

20 *Ibid.*

21 The *Māhele* or "Division" was the culmination of a series of land reforms at the end of which the lands were divided into roughly three parts: (1) the King's or Crown Lands, (2) the Chiefs', and (3) the government's. For a full discussion of the subject, see Kuykendall, I, pp. 269-298.

22 Kanahele, *Kū Kanaka: Stand Tall, A Search for Hawaiian Values* (Honolulu: University of Hawaii Press, 1986) pp. 184-88. This view of Earth was common among many primal peoples and today it has gained currency in the modern scientific community, especially among the advocates of General Systems Theory.

23 Kelly, p. 9.

24 Kanahele, *Kū Kanaka*, p. 182.

25 Mrs. W. F. Allen, "A Reminiscence of Mrs. Bishop," in *Blue and White*, Founder's Day edition, Dec. 19, 1904.

26 Henry H. Parker, "Bernice Pauahi Bishop Reminiscences," Hawaiian Mission Children's Society Library.

27 Krout, p. 114.

28 *Ibid.*

29 Parker.

30 *Ibid.*

31 As told to Dr. Donald Kilolani Mitchell by Mrs. A. F. Cooke, Nov. 20, 1942.

32 Following his father's funeral, Lot reportedly told his retainers that they would have to go to work and not be idle. Rufus A. Lyman, "Recollections of Kamehameha V...," Hawaiian Historical Society (1895), pp. 12-19.

33 The "33" includes 30 servants and families plus Pauahi, Lili'u and Charles.

34 Krout, p. 111.

35 *Memories of Pauahi Ke Alii, Dec. 21, 1916.* Nakuina was born on Mar. 5, 1847 and lived to 1929. She was the mother of Fred Beckley, a member of the first graduating class, 1891, of the Kamehameha School for Boys.

36 Mrs. A. F. Cooke to Dr. Mitchell.

37 Nakuina.

38 W. F. Allen.

39 *Ibid.*

40 Damon, p. 76.

41 Krout, p. 117.

42 Charles De Varigny, *Fourteen Years in the Sandwich Islands 1855-1868* (Honolulu: University Press of Hawaii and the Hawaiian Historical Society, 1981), p. 266.

43 Krout, p. 117.

44 Nakuina.

45 Mrs. Pierre Jones, "Bernice Pauahi Bishop," An Address on the Occasion of Founder's Day, December 19, 1923.

46 Ethel M. Damon, *Sanford Ballard Dole and His Hawaii* (Palo Alto, California: Hawaiian Historical Society, 1957), p. 185.

47 Krout, p. 113.
48 De Varigny, p. 266.
49 *Ibid.*
50 Niklaus R. Schweizer, *Hawai'i and the German Speaking Peoples* (Honolulu: Topgallant Publishing Co., 1982), p. 141.
51 De Varigny, p. 267.
52 *Ibid.*
53 For a full discussion of historical development of Hawaiian music, see Kanahele, *Hawaiian Music and Musicians.*
54 For a full discussion of hospitality, see George S. Kanahele, ed., *Hawaiian Values, Series I* (Honolulu: Project WAIAHA, 1982), pp. 18-25.
55 Damon, *Sanford Dole...*, p. 184.
56 Thrum's Annual, 1916, p. 65.
57 Krout, p. 115.
58 Damon, p. 184.
59 Mrs. Pierre Jones.
60 Krout, p. 118.
61 Masakiyo Yanagawa, *The First Japanese Mission to America (1860) Being a Diary Kept by a Member of the Embassy,* edited with an Introduction by M. G. Mori (Kobe, Japan: J. L. Thompson & Co., 1937), pp. 10-11. See also Shinnichi Watanabe, *Diplomatic Relations Between the Hawaiian Kingdom and the Empire of Japan 1860-1893,* M.A. thesis, University of Hawaii, 1944, pp. 1-2.
62 Watanabe, p. 1.
63 Yanagawa, p. 16.
64 Krout, p. 118.
65 Damon, p. 185.
66 Lili'uokalani, p. 11.
67 *Ibid.,* p. 15.
68 Helena G. Allen, *The Betrayal of Liliuokalani, Last Queen of Hawaii 1838-1917* (Glendale, California: Arthur H. Clark Co., 1982), p. 104.
69 *Thrums,* p. 67.
70 *Ibid.*
71 *Ibid.*
72 Krout, p. 118.
73 Lili'uokalani, p. 33.
74 Krout, p. 119.
75 Joesting, p. 30.
76 *Ibid.,* p. 28.
77 *Ibid.,* p. 32.
78 *Ibid.*
79 *Ibid.,* p. 36.
80 Kent, p. 99.
81 *Ibid.,* p. 108.
82 *Ibid.,* p. 109.
83 Joesting, p. 46.
84 *Ibid.,* pp. 46-47.
85 Allen, p. 97.
86 Kristin Zambucka, *The High Chiefess Ruth Keelikolani* (Honolulu: Mana Publishing Co., 1977), p. 25.
87 Lili'uokalani, p. 26.
88 Clarice B. Taylor in *Honolulu Star-Bulletin,* Nov. 17, 1955.
89 Lili'uokalani, p. 27.
90 *Star-Bulletin,* Nov. 22, 1955.
91 *Ibid.*

5/A Captive of the Politics of Fate

1 Kuykendall, II, p. 195.
2 For demographic statistics, see Robert C. Schmitt, *Demographic Statistics of Hawaii, 1778-1965* (Honolulu: University of Hawaii Press, 1968), pp. 11, 42, 74 and 75.
3 Kuykendall, II, p. 178.
4 *Pacific Commercial Advertiser,* October 23, 1869.
5 *Pacific Commercial Advertiser,* October 20, 1889. Not all Hawaiians agreed with this verdict, however. As one Hawaiian tūtū put it: "Chinese men were highly regarded by the Hawaiians as the most desirable husbands. Not only were they good providers, but they cared for their in-laws..." Annie Kanahele, *Annie, Life of A Hawaiian* (Honolulu: Fisher Printing Co., Inc., 1976), p. 2.
6 Kuykendall, II, p. 36.
7 *Ibid.,* p. 227.
8 Daws, *Shoal of Time,* pp. 186-87.
9 Damon, *Sanford Dole...*, pp. 107-08.
10 Rufus A. Lyman, "Recollections of Kamehameha V," *Third Annual Report of the Hawaiian Historical Society for the Year 1895* (Honolulu, 1896), p. 19. Lyman was the *kahu* or guardian of Lot's estates on the Island of Hawai'i.
11 Damon, *Sanford Dole...*, p. 108.
12 Lili'uokalani, *Hawaii's Story,* p. 35.
13 Letter from Governor John Dominis to Charles R. Bishop, January 7, 1873. Dominis wrote the letter to clear up the "many unfounded rumors and misrepresentations" that had been circulating since the King's death. A corroborating letter by Stephen H. Philips dated December 7, 1872, which he wrote a few hours after the King's death, was also sent to Charles. Both letters were published in the *Sixth Annual Report of the Hawaiian Historical Society for the Year 1898* (Honolulu, 1898), pp. 11-16.
14 This and other quotations that follow are taken verbatim from Governor Dominis' letter. *Ibid.,* pp. 14-15.

15 Sanford B. Dole, "Thirty Days of Hawaiian History," in Damon, *Sanford Dole...*, p. 109.

16 David L. Gregg, July 30, 1857, Private Papers, Hawaii State Archives.

17 Kuykendall, II, 242.

18 Alfons L. Korn, *News from Molokai, Letters Between Peter Kaeo & Queen Emma, 1873-1876* (Honolulu: University Press of Hawaii, 1976), p. 46.

19 *Ibid.*, p. 126.

20 Kuykendall, II, pp. 242-43.

21 Elisha H. Allen, December 14, 1872, Allen Papers, cited in Rhoda Hackler, *Elisha Hunt Allen,* M.A. thesis, University of Hawaii, 1972, p. 178.

22 Lili'uokalani, *Hawaii's Story,* p. 37.

23 A. Francis Judd, "Sketch of Lunalilo's Life," *Forty-third Annual Report of the Hawaiian Historical Society for the Year 1934* (Honolulu, 1935), pp. 36-43.

24 Kent, p. 61.

25 Varigny, pp. 251-52.

26 *Nuhou,* August 19, 1873.

27 *Nuhou,* July 18, 1873.

28 August 8, 1973.

29 Kuykendall, II, p. 221.

30 "The Turrill Collection," *Sixty-sixth Annual Report of the Hawaiian Historical Society for the Year 1957* (Honolulu, 1958), p. 59.

31 *Ibid.*, p. 71.

32 Korn, p. 142.

33 "An Inside View of the Reign of Lunalilo," *Forty-ninth Annual Report of the Hawaiian Historical Society* (Honolulu, 1941), p. 20.

34 Kuykendall, II, p. 256.

35 Korn, p. 68.

36 Kuykendall, II, p. 259.

37 "An Inside View of the Reign of Lunalilo," *Forty-ninth Annual Report...*, p. 13.

38 Korn, pp. 92-93.

39 *Ibid.*

40 *Ibid.*, p. 86.

41 *Ibid.*, p. 93.

42 *Ibid.*, p. 143.

43 *Ibid.*

44 *Ibid.*

45 *Ibid.*

46 "An Inside View of the Reign of Lunalilo, *Forty-ninth Annual Report...*, pp. 20-22.

47 Korn, p. 144.

48 "An Inside View of the Reign of Lunalilo," *Forty-ninth Annual Report of the Hawaiian Historical Society for the Year 1940* (Honolulu, 1941), p. 20.

49 Alfred Stedman Hartwell, "Forty Years of Hawaii Nei," *Fifty-fourth Annual Report of the Hawaiian Historical Society for the Year 1945* (Honolulu, 1947), p. 16.

50 "An Inside View of the Reign of Lunalilo...," p. 26.

51 *Ibid.*, p. 27.

52 Lunalilo apparently died of "consumption" or tuberculosis.

6 / Revelations of an Odyssey

1 Krout, p. 133.

2 Kent, p. 37.

3 Theodore Morgan, *Hawaii, A Century of Economic Change 1778-1876* (Cambridge, Mass.: Harvard University Press, 1948), pp. 227-231.

4 Krout, p. 132.

5 Morton Dauwen Zabel, ed., *The Art of Travel, Scenes and Journeys in America, England, France and Italy from the Travel Writings of Henry James* (Garden City, New York: Doubleday & Co., Inc., 1958), pp. 1-48.

6 Krout, p. 140.

7 The entry in her diary dated November 25, 1875, reads as follows: "After two o'clock we drove to the National Museum (in Munich) — a most wonder place...as Baedeker's says...."

8 Krout, p. 136.

9 July 16, 1875.

10 *Ibid.*, July 19, 1875.

11 *Ibid.*, July 18, 1875.

12 *Ibid.*, July 19, 1875.

13 *Ibid.*, July 20, 1875. It should be noted that Ireland was by the 1850s the most overcrowded and poorest country in Europe and that the people, particularly in the poorer counties like Cork, had not yet recovered from the terrible famines that ravaged the land in the late 1840s and 1850s.

14 Krout, p. 143.

15 Diary, July 23, 1875.

16 Krout, p. 144.

17 Krout, p. 147.

18 *Ibid.*, p. 153.

19 Diary, August 4, 1875.

20 *Ibid.*, August 8, 1875.

21 Krout, p. 148.

22 *Ibid.*

23 *Ibid.*, p. 149.

24 *Ibid.*, p. 159.

25 *Ibid.*, p. 156.

26 *Ibid.*, pp. 159-60.

27 Diary, November 5, 1875.

28 *Ibid.*, November 9, 1875.

29 *Ibid.*

30 *Ibid.*

31 *Ibid.*, November 11, 1875.

32 *Ibid.*, November 14, 1875.

33 *Ibid.*, November 21, 1875.

34 *Ibid.*, November 25, 1875.

35 *Ibid.*, November 25, 1875. Pauahi probably erred on the date of this entry. Since the visit to the New Pinakothek took place the day after their visit to the Old Pinakothek, the date should be November 26.

36 *Ibid.*, November 25, 1875.

37 *Ibid.*, November 27, 1875.

38 *Ibid.*, December 1, 1875.

39 *Ibid.*

40 Krout, p. 167.

41 Diary, December 5, 1875.

42 Krout, p. 172.

43 Diary, December 8, 1875.

44 *Ibid.*

45 *Ibid.*, December 11, 1875.

46 Krout, p. 169.

47 *Ibid.*, p. 172.

48 Diary, December 19, 1875.

49 *Ibid.*, December 16, 1875.

50 *Ibid.*, January 24, 1876.

51 *Ibid.*, December 27, 1875.

52 *Ibid.*, January 23, 1875.

53 *Ibid.*, January 10, 1876. A fuller and somewhat humorous account is given in Krout, pp. 180-81.

54 Krout, p. 178.

55 *Ibid.*

56 Diary, January 6, 1876.

57 *Ibid.*

58 *Ibid.*, January 31, 1875.

59 *Ibid.*, February 4, 1876.

60 *Ibid.*, February 5, 1876.

61 *Ibid.*, February 23, 1876.

62 Mr. Bishop recalled the event in a letter he had written to Princess Ka'iulani dated January 22, 1896. Kent, p. 31.

63 Diary, March 3, 1876.

64 *Ibid.*, March 6, 1876.

65 *Ibid.*, March 9, 1876.

66 Krout, p. 186.

67 *Ibid.*, p. 187.

68 Pauahi did not keep a daily journal in Paris. On her return to London, she wrote several pages in her diary recounting what she did in Paris. This part of her diary is dated May 13, 1876.

69 Krout, p. 191.

70 *Ibid.*, p. 189.

71 Diary, May 13, 1976.

72 Krout, p. 193.

73 *Ibid.*

74 *Ibid.*, p. 192.

75 Kent, pp. 38-39.

76 Joesting, p. 60.

7 / The Seeds and the Corpus

1 Joesting, p. 66.

2 Krout, p. 198.

3 For details of the cultural life of the city, see Margaret Mary Frowe, *The History of the Theater During the Reign of King Kalakaua, 1875-1891.* M.A. thesis, University of Hawaii, 1937.

4 Zambucka, *Ruth Keelikolani*, p. 50.

5 Lili'uokalani, p. 55.

6 Based on *Māhele* Awards as in *Indices of Awards* ... p. 58.

7 Donald Kilolani Mitchell, "The Chiefess 'Akahi," May 1, 1979.

8 *Biennial Report of the President of the Board of Education, to the Legislative Assembly of 1878, Reign of His Majesty Kalakaua—Fifth Year.* Honolulu: Printed by H. L. Sheldon, p. 2.

9 *Ibid.*, p. 3.

10 *Ibid.*, p. 4.

11 George Allen Odgers, *Education in Hawaii, 1820-1893.* Ph.D. thesis, Stanford University, 1933, p. 178.

12 *Ibid.*, p. 176.

13 *Biennial Report of the President of the Board of Education, to Legislative Assembly of 1874...*, p. 18.

14 *Biennial Report...1878*, p. 6.

15 C. M. Woodward, *The Manual Training School*, New York: Arno Press and The New York Times, 1969, p. 217.

16 Kelley, *Loko I'a O He'eia*, p. 41.

17 *Ibid.*, p. 42.

18 Damon, *Sanford Dole*, p. 150.

19 *Handicraft*, Jan. 1889, Vol. 1, No. 1, p. 3.

20 Rev. Henry H. Parker, "Bernice Pauahi Reminiscences," from Mrs. W. W. Thayer, October 9, 1958, Hawaiian Mission Children's Society Library.

21 *Handicraft*, January 1889, Vol. 1, No. 1, p. 3. See also, Ethel M. Damon, *The Stone Church at Kawaiahao, 1820-1944*, Honolulu: Trustees of Kawaiaha'o Church, 1945.

22 Krout, pp. 122-23.

23 Elisha H. Allen, Feb. 14, 1880.

24 Damon, *Sanford Dole*, p. 154.

25 Lili'uokalani, *Hawaii's Story*, pp. 69-74.

26 Kuykendall, III, pp. 236-237.

27 Cited in Zambucka, pp. 69-70.

28 Lili'uokalani, p. 72.

29 Zambucka, p. 74.

30 Charles R. Bishop to Albert F. Judd, Sept. 28, 1882.

31 *Hawaiian Gazette*, Feb. 15, 1883.

32 Zambucka, p. 82.

33 Cited in *ibid.*

34 *Ibid.*

35 Zambucka, p. 71.

36 *Hawaiian Gazette*, May 30, 1883.

37 *Wills and Deeds of Trust, Bernice P. Bishop Estate, Bernice P. Bishop Museum, Charles R. Bishop Estate.* (Honolulu: Bishop Estate Trustees, 1957), pp. 12-13.

38 *Ibid.,* p. 9.

39 *List of Lands Belonging to the Estate of H. R. H. Ruth Keelikolani* (Handwritten document, ca. 1883(?)).

40 Midkiff, *Origin, Objectives...*, pp. 22-23.

8 / Hele Lā O Kaiona

1 Kent, p. 145.

2 Clarice B. Taylor, *Star-Bulletin,* June 24, 25, and 27, 1949. Also, *Advertiser,* Dec. 13, 1955 and May 21, 1956. Interview with Namahana Lydia Maioho, the daughter of William Taylor, November 9, 1984, Honolulu. Cf. Kent, pp. 27-28.

3 Bishop's official statement to the Trustees Under the Will of Bernice Pauahi Bishop, April 6, 1910. Cited in Kent, p. 145.

4 Kent, pp. 274-77.

5 Robert C. Schmitt, *Demographic Statistics of Hawaii: 1778-1965* (Honolulu: University of Hawaii Press, 1968), p. 74.

6 Odgers, pp. 177-78.

7 Bishop to S. M. Damon, October 9, 1911, cited in Kent, p. 145.

8 *Wills and Deeds...*, pp. 17-19.

9 *Ibid.,* p. 19.

10 *Ibid.,* p. 20.

11 Queen Emma's Will.

12 Queen Kapi'olani's Will.

13 Lili'uokalani's Will in Queen Lili'uokalani Trust files.

14 Bishop to Charles M. Hyde, February 11, 1897. Cited in Kent, p. 162.

15 Odgers, p. 179.

16 *Ibid.,* p. 213.

17 After the schools were established, the boys' school became known for its manual or industrial training.

18 Punahou or Oahu College, which was founded in 1841, served as a college preparatory high school. Pauahi may not have wanted her schools to be competing necessarily with Punahou.

19 Bishop to Uldrick Thompson, April 19, 1899. Cited in Kent, 254.

20 Bishop to Meyer, October 29, 1883.

21 Damon to George Clark, November 3, 1883.

22 Damon to Meyer, December 28, 1883.

23 Damon to W. H. Rice, January 14, 1884.

24 Krout, p. 218.

25 Bishop to Meyer, February 9, 1884.

26 Bishop to Meyer, March 10, 1884.

27 Krout, p. 219.

28 Lili'uokalani, *Hawaii's Story,* p. 108.

29 Krout, p. 221.

30 Damon to Meyer, May 10, 1884.

31 Harriet B. Damon to SC Damon, Frank & Mary, June 15, 1884, in Damon File, HMCS Library.

32 Bishop to Meyer, May 10, 1884.

33 Krout, p. 221.

34 Damon to George Campbell, June 16, 1884.

35 Bishop, April 26, 1884.

36 April 28, 1884.

37 Damon to Lyman, June 6, 1884.

38 Damon to Lyman, February 4, 1884.

39 Bishop, May 8, 1884.

40 Damon to Charles T. Gulick, July 28, 1884.

41 Damon to George Campbell, June 6, 1884.

42 Bishop to Meyer, July 7, 1884.

43 Bishop to Meyer, August 12, 1884.

44 *Hawaii's Story,* p. 108.

45 Letter from Juliette Montague Cooke to Juliette Cooke, October 6, 1884, HMCL.

46 *Wills and Deeds...*, pp. 21-25.

47 *Ibid.,* p. 23.

48 Damon to Edward Damon from London, June 10, 1897. Damon File, HMSC Library. Damon wrote: "When you visit your Chief at [manuscript unclear], as he is somewhat the same relation to you as Mrs. Bishop was to me and I always think of her as my chiefess, I hope you will express to him whole souled thoughtfulness—All men have souls but it is only the few who have enough to spare for others."

49 *Wills and Deeds...*, p. 21.

50 Lili'uokalani, *Hawaii's Story,* p. 110.

51 *Wills and Deeds...*, p. 24.

52 Master's Report, November 29, 1884 and January 30, 1885. First Circuit Court, Probate No. 2414. Archives, State of Hawaii.

53 Letter from Juliette Montague Cooke to Juliette Cooke, October 8, 1884.

54 *Wills and Deeds...*, pp. 26-27.

55 *Ibid.,* p. 27.

56 Damon to George Campbell, October 11, 1884.

57 Damon to Meyer, October 12(?), 1884.

58 Damon to Meyer, October 14, 1884.

59 A different time for her death is given as "eight minutes after 12 noon" by the *Pacific Commercial Advertiser,* October 17, 1884.

60 Kawena Pūku'i, *'Ōlelo No'eau, Hawaiian Proverbs & Poetical Sayings,* Bernice Pauahi Bishop Museum Special Publication No. 71, Bishop Museum Press, Honolulu, 1983, p. 206.

61 *Hawaiian Gazette,* November 5, 1884.

62 *Pacific Commercial Advertiser,* November 3, 1884.
63 Krout, p. 233.
64 *Hawaiian Gazette,* November 5, 1884.

65 *The Friend,* November 1884, Vol. 33, No. 11, p. 1.
66 *Pacific Commercial Advertiser,* October 20, 1884.

APPENDIX

The Birth Chant of Bernice Pauahi Bishop

He Inoa no Pauahi (Ka lehua o Konia me ke oni ana opio—) Birth chant. (The Hawaiian original from the "Meles from Mrs. AP Taylor" by Helen Roberts, and is found in the *Roberts Collection of Meles, No. 24, 1923-24,* in the Bishop Museum Library.)

Kulia kalani e Uli
Kulia ka pule ia Ku
Wahia ka lani e Kane
Oa ka moku ia ka ihi
O pa'ihi ka lani ke ali'i
Ninau o Kane, Kanaloa
Eia ka hoaka o na 'li'i
Eia ka eu o ka la'i kapu
Ke kupua nana i hele ke kai uli ke kai kea
Ke kai ka popolohua a Kane-honua-mea
Eia kalani ka haku ko'i alamea
He kapu he moe wai no ka uka
Nona ke ka nani ula i loa'a
E kuana me ka hala-o-mapuana
Hanupa oa i hono papu no paka'alana
Uiliwili ao a ka mo'o ali'i
He'e i ka nalu kai'a kau hola
Moku ka piko o ke li'i lele i ka lani
Kani uina a kula o Paka'alana
Hanau kalani ke kani nei ka pahu
Ku'i ka he kili lapa ka uila
I ho mai kaua koko ka a lewalewa
Ka punohu ka ha'o wale i ka moana
Ua ikea ka lani me ka malama

Pii ka Pi'ilani a ma lo'e lo'e
Oi oi ka iwi kua mo'o o na lani nui
He maulani ia na Makaalaneo
Hanau ia mai i la ua a loa'a
Maloko mai o ka makuahine
Hanau ka ouli ho'okea lani
He ali'i he pu ko'a Ku
He papa una oa a Lono
He a hua Ku no ke kai hohonu
O ka lani nui i mamao
O ka keawe hiapo kapu no ia
Oke kulu o ka hinu o ka hou o ke kapu la ho'i ia ia
Kulia mai e ka lani ka honua
Ho'oahua ia mai ko'oka a ka moku
Pa'apa'u ia ka holo loa ke ali'i noha mai ka lua
U leo haha ole Kaalaihi
Kanaloa kaia kuku pau ai na lima i ka ekaeka
Kalalahea, ka mano ka ahiale, ka niuhi moelawa
Kalani pu'uhono ka moku
O Kahoe lowela-o-ki-ao-ka-maka
O ka ulu nana e hahao ka enaena
O ka wela la'i a nana e hoelieli a ha'aha'a ka lani
Ka huli hiwa a Kama
U lalapa no ka la ua keiki
O Ka-pu-likoliko ia ka lani
He mano hai lepo ka hahalua kaia nui hihimanu
Ke ko'a'e lele uka a ke aku lele kai
O ka manu kinana i ia Pa'e
O Kalani-kau-maka-a-mano
Ka makalapua
O Ka lanalana-i-o-a'e-o Kaiwa-nui-kilau-kapu ia he li'i
O Kalani-wai-akua wai kanaka ole
O Ka-lau-a-keakea i puka keaka ahuula
I lohia mai ka'i ka pano ohiohi o ka na'o hala'a
O ka hu o ka ihe pa'a ko aina
I a'u kahi ka hole ma waho
O ka'a lae a nana e ke'u kaoha lile
O kapakaua ia mana e Kua
E uei na ai la ho'i ka lana ola'o
O ka Ehu ia nana e ho'onana

O Ka-naʻe-o-lau o Iku ke kane o kawalele
Loaʻa ka puʼlolena ula
Kapu kani wala heʻe-ka moana kai elele
Loli ma koko i ka pali ala
E moe ana i ke ala nui i ka ale ula
I ka ula a weoweo o kukuna
O a o e ma kukula o Kahiki e
E ka la — ni
E Kalani-nui-kua-hilo-hilo
I ke kapu e he — liʻi
I hoa ka huli i malama i — o — eha
O ka lele hakanuʻa haʻi-na-kolo
O ka hihiʻi lei a Maheha
O ke kolo a hiu wai naua e ka kaʻe
O Kauhi ka manu nana e poʻo ka wai la
Ke kahu
Kahu ka ena kaimu i kaikoʻo o Nauahi loa
Mai kama no a Waialua
A ole i pili ia mai e ka lae o ka huku
Ka au kuku kai walu o ke Koʻolau
I Waialua no kapo i na mai
He leo kai ka kai o Ewa e hoʻolano
e — eo — e.

The Birth Chant of Princess Bernice Pauahi Bishop
English Translation by Ahuena Taylor

The Royal Princess is desired by "Uli" (Eternity)
The prayer of supplication for her was desired by "Ku."
Break the heavens O "Kane"
The islands are crashed by "Kaihi."
"Paihikalani" was the chief.
When "Kane" inquired of "Kanaloa:"
"Here is the symbol crescent of chiefs!"
Here is the urchin of the still atmosphere of Kapus!
The one that sends the white sea
And the dark blue sea running.
The dark green sea of "Kane" — foundation of that someone.
Here is the heaven, the star, the hard volcanic stone,

The water bed for a man!

"She is sacred!" answered "Kaihi."

The sweet scented single gardenia (Kiele) is hers

Where one stands and gazes for the branches of "Mapuana" (permeating scent)

The fragrant cove in the center of the fort of "Pakaaiana"

The twisted branches of the chiefly tree

The fish that rests above, receding with the surf is hers.

And "Pakaalana" sounded.

The Royal one is born, the drums are sounding,

The thunder resounds and the lightning is flashing.

The blood rain is falling and is moving along with the floating clouds

The wondrous rainbow pillar stands alone in the ocean.

The Royal one is acknowledged warmly.

The Royal ladder climbs until it is substantial

Expanding the spinal column of the chiefs

They are the Royal ones of "Kamaka-ala-neo"

That was begat by those two,

Born was the God-like white bosun bird

A chiefess a rock that stands

A foundation, a barnacle of Ku.

A great standing billow of the deep ocean,

Of Kalani-nui-ia-mamao

Who was "Keawe's" Kapu first born

The sheen of the sweat of the Kapu was his.

Desired from heaven and by earth.

That was piled up and backed by the Kingdom,

Which crouched on the long reef.

The chiefess who burst forth from the depth

The voice of the "Alaihi" is scarce.

"Kanaloa" was the fish,

Spreading the length,

With hands out-stretched in the turbulent waters,

Of the shark of the fair branch,

The "Ahi" of the ripping waves,

And the King of sharks.

That is the line that will bring joy.

And make humble the Royal line.

The young taro top of "Kama"

"Lalapu" was their child.

The deep cloud cluster from Heaven.
The shark that stirs up the dirt in the sea
The white bosun bird (Koae) that flies to the land heights.
The bonito that flies at sea.
And the fine feathered bird that lands is the mother.
She is the Royal one "Kau-maka-o-mano" the favorite flower.
Who is "Kalani-wai-akua-wai-kanaka-ole"
That was made a Kapu chiefess.
The "Alae" bird who scolds the count of chiefs,
Whose power is the Fort of "Ku"
That controls the surging of life.
Is the "Ehu" (Abner Paki) that will make mail,
"Kanaealau" and "Iku" the husbands of the diving one.
The wild duck that leads in rows.
With "Kauhi" the bird that digs the water in the dividing line.
Who builds the heat, the oven, until the long fires
Become like a wild sea.
From "Kama" to "Waialua."
And comes close the head lands of "Kahuku,"
And the hawk-like scratching sea of "Kahuku,"
The night was spent at "Waialua,"
For a voice was at the sea of "Ewa."
Listening for the response.
Respond! Oh Heavenly one.

BIBLIOGRAPHY

Allen, Helena G. *The Betrayal of Liliuokalani, Last Queen of Hawaii 1838-1917.* Glendale, California: Arthur H. Clark Co., 1982.

Allen, William F. "A Reminiscence of Mrs. Bishop," *Blue and White* (Founder's Day Edition), December 19, 1904, Kamehameha Schools.

Baker, Ray Jerome. *Honolulu in 1853.* Honolulu: R. J. Baker, 1950.

Bishop, Bernice Pauahi. *A Report of Voyages to and Travels on Hawaii, Maui, and Molokai Undertaken by the Students of the Chiefs' Children's School in the Summer of 1846.* Honolulu: Bernice P. Bishop Museum Press, 1981.

_____. *The Diary of Bernice Pauahi Bishop.* Manuscript and Transcription in Bishop Museum Library.

Bishop, Charles R. *Biennial Report of the President of the Board of Education, to the Legislative Assembly of 1878, Reign of His Majesty Kalakaua — Fifth Year.* Honolulu: H. L. Sheldon.

_____. *Correspondence.* H. W. Kent Collection, Masonic Public Library.

Cooke, Amos Starr and Juliette Montague. *Correspondence.* Missionary Letters Collection, Hawaiian Mission Children's Society Library (HMCSL).

Damon, Ethel M. *Samuel Chenery Damon.* Honolulu: The Hawaiian Mission Children's Society, 1966.

_____. *Sanford Ballard Dole and His Hawaii.* Palo Alto, California: Hawaiian Historical Society, 1957.

_____. *The Stone Church at Kawaiahao, 1820-1944.* Honolulu: Trustees of Kawaiahao Church, 1945.

Damon, Samuel M. *Correspondence.* Missionary Letters Collection, Hawaiian Mission Children's Society, and Bishop Estate Collection, Bernice P. Bishop Museum.

Daws, Gavan. *Shoal of Time, A History of the Hawaiian Islands.* Honolulu: University Press of Hawaii, 1968.

Dominis, John. Letter to Charles R. Bishop in *Sixth Annual Report of the Hawaiian Historical Society for the Year 1898*. Honolulu: 1898.

Fornander, Abraham. *An Account of the Polynesian Race; Its Origin and Migrations and the Ancient History of the Hawaiian People to the Times of Kamehameha I*, 3 vols., 1878-1885. New ed. (3 vols. in 1). Rutland, Vermont: Charles E. Tuttle Co., 1969.

_____. *Fornander Collection of Hawaiian Antiquities and Folk-Lore: The Hawaiian Account of the Formation of Their Islands and Origin of Their Race with the Traditions of Their Migrations, etc. as Gathered from Original Sources*. Bernice P. Bishop Museum Memoirs, v. 4-6. Honolulu: Bishop Museum Press, 1917-18.

The Friend.

Frowe, Margaret Mary. *The History of the Theater During the Reign of King Kalakaua, 1875-1891*. Master's thesis, University of Hawaii, 1937.

Gregg, David L. *Private Papers*, Hawaii State Archives.

Griffin, Donald W. *The Life of William L. Lee, First Chief Justice of the Supreme Court of the Hawaiian Kingdom*. Master's thesis, Vanderbilt University, 1956.

Hackler, Rhoda. *Elisha Hunt Allen*. M.A. thesis, University of Hawaii, 1972.

Handicraft.

Handy, E. S. Craighill and Mary Kawena Pūku'i. *The Polynesian Family System in Ka'u, Hawai'i*. Rutland, Vermont: Charles E. Tuttle Co., 1972.

Hartwell, Alfred Stedman. "Forty Years of Hawaii Nei." *Fifty-fourth Annual Report of the Hawaiian Historical Society for the Year 1945*. Honolulu: 1947, pp. 9-24.

Hawaiian Gazette.

Hawaiian Historical Society. "An Inside View of the Reign of Lunalilo." *Forty-ninth Annual Report of the Hawaiian Historical Society for the Year 1940*. Honolulu: 1941, pp. 12-28.

He Inoa no Pauahi — Birth Chant. Unpublished chant, in *Helen Roberts Collection of Meles*, No. 24, 1923-24. Bernice Pauahi Bishop Museum Library. An English translation of the chant done by Mrs. Emma Ahuena Taylor appeared in the *Paradise of the Pacific Magazine*, April 1934.

Honolulu Star-Bulletin.

I'i, John Papa. *Fragments of Hawaiian History*. Honolulu: Bernice P. Bishop Museum Press, 1959.

Joesting, Edward. *Tides of Commerce*. Honolulu: First Hawaiian Bank, 1983.

Jones, Pierre. *Bernice Pauahi Bishop, An Address on the Occasion of Founder's Day,* *December 19, 1923.*

Judd, Francis A. "Sketch of Lunalilo's Life." *Forty-third Annual Report of the Hawaiian Historical Society for the Year 1934,* Honolulu, 1935, pp. 36-43.

Judd, Gerrit P., IV. *Dr. Judd, Hawaii's Friend.* Honolulu: University of Hawaii Press, 1960.

Judd, Laura Fish. *Honolulu, Sketches of the Life; Social, Political and Religious, In the Hawaiian Islands, From 1828 to 1861.* Honolulu: *Star-Bulletin,* 1928.

Kamakau, Samuel M. *Ruling Chiefs of Hawaii.* Honolulu: Kamehameha Schools Press, 1961.

Kanahele, Annie. *Annie, Life of a Hawaiian.* Honolulu: Fisher Printing Co., Inc., 1976.

Kanahele, George S., ed. *Hawaiian Music and Musicians, An Illustrated History.* Honolulu: The University Press of Hawaii, 1979.

_____. *Kū Kanaka: Stand Tall, A Search for Hawaiian Values.* Honolulu: University Press of Hawaii, 1986.

_____. *Hawaiian Values, Series I.* Honolulu: Project WAIAHA, 1982.

Ka Nupepa Ku'oko'a

Kelly, Marion. *Loko I'a O He'eia: He'eia Fishpond.* (For the Bernice Pauahi Bishop Estate.) Department of Anthropology, Bernice Pauahi Bishop Museum, Honolulu, September 1975.

Kent, Harold W. *Charles Reed Bishop Man of Hawaii.* Palo Alto, California: Pacific Books, 1965.

Korn, Alfons L. *News from Molokai, Letters Between Peter Kaeo & Queen Emma, 1873-1876.* Honolulu: University Press of Hawaii, 1976.

Krout, Mary H. *The Memoirs of Honorable Bernice Pauahi Bishop.* New York: The Knickerbocker Press, 1908.

Kuykendall, Ralph S. *The Hawaiian Kingdom,* 3 vols. Honolulu: University of Hawaii Press, 1938-1967.

Lili'uokalani, Queen. *Hawaii's Story by Hawaii's Queen.* Rutland, Vermont: Charles E. Tuttle Co., 1964.

Lyman, Henry M. *Hawaiian Yesterdays.* Chicago: A. C. McCurg & Co., 1906.

Lyman, Rufus A. "Recollections of Kamehameha V," *Third Annual Report of the Hawaiian Historical Society for the Year 1895.* Honolulu, 1896, pp. 12-19.

McKinzie, Edith K. *An Original Narrative of Kamehameha the Great Written in Ka Na'i Aupuni (1905-1906) by Joseph M. Poepoe: Hawaiian Text with English Translation and Brief Comparative Reviews of Earlier Historical Biographers of Kamehameha I.* A paper submitted in partial fulfillment of the requirements for Master of Education degree, University of Hawaii, 1982.

_____. *Hawaiian Genealogies Extracted From Hawaiian Language Newspapers*, vol. 1, ed. by Ishmael W. Stagner, II. Laie, Hawaii: The Institute for Polynesian Studies, Brigham Young University-Hawaii Campus, 1983.

Mellen, Kathleen D. *The Lonely Warrior, The Life and Times of Kamehameha the Great of Hawaii*. New York: Hastings House, Publishers, Inc., 1949.

_____. *The Magnificent Matriarch, Ka'ahumanu Queen of Hawai'i*. New York: Hastings House, Publishers, Inc., 1952.

Menton, Linda K. *"Everything Lovely and of Good Report" The Chiefs' Children's School 1839-1850*. Ph.D. thesis, University of Hawaii, 1983.

Midkiff, Frank E. *The Origin, Objectives, and Development of the Bernice Pauahi Bishop Estate*. Unpublished report, July 7, 1961.

Mitchell, Donald K. *The Chiefess 'Akahi*, May 1, 1979.

Morgan, Theodore. *Hawaii, a Century of Economic Change 1778-1876*. Cambridge, Mass.: Harvard University Press, 1948.

Morse, Marion. *The Father of Kings: The Story of Keku-ana-oa*. Unpublished manuscript. Donald K. Mitchell Collection.

Nakuina, Emma. *Memories of Pauahi Ke Ali'i, December 21, 1916*. Donald K. Mitchell Collection.

Nuhou.

Odgers, George A. *Education in Hawaii, 1820-1893*. Ed.D. thesis, Stanford University, 1933.

Office of the Commissioner of Public Lands of the Territory of Hawaii, *Indices of Awards Made by the Board of Commissioners to Quiet Land Titles in the Hawaiian Islands*. Honolulu: Star-Bulletin Press, 1929. *Pacific Commercial Advertiser.*

Paradise of the Pacific Magazine, April 1934.

Parker, Henry H. *Bernice Pauahi Bishop Reminiscences*. Hawaiian Mission Children's Society Library.

Polynesian.

Pūku'i, Mary Kawena, E. W. Haertig, and Catherine A. Lee. *Nānā I Ke Kumu* (Look to the Source), Vol. II. Honolulu: Hui Hānai, Queen Lili'uokalani Children's Center, 1972.

Pūku'i, Mary Kawena. *'Ōlelo No'eau, Hawaiian Proverbs & Poetical Sayings*. Bernice P. Bishop Museum Special Publication No. 71. Honolulu: Bernice P. Bishop Museum Press, 1983.

_____, Samuel H. Elbert, and Esther T. Mo'okini. *Place Names of Hawai'i*. Honolulu: The University Press of Hawaii, 1974.

Richards, Mary Atherton. *The Chiefs' Children's School*. Honolulu: *Honolulu Star-Bulletin*, 1937.

Schmitt, Robert C. *Demographic Statistics of Hawaii, 1778-1965*. Honolulu: University of Hawaii Press, 1968.

_____. "The Missionary Censuses of Hawaii." *Pacific Anthropological Records,* No. 29, May 19, 1973. Bernice P. Bishop Museum.

Schweizer, Niklaus R. *Hawai'i and the German Speaking Peoples*. Honolulu: Topgallant Publishing Co., 1982.

Stokes, John F. B. "Kaoleioku, Paternity and Biographical Sketch." *Forty-third Annual Report of the Hawaiian Historical Society for the Year 1934,* Honolulu, 1935, pp. 1-32.

Sullivan, Josephine. *The History of C. Brewer & Company, Limited, One Hundred Years in the Hawaiian Islands 1826 to 1926*. Boston: Walton Advertising & Printing Co., 1926.

Taylor, Clarice B. "Tales About Hawaii." *Honolulu Star-Bulletin*.

"The Turrill Collection." *Sixty-sixth Annual Report of the Hawaiian Historical Society for the Year 1957*. Honolulu, 1958.

Varigny, Charles de. *Fourteen Years in the Sandwich Islands, 1855-1868*. Honolulu: University Press of Hawaii and the Hawaiian Historical Society, 1981.

Watanabe, Shinnichi. *Diplomatic Relations Between the Hawaiian Kingdom and the Empire of Japan 1860-1893*. M.A. thesis, University of Hawaii, 1944.

Wilder, Kinau. *The Wilders of Waikiki*. Honolulu: Topgallant Publishing Co., 1978.

Wills and Deeds of Trust, Bernice P. Bishop Estate, Bernice P. Bishop Museum, Charles R. Bishop Estate. Honolulu: The Trustees, 1957.

Woodward, C. M. *The Manual Training School*. New York: Arno Press & The New York Times, 1969.

Yanagawa, Masakiyo. *The First Japanese Mission to America (1860) Being a Diary Kept by a Member of the Embassy*. Edited with an introduction by M. G. Mori. Kobe, Japan: J. L. Thompson & Co., 1937.

Zabel, Morton Dauwen, ed. *The Art of Travel, Scenes and Journeys in America, England, France and Italy from the Travel Writings of Henry James*. Garden City, New York: Doubleday & Co., Inc., 1958.

Zambucka, Kristin. *The High Chiefess Ruth Keelikolani*. Honolulu: Mana Publishing Co., 1977.

INDEX